DIVINE SERVICE?

Religion and International Security

Series Editor: Lee Marsden, University of East Anglia

In the twenty-first century religion has become an increasingly important factor in international relations and international security. Religion is seen by policy makers and academics as being a major contributor in conflict and its successful resolution. The role of the Ashgate series in Religion and International Security is to provide such policy makers, practitioners, researchers and students with a first port of call in seeking to find the latest and most comprehensive research on religion and security. The series provides established and emerging authors with an opportunity to publish in a series with a reputation for high quality and cutting edge research in this field. The series produces analytical and scholarly works from around the world that demonstrate the relevance of religion in security and international relations. The intention is not to be prescriptive or reductionist in restricting the types of books that would be appropriate for the series and as such encourages a variety of theoretical and empirical approaches. International security is broadly defined to incorporate inter and intra-state conflict, human security, terrorism, genocide, religious freedom, human rights, environmental security, the arms trade, securitisation, gender security, peace keeping, conflict resolution and humanitarian intervention. The distinguishing feature is the religious element in any security or conflict issue.

Other titles in the series

Religious Transnational Actors and Soft Power
Jeffrey Haynes

Religion, Conflict and Military Intervention
Edited by Rosemary Durward and Lee Marsden

Media, Religion and Conflict
Edited by Lee Marsden and Heather Savigny

Radicalism Unveiled
Farhaan Wali

The Ashgate Research Companion to Religion and Conflict Resolution
Edited by Lee Marsden

Divine Service?
Judaism and Israel's Armed Forces

STUART A. COHEN
Ashkelon Academic College, Israel

ASHGATE

Published by
Ashgate Publishing Limited
Wey Court East
Union Road
Farnham
Surrey, GU9 7PT
England

Ashgate Publishing Company
110 Cherry Street
Suite 3-1
Burlington, VT 05401-3818
USA

www.ashgate.com

British Library Cataloguing in Publication Data
Cohen, Stuart, 1946-
Divine service? : Judaism and Israel's Armed Forces. –
(Religion and international security)
 1. National security–Religious aspects–Judaism.
 2. National security–Israel. 3. Draft–Israel. 4. War–
 Religious aspects–Judaism. 5. War (Jewish law)
 I. Title II. Series
 296.3'827-dc23

The Library of Congress has cataloged the printed edition as follows:
Cohen, Stuart, 1946-
Divine service? : Judaism and Israel's armed forces / by Stuart A Cohen.
    pages cm. – (Religion and international security)
 Includes bibliographical references and index.
 ISBN 978-1-4094-6637-6 (hardback) – ISBN 978-1-4094-6639-0
 (ebook) – ISBN 978-1-4094-6638-3 (epub) 1. Judaism and state. 2.
 Civil-military relations–Israel. 3. Military law (Jewish law) 4. War
 (Jewish law) 5. War–Religious aspects–Judaism. 6. Israel–Armed Forces.
 I. Title.
 BM538.S7C64 2013
 296.3'827--dc23
                                                                    2012048050
ISBN 9781409466376 (hbk)
ISBN 9781409466383 (ebk – PDF
ISBN 9781409466390 (ePUB – PDF)

Printed and bound in Great Britain
by MPG PRINTGROUP

Contents

Acknowledgements

The initiative for this book came from Professor Lee Marsden, the editor of Ashgate's series on Religion and International Security. It is a pleasure as well as a duty to thank him for his interest, and to express my gratitude to the entire staff at Ashgate for helping to bring the work to fruition.

Earlier versions of several chapters in this book originally appeared elsewhere, and thanks are due to those venues for their consideration. I also gratefully acknowledge the hospitality extended by both the University of Michigan's Frankel Center, where I presented an oral version of Chapter 9 in March 2012, and the conveners of the British International Studies Association Conference held at Edinburgh in June 2012, where I presented an oral version of Chapter 1.

Without in any way absolving myself of responsibility for the content of the following pages, this book attempts to incorporate the comments and criticisms received over the years to my analyses of the intersection between Judaism and Israel's armed forces. It also seeks to give due acknowledgement to the insights that I have derived from the work of other scholars who have also analyzed this fascinating phenomenon. I trust that I have done justice to them all.

I completed revising this manuscript in the summer of 2012, whilst also transferring to a new academic home. Far from interfering with my writing, the move to the recently founded Academic College at Ashkelon, Israel, acted as a stimulus, and I am indebted to my colleagues there for creating the ambience that makes it so.

My greatest debt, however, is to my wife and our family, who – not for the first time – have proven to be stimulating sources of information as well as encouragement. Hence, this book is dedicated to them.

To Tova and our family

May the Lord bless you and watch over you;
May the Lord make his face shine on you and be gracious to you;
May the Lord look kindly on you and grant you peace.

Numbers 6:24–6.

Chapter 1
Judaism in the IDF:
Parameters, Dynamics and Paradoxes

From a sociological perspective, the defining characteristic of the Israel Defense Force (IDF) is that it consists almost entirely of Jewish men and women. Nominally, all Israeli citizens are liable for conscript terms of two to three years at age 18 and, after their discharge, are also required to report for spells of reserve duty until middle age. In fact, however, military service by non-Jewish segments (Bedouin, Druze and Christians of varying denominations, who together comprise about 5 percent of Israel's total citizenry) is statistically immaterial. Muslim Arabs, who make up a quarter of the population and thus constitute the one gentile group with the potential to exert a significant impact on the IDF's religious demography, receive blanket draft exemptions and, a handful of volunteers apart, are consequently entirely absent from the ranks. Hence, to all intents and purposes, the IDF is an army of Jews.

The IDF is also a 'Jewish' army, in the sense that traditional Jewish themes and motifs form integral parts of its very texture. All military kitchens in Israel conform to traditional Jewish dietary requirements; the sabbath and Jewish holy days shape military schedules with respect to training and vacations; all burials in Jewish sections of official military cemeteries are conducted in accordance with traditional religious practice.[1] Almost every other major rite of passage in the Israeli military experience is also deliberately suffused with ceremonies and pageants designed to arouse profound Jewish connotations. For instance, at induction, new recruits receive a copy of the Old Testament, which religious conscripts necessarily consider to contain the word of God and which non-believers have been taught at school to regard as the formative text of Jewish civilization. Similarly evocative are the venues selected for the staging of passing out parades. On completion of basic training, for instance, each new cohort of paratroops is formally enrolled during the course of a torchlight ceremony held at 'the western wall' in Jerusalem. Since 2010, the same venue has also been used by the Golani infantry brigade. The location is well chosen. Quite apart from being located at the heart of the Old City where IDF troops covered themselves in glory during the Six Days War of 1967, the wall is also the sole remaining relic of the second temple destroyed by Roman legionnaires in the year 70ce, and hence a site of religious pilgrimage.

---

1   Families who desire a non-denominational burial have to intern the deceased in a private cemetery, such as those administered by some secular kibbutzim.

It is impossible to exaggerate the uniqueness of such phenomena, or indeed to disregard the revolution in Jewish history that they signify. In the period 1920–1940, when the Zionist movement established the embryonic fighting forces out of which the IDF was to emerge in 1948, 1,900 years had passed since the last previous occasion on which Jews had resorted to force in defense of their own polity: the ill-fated and short-lived Judean uprising against Rome launched in 135ce. Traumatized by the devastation and displacement which followed that military debacle, rabbinic scholars and spiritual guides had during the intervening centuries transformed the necessity for Jewish passivity into a virtue. Jewry's mission, they insisted with undiminished conviction, was to be entirely non-bellicose – even when threatened with physical destruction. Exile and powerlessness, after all, constituted Divine punishments for Israel's sins. Redemption, therefore, had to await the Almighty's pleasure, which would be signified by the advent of the Messiah. Any attempt to 'hasten the end of days' by taking up arms, even in self-defense, was ipso facto sinful and doomed to failure. Instead, as one fourteenth-century rabbi put it, the model for all Jewish action had to be the conciliatory strategy that, according to Genesis Chapter 33, was adopted by the patriarch Jacob prior to meeting his brother Esau. Hence:

> We should follow in the footsteps of our forefathers, that is, prepare to approach the children of Esau [i.e. gentiles] with gifts, and with humble language, and with prayer to God, may He be blessed. It is impossible for us to meet them in war, as it is said [Song of Songs 2:7; 3:5; 8:4]: 'I have abjured you, O daughters of Jerusalem, not to provoke war with the nations (cited, Ravitzky 1996: 227–8).

In the modern state of Israel, Jewish responses to that tradition have been disparate. Broadly speaking, four principal attitudes can be identified.

One is posited by the burgeoning 'ultra-orthodox' and fundamentalist (*haredi*) communities, a mélange of varying approaches to the State and its institutions that together make up about 11 percent of the Jewish population. Altogether committed to a lifestyle that is anti-modernist in its fidelity to time-honored practices and norms, *haredim* have for several decades now embellished traditional Judaism's non-martial teachings, especially by espousing doctrines that view study of the sacred texts to be a Jew's sole guarantee of God's protection. Translated into the language of political action, this tenet lies at the root of *haredi* demands that the Government of Israel continue to grant indefinite draft deferments to persons for whom '*torah* scholarship is their profession'.

That position is fiercely opposed by a second camp, consisting of 'secularists', who comprise less than 10 percent of Israel's Jewish population. Ideologically opposed to all intrusions of religion into public life, secularists are especially suspicious of any attempt to attach traditional Jewish meanings – positive or negative – to modern Israel's conscription policies. As far as they are concerned, soldiering is a civic obligation tout court, and as such one of the characteristics of the 'new Jew' that many of Zionism's founding fathers set out to fashion through a deliberate effort at social engineering.

Two groups contest the middle ground between the *haredi* and secularist extremities. One consists of persons identified in Israel as 'religious Zionists', who comprise some 12 to 15 percent of the Israeli Jewish population. Like 'modern orthodox' Jews in western diasporas, 'religious Zionists' are committed to the belief that the observance of traditional religious practices need not be inconsistent with integration into modern society. With specific reference to participation in Israel's defense, they accordingly explicitly reject the *haredi* hypothesis that national security is best guaranteed by devotion to study. At the same time, however, they also reject secularist efforts to empty military duty of all religious meaning. On the contrary, their belief that the establishment of the State of Israel constitutes a definitive sign of Divine grace ('the beginning of the flowering of our Redemption'), has led religious Zionists to argue that service in a framework designed to defend God's handiwork must ipso facto be considered a primary religious obligation. All that has to be ensured is that the IDF will create the conditions that will enable orthodox Jews to perform their service without compromising their adherence to the everyday practices and rituals (such as dietary laws and prayer) that are integral to traditional Jewish identity.

The latter, finally, is also of some concern to 'traditionalists', the remaining 50 to 55 percent of Jews, who in varying degrees retain an attachment to religious customs and rituals, even though they do not observe them with particular rigidity. Without necessarily sharing national–religious beliefs in the inherent sanctity of the IDF (although some do), they too expect the Force to display characteristics that are identifiably 'Jewish' and, even more, to operate in accordance with the mores that owe their origin to religious instruction.

Embryonic versions of these four approaches to military service were articulated in Israel from the very moment that the state came into existence in 1948. Ever since, politicians and ideologues have attempted to formulate accommodations between the rival camps – and have wrestled with the consequences of their failure to find a universally acceptable modus vivendi. However, whereas disputes over the intersection between religion and military service were once considered to be no more than a relatively subsidiary irritant to Israel's societal cohesion, troublesome but certainly not an issue of primary and pressing national importance, they have in recent decades assumed far greater and more urgent proportions. This book seeks to account for that transformation and to identify the reasons for the contemporary prominence of religious dimensions in the national security discourse. In that sense, the present study constitutes a sequel to my previous book on this topic (S. Cohen 1997), which inevitably requires updating.

Over the years, I have attempted to accomplish that task by writing several discreet studies on individual topics of relevance, most of which have appeared in either academic journals or edited volumes of essays. A selection of those papers is reproduced here, albeit with occasional editorial changes, not because they remain the latest word on their subjects, but because they serve two complementary purposes. First, they convey authentic echoes of the ticking clock and provide cameo portraits of the tensions that in Israel – as elsewhere – have periodically been injected into the public discourse by what some observers have termed the growing 'sacralization' of international politics (Sheikh 2012). Secondly, the individual papers also reflect the extent to which, since the mid-1990s, the meanings attached to Judaism have likewise been affected from time to time by the twists and turns of contemporary Israel's erratic path from war to peace – and back again. At that level, the book traces the way in which Judaism is arguably losing much of its singularity amongst the world's great religions. Once almost entirely quarantined from the influences exerted on doctrines and beliefs by the temptation to resort to armed force, Jews the world over now feel the effects of what most Israelis consider to be their need to resort to terrestrial power and military operations.

In many respects, that extended and still ongoing process can be attributed to influences that are transnational in scope (Fox and Sandler 2004: 83–111, Shah, Stepan and Duffy Toft 2012). Nevertheless, the idiosyncrasy of its expression has been shaped by the specific dynamics of the Israeli domestic context. The purpose of the remainder of this introduction is to indicate those which are especially relevant. It does not aim, therefore, to compress a survey of all Israeli society and its recent history into the space of a few pages. Rather, it seeks to highlight the developments that have exerted the most profound influences on the twin, and indeed mirror-like, processes discussed in greater detail in ensuing chapters: the growing intrusion of religion into Israel's security discourse; and the growing prominence of security-related issues in Israeli Judaism's religious thought.

Three trends deserve particular attention. One is the changing demographics of religious affiliation within the IDF; the second is the development of an entirely new corpus of military-related religious teachings and of an equally novel framework of military-related religious institutions explicitly tailored to meet the needs of observant members of Israel's armed forces; and the third is the emergence of several issues of religiously-based contention that threaten the IDF's long-term cohesion. Whilst necessarily related, these topics will here be treated sequentially.

The Changing Demographics of Religion in the IDF

Although the IDF Manpower Directorate, the body responsible for military personnel issues in Israel, does occasionally release random reports on the size and composition of the Force, it persistently refuses to comment on the proportions of Jewish conscripts, men and women, who can be categorized as 'religious' and 'secular'. Necessarily, therefore, assessments are in this area tentative and largely derived from other sources. Some figures are provided by the Ministry of Education, which publicizes the annual numbers of graduates from 'national–religious' and 'national' (that is, secular) high schools. More morbid and less comprehensive is the information that can be gleaned from the memorial biographies published in the national media whenever a soldier falls in battle or is otherwise killed. And then, of course, there is the simpler tool of personal observation which, although necessarily impressionistic, is especially useful in this case thanks to the conspicuity of the dress codes habitually observed by religious men (especially the skullcap) and women (skirts rather than slacks).

Superficially, these sources tell a tale of remarkable continuity. They indicate that, notwithstanding the fluctuations in overall Israeli demographics, as far as males are concerned, the proportion of 'religious' to 'non-religious' conscripts in the overall IDF complement has remained more or less constant ever since the 1950s, hovering between 13 and 17 percent. In other words, the contradictory effects produced by changing birth rates and immigration (whereas 'religious' couples tend to have larger than average families, most new immigrants since the 1980s have been non-observant) cancel each other out. At the end of 2012, and in keeping with overall population trends, 'secular' Jewish troops in the IDF seem still to outnumber those who are 'religious' by over five to one.

Closer inspection, however, reveals that the impression of consistency is deceptive. First, this is because the focus on the 'religious/secular' ratio amongst young males who do enlist masks the truly massive changes in the percentages of those who do *not* do so. In the 'secular' segment, the changes have been marginal. Certainly, 'draft avoidance' – a portmanteaux term that covers phenomena as different as conscientious objection, pleas of 'psychological unsuitability' and claims of 'physical incapacity' – became more common amongst secular high school graduates during and after the 1990s than had been the case in earlier decades. Even so, it remained a decidedly minority phenomenon. Whereas in the 1980s and 1990s all such categories – combined – amounted to 4 percent of the total number of non-draftees (that is, roughly 1 percent of the total of young males summonsed to duty), in 2009 the respective figures were still no more than 4 and 1.5 percent respectively (S. Cohen 2009: 65–6).

By contrast, the same period had witnessed nothing less than an explosion in the numbers of 'ultra-orthodox' (*haredi*) males who declare '[the study of] the *Torah* [the generic term for sacred Jewish texts] to be their profession' and on those grounds are excused by the Minister of Defense from the draft for an indefinite time. When originally sanctioned by David Ben-Gurion, Israel's first and most influential Prime Minister and Minister of Defense (he held both posts for most of the period 1948–1963), that concession to *haredi* priorities was considered to be only a minor infringement of the rule of universal conscription. Especially was that so since it could be justified by two extenuating circumstances. One was the need to repair some of the ravages that the Holocaust had recently wreaked on Jewry's scholarly traditions. Another was that the concession was originally restricted to just 400 male students. But, in a trajectory that parallels the growing power and cohesion of political parties representing *haredi* interests, a revival that Ben-Gurion never envisaged, the numbers have grown exponentially. The sum total of *haredi* deferments rose to 8,257 in 1977, the year that *haredi* parties first joined a government coalition, and jumped to 16,000 in 1985, to 30,000 in 1999 and to over 50,000 (over half aged 18–21) by 2011 (The Knesset Center for Research and Information 2012: 23). At the end of the first decade of the millennium, persons in this category accounted for over half of the *total* number of Jewish non-draftees, equivalent to 13 percent of the overall potential recruitment pool.[2] Extrapolations from junior and high school registration statistics show that the latter figure could reach 25 percent by 2020 (Ben-David 2009: 141).

True, several attempts have been made to reverse that trend. For instance, in 1999 the IDF agreed that *haredi* males who wished to retain their traditional lifestyles and yet not apply for draft exemptions (principally because they lacked the intellectual and psychological prerequisites for devotion to a life of uninterrupted scholarship in Talmudic academies) would be allowed to enlist in their own segregated unit. In practice, what this meant was that soldiers in 'Battalion 97', otherwise designated *Netzach Yehudah* ('Eternal Judah') or, more popularly, the *Nachal Haredi*, serve under conditions unknown anywhere else in the IDF. They are entirely sequestered from females, allowed regular contact with *haredi* religious mentors, supplied with food that meets the most stringent standards of conformity with orthodox Jewish dietary laws, and permitted to retain elements of their own dress code (Drori 2005b). A second initiative has been the establishment of a service track known as *Shachar* (an acronym for *sherut haredim*; 'haredi service', but which also translates as 'dawn'), which assures more mature *haredi* men (generally aged 24–27) that they will be given military assignments that also provide them with a technical training which, on discharge, they can put to use in the civilian market. Yet a third option, contained in legislation passed by the *Knesset* in 2002 (the 'Tal Law'), and renewed in a slightly revised form in 2011, allowed *haredim* to enlist as individuals in regular units at the age of 24 for drastically abbreviated terms of service.

Optimists take considerable heart from reports indicating a growing willingness amongst *haredi* young men to take advantage of the offers thus presented. According to figures compiled on the basis of reports submitted by the IDF's Manpower Directorate, an audit compiled by the Israeli parliament's Research and Information Center found that enlistment in the *Nachal Haredi*, for instance, had climbed from 90 per annum in the first years of the new millennium to 250 in 2007, 347 in 2009 and 380 in 2011. *Shachar*'s popularity rose even more sharply. This service model, which began as the brainchild of the commander of the Israel Air Force in 2007, when it catered to just 38 conscripts who enlisted as technicians, has since been adopted by several other branches, including Intelligence, Computer Services and the Navy. As a result, enlistment in *Shachar* jumped to 382 in 2009 and to 608 in 2010. The following year, 450 *haredi* youngsters aged 15 to 18 also registered for a pre-conscription program entitled *Shachar Tov* (lit: 'good dawn'; The Knesset Center for Research 2012: 19).

---

2   Whilst the proportion of *haredim* in the total number of non-serving Israeli males rose from 8.4 percent to 13 percent between 2005 and 2011, the equivalent figures for all other categories (including persons resident abroad and excused service for health reasons or because they possessed a criminal record) declined in the same period from 14.8 percent to 12.1 percent. The Knesset Center for Research and Information 2012: 12.

Enthusiasts in the IDF are confident that these figures can be doubled during the course of the next decade. But even if that projection proves true, and even if all the current statistics are correct (a matter very much complicated by difficulties in determining who is a 'true' *haredi*, who is a fellow traveler, and who a dropout from that community), birth rates will ensure that the overall demographics of the IDF will become yet more lopsided than they already are. Even as matters stand, the rate of *haredi* non-enlistment makes a mockery of the entire notion of equitable burden sharing inherent in conscription. Specifically, of the estimated 7,500 *haredi* 18 year-old males officially liable for service in 2011, just 1,282 were in fact drafted. Confronted with that situation, in February 2012 most members of Israel's Supreme Court considered that they had no option but to declare intolerable the inequalities embedded in the Tal Law. By a majority of nine to six, the judges gave the Government less than a year to come up with alternative provisions. As the Epilogue to this book argues (below pp. 169–179), the repercussions of the failure to meet that deadline could – in the long-term – affect Israel's draft policies in their entirety.

A gender breakdown of recent enlistment figures likewise undermines the impression of continuity in service patters over the last 60 years. Overall, it is true, today – as in the past – by far the majority of females drafted into the IDF come from 'secular' backgrounds. Nevertheless, the proportions are changing. Until the late 1990s, on average some 90 to 95 percent of the annual total of Jewish female graduates from 'national–religious' high schools, like their *haredi* counterparts, performed no military service whatsoever. Instead, and often under instruction from their rabbinic mentors (who on this point very much agreed with *haredi* religious authorities), women from this sector claimed – and were granted – exemption from the draft on the grounds that military duty would conflict with their religious lifestyles. As an alternative, a high percentage performed a year or two of voluntary civic service, an example that very few *haredi* women followed.

In recent years, however, two new trends have become apparent. For one thing, increasing numbers of female graduates of 'national [that is, secular]' high schools are claiming, and receiving, exemptions from service on 'incompatibility' grounds (IDF sources report that the figure is as high as 40 percent). On the other hand, and far more remarkably, despite the persistence of mainstream orthodox rabbinic objections to female conscription, by 2010 between a quarter and a third of female graduates of 'national–religious' high schools were nevertheless enlisting in the IDF in one capacity or another (Budai-Heiman 2012, Sela 2012). In 2013, the proportion was expected to rise to almost 50 percent. One result of this development was a significant rise in requests from women on service for spiritual guidance and religious instruction. In response, ever since 2005 the IDF chaplaincy has added females (albeit in very limited numbers) to its complement of 'religious affairs officers'.

In the male segment, too, the figures repay closer scrutiny. What the bare statistics report is that impressively high proportions – some 85 percent – of graduates of 'national' (secular) as well as 'national–religious' high schools continue to answer the call to duty (Soen 2008). In other words, both segments have proved remarkably immune to the mood of post-modernism/post-materialism/

post-Zionism thought to be sweeping the country when, in April 1997, the IDF released a panic-stricken warning on a dip in 'motivation to service'.

What the reports on the recovery of the conscription rates do not tell us, however, is in which capacities 'religious' and 'secular' troops tend to serve. The answer to that question can only be obtained through observation – but nevertheless seems to be unequivocal. Over the past quarter of a century, a shift of truly massive proportions has taken place in the sociological architecture of the IDF. Prior to the 1980s, its combat units were for the most part manned – and, even more so, commanded – by graduates of the secular school system, most of whom were of *ashkenazi* (that is, western and European) Jewish families. Moreover, sons of secular *kibbutzim* figured especially prominently – and in vastly disproportionate numbers – in the ranks of junior officers in the ground forces, in training courses for fighter pilots, parachutists, and commando units, and in the rosters of persons killed in action whilst 'commanding from the front' during battle (Gal 1986: 83). That is no longer the case. 'Secular' troops from *ashkenazi* and bourgeois backgrounds seem now be under represented in IDF combat units. Instead, and in increasing numbers, they have gravitated towards 'hi-tech' and white-collar logistical and combat support units, which have of late enormously expanded in size and prominence thanks to the IDF's growing (over?) reliance on state-of-the-art C4I systems.

Casualty figures, especially as audited by Levy (2006, 2009, 2012), show that as from the mid-1990s the gaps thus created in frontline ranks began to be filled by groups that were once considered 'peripheral' components of the IDF's complement. These consisted of population segments whose contribution to Israel's battlefield victories had for long been considered subsidiary: oriental (*mizrachi*) Jews; Druze soldiers; new immigrants (both from the former USSR and from Ethiopia); and – above all – graduates (*ashkenazi* and *mizrachi* alike) of the 'national–religious' educational system. More recently, that development has gathered even greater momentum, especially with respect to 'national–religious' youngsters. Long gone are the days when Zionist leaders could charge that members of this community were noticeable by their absence from the rosters of the persons who had given their lives to defend the *Yishuv*.[3] On the contrary, the sight of a knitted skullcap (*kippah serugah*), the most recognizable hallmark of male national–religious Jewry, has become common throughout the IDF. It is especially conspicuous at graduation parades of junior officers in infantry brigades where a rough count indicates that national–religious males now constitute about half of the total (that is, three times their demographic proportion). Their presence in senior echelons of the IDF, although not as dominant, is also obtrusive. The promotion of religiously observant officers to the General Staff, unheard of before 1998, now raises few eyebrows. One (Major General Yair Naveh) was in 2010 appointed deputy Chief of Staff. Female

---

3   Thirty years after they were first enunciated, religious Zionist leaders still winced at Ben-Gurion's remarks to that effect. See the introduction by one of the formative influences on national–religious pre-military education (Rabbi M.Z. Nerya, 1913–1995) to Raz 1966. I am indebted to Rabbi Yonatan Cohen for this reference.

members of the national religious community have likewise been promoted to high military station. In 2011, Brigadier General Rachel Tevet-Wiesel, thereto president of the Central and Air Force District Military Tribunal, became the first orthodox Jewess to be appointed the Chief of Staff's Advisor on Women's Issues, a post originally created 11 years earlier to replace the office of CO the Women's Corps.

Intellectual and Institutional Innovations

Adopting what is essentially a *cui bono?* focus, one prominent school of Israeli sociology attributes current changes in the IDF's demographic profile to an amalgam whose primary ingredients are economic interests and political ambitions (Levy 2007a). By contrast, the present analysis stresses the role played by intellectual and institutional developments as agencies of change, in religious and secular communities alike. The exponential growth in the numbers of *haredi* draft deferments, for instance, cannot be understood without reference to the refinement of traditional doctrines that prioritize *torah* study over any other occupation (not least, military service) and to the consequent establishment and expansion of the massive Talmudic seminaries, both developments that have facilitated the emergence of 'a society of scholars' in that community (Friedman 1991). The dramatic drop in the proportion of *kibbutz* youngsters serving in combat units must be contextualized along similar intellectual and institutional lines, in this case by noting the dilution of the collectivist ideology that once fuelled the *kibbutz* movement and the dismantlement in Israel of many of the other structures traditionally associated with the construction of a socialist society. Precisely the same parameters need to be employed in order to understand the shifts that have taken place in the service patterns of national religious youth.

Amongst this segment, changes in intellectual attitudes towards military service have been especially remarkable. For almost two millennia, after all, the greatest minds in Jewry's crowded gallery of religious codifiers and philosophers had overwhelmingly avoided passing any comment whatsoever on matters military. As Chapter 6 (below pp. 85–106) illustrates, a review of the current scholarship being produced by the spiritual leaders of Israel's national religious community reveals an entirely different picture. Deliberately overthrowing traditional bounds of restraint in this area, rabbis – many of whom possess extensive military experience of their own – have in recent decades added an entire corpus of military-related decisions and commentaries to the traditional orthodox canon. Given both the comparative novelty of this endeavor and the dearth of traditional precedents, it comes as little surprise to discover that rabbinic approaches to subjects of military concern are especially disparate (below pp. 143–168). Lack of unanimity, however, has often acted as a spur to further enquiry. In so doing, it has also had practical consequences. By providing a mass of spiritual guidance and ritual instruction in an area long virtually devoid of both, those scholars have removed what had once been a major brake on whatever enthusiasm national–religious youngsters, and their parents, may have otherwise felt about the prospect of military service (S. Cohen 2012).

Institutional developments, many of them simultaneous, have exerted the same effect. This particular strand in our story begins with the establishment of the IDF's military chaplaincy, which after some initial experimentation assumed its present form as early as 1949 (Kampinsky 2008). From its inception, this framework was expected to perform two parallel but distinct roles. One was to communicate the rudiments of Jewish values and teachings to the complement as a whole, secular as well as religious, and thereby serve as a mechanism for troop cohesion. At the same time, however, the IDF chaplaincy was expected to serve the specific interests of the minority of troops who desire to be religiously observant. These did not require 'outreach' programs that focused on basic courses of instruction in Jewish values and customs. Rather, what orthodox soldiers needed were proofs that enlistment would not prevent them from maintaining basic standards of observance. Hence, the chaplaincy had to ensure that kitchens on every military installation would observe Jewish dietary laws and that every military base would contain the facilities (synagogues, prayer books, etcetera) that observant soldiers require on a regular basis. Absent assurances to that effect, there was always the danger that they might resist the entire notion of a 'people's army' – either by downing arms (as did two military orderlies as early as September 1948, when commanded to cook a hot meal on the sabbath; Ostfeld 1994: 278) or by renewing demands for the establishment of segregated 'religious' units.

During its formative period, the IDF chaplaincy focused most of its attention on the second of those priorities. Primarily, that choice was made by Rabbi (hereafter R.) Shlomo Goren, the first and most influential of all IDF Chief Rabbis, who held the office from 1949 until 1971. Although certainly not insensitive to the needs of the non-observant majority, Goren considered it is duty to devote most of the limited resources at his disposal to satisfying the interests of the observant minority and ensuring that religious troops could serve, as equals, in as wide a range of IDF units as possible. Two of Goren's most recent successors, R. Yisrael Weiss (IDF Chief Rabbi 2003–2006) and R. Avichai Rontski (2007–2010), by contrast, sought to pursue a more even-handed approach. Goren's battles, they maintained, had in fact been won. What was now required was a program of instruction and leadership that would ensure that the rabbinate also addressed the needs of traditionalists, that large bloc of the complement who required the provision, not just of physical facilities for religious observance but, more insistently, spiritual guidance and comfort before, during and after battle. R. Weiss responded by establishing in 2004 a 'Combat Values Branch' (*Anaf Erkhei Torat Ha-Lekhimah*) largely staffed by charismatic lecturers (in 2006 it was more modestly re-designated the 'Jewish Awareness Department'; *Ha-Makhlakah le-Toda'ah Yehudit*; Kampinsky 2012).

With even greater success, R. Rontski recruited a new breed of military chaplains, deliberately headhunting ordained rabbis who were also graduates of combat units, and hence capable of empathizing directly with the troops in the field – an attribute emphasized by the fact that IDF rabbis do not observe the Geneva Convention's rules prohibiting military chaplains from bearing arms. During the course of a lengthy interview that he gave to the popular IDF weekly *Ba-Machaneh* ('In Camp'), the current IDF Chief Rabbi, General Rafi Peretz, a qualified combat pilot, whilst vigorously denying charges of 'missionary' activity, nevertheless made it clear that he too intends to maintain 'a dialogue' with all shades of religious opinion in the ranks (Peretz 2011).

One of the circumstances that has allowed the IDF chaplaincy in recent years to shift so much of its attention to 'traditionalists' and even 'secularists' within the Force is that soldiers who come from religiously observant backgrounds are now being serviced by alternative frameworks. Especially influential in this respect are two sets of educational institutions: 'arrangement' academies of Jewish study (*yeshivot hesder*) and 'pre-conscription Torah colleges' (*mekhinot ha-kedam tzeva'iyot ha-toraniyot*), both of which enjoy IDF sanction and cooperation.

The *hesder* (lit. 'arrangement') academies, whose five-year timetable (involving less than two years of conscript duty and more than three years of academic study) is described in some detail in Chapter 4 (below pp. 59–72), is the older of these two sets of institutions, and was initiated in 1964. However, what began as an experiment, limited to just one academy with a total enrolment of 20 students, has over time mushroomed into a much larger program. Nine such establishments were founded between 1967 and 1979; three more in the 1980s; and another 40 since 1990. Official government websites now list 65 *hesder yeshivot*, located across the length and breadth of the land, with an annual intake of 1,600 students, who together thus comprise about 20 percent of the total numbers of all national–religious high school male graduates (The Knesset Center for Research 2012: 20). During the past decade, a similar program has been instituted for women, who are now able to choose between three academies (termed *midrashot*) of their own (Rossman-Stollman 2005).

Even more precipitous has been the growth of the pre-conscription (*mekhinah*) program. This requires graduates of national–religious high schools to serve full three-year conscript terms as regular soldiers, but permits them to postpone their enlistment for a calendar year – during which time they undergo an intensive course of training in both physical fitness and Jewish values in the *mekhinah* of their choice. Although the first *mekhinah* did not open its doors until 1988, with an enrolment of barely a dozen students, this program now rivals the *hesder* in popularity. By the year 2000 there already existed 15 *mekhinot*, since when a further dozen have been added (as have 12 others that cater to secular or mixed religious–secular youth). Annual enrolment in the religious *mekhinot* now tops 1,800 males per year, almost a third of the annual sum total of male graduates of the national–religious high school system. Moreover, here too changes in the service preferences of women graduates of national–religious schools are also beginning to have an effect and 2006 saw the foundation of the first *mekhinah* for religious women intending to enlist in the IDF.

Although most male graduates of national–religious high schools still enlist individually, and hence not through either the *hesder* or *mekhinah* tracks, the two programs have clearly impacted on service patterns throughout this segment of the population. *Hesder* conscripts, who were originally assigned to units in largely homogeneous groups, have traditionally been conspicuous components of the IDF armored corps and of its four principal infantry brigades. In each case, their presence has acted as a magnet for other religious soldiers, whose willingness to volunteer for those formations has been augmented by the knowledge that they will be serving in the company of a large number of persons who come from a similar background and who share similar interests and lifestyles.

Mekhinah graduates, whose timetable does not require them to enlist in groups, fulfill a different function. They act as individual role models, whose record of excellence as new recruits, NCOs and junior officers sets standards which all their brothers-in-arms – especially those who likewise come from religious backgrounds – strive to emulate. The bar is very high indeed. An internal IDF study published in 2010 revealed that that almost 80 percent of the graduates of religious *mekhinot* volunteer for service in combat units (twice the national average) and that 45 percent (nine times the national average!) accept invitations to attend the IDF junior officers' course, a commitment that requires them to 'sign on' for an extra year of (salaried) duty ('B' 2010: 55). The record of *Bnei David*, the flagship religious *mekhinah*, is especially remarkable. On its twentieth anniversary, celebrated in 2008, its secretariat reported that of its first 1,000 graduates 41 had served as pilots, 70 in reconnaissance squads, 400 in other elite field units and 200 in the armor or artillery corps. Half of all graduates had become junior officers.

Issues of Contention

In 1993, when Chapter 4 (below pp. 59–72) was first published, public reactions to the *hesder* program provided little inkling of the storm of controversy that the framework was soon to arise. On the contrary, the dominant tone of most comments on the *hesder* was acclaim, which reached an apogee in 1991 when a committee established by the Minister of Education awarded the *hesder* framework the prestigious Israel Prize, the country's highest award for contributions to the texture of national life. The citation, proclaimed at a ceremony held on Independence Day in the presence of the President, the Prime Minister and numerous other dignitaries, applauded the degree to which *hesder* troops

> fulfill the Zionist vision in their own unique fashion, by combining the scroll [i.e. study of the sacred texts] with the sword and are sons of the *torah* as well as men of valor. Graduates of the program have excelled in their self-sacrifice and play a full role in the life of the country and in carrying out whatever missions the state demands (Ministry of Education 1991: 24–5).

Since the mid-1990s, however, much of the tide of opinion has turned. True, the military competence displayed by individual national–religious troops and officers still commands considerable respect, as does the image of the *hesder* soldier who combines study and military service.[4] Nevertheless, the *hesder* and *mekhinah* programs have become subjects of increasingly vocal criticism. Repeatedly, senior figures in public life, including some retired senior officers, have explicitly warned that the high profile of national–religious soldiers in the IDF, together with their concentration in homogeneous *hesder* units, constitutes a threat to the military's character as a non-denominational agency of government (Ash. Cohen 2009).

Swings of that dimension in the pendulum of attitudes cannot be attributed merely to the vagaries of mood to which Israeli politicians and their public are notoriously prone. They also reflect several more deep-seated fears, primary amongst which is the negative influence that religious practices and themes might be exerting on the military's integrative societal function. This is an especially sensitive issue, not least because it touches on what is widely considered to be the IDF's cardinal ethos: its status as a 'people's army' which, by virtue of universal conscription, serves to unite all classes of Israel's divergent (Jewish) population. As Chapter 8 (below pp. 127–142) shows, Ben-Gurion was from the first insistent on the retention of that character, and as early as 1949 dismissed with notable asperity all suggestions to reconsider the integration of religious and non-religious troops in common combat units. Sixty years later, however, the very fulfillment of Ben-Gurion's vision, as indicated by the growing proportion of national–religious combat troops, is causing it to be subject to increasing review.

One cause of concern is the possible political implications of the high proportion of ideologically committed troops; another, their alleged impact on IDF operational behavior; and yet a third their relations with non-observant servicemen and servicewomen who still constitute the majority of the overall complement. The concluding paragraphs of this introduction will briefly summarize each of those issues and provide an assessment of their viability.

The Political Implications

Observers began to ponder the possible political implications of the growing prominence of religion as a factor in the IDF's comportment in September 1993, when the government led by Yitzchak Rabin revolutionized Israel's security policy by publicly recognizing the PLO as a negotiating partner to which, in the form of the Palestine Authority, it was prepared to grant autonomous control over portions of the West Bank and Gaza Strip. National–religious reactions were especially critical. No

---

4　Indeed, in February 2003 the Israeli philatelic service marked the fortieth anniversary of the founding of the programme by issuing a stamp depicting both the main campus of the first *yeshivat hesder* and two young men, one in uniform the other draped in a prayer shawl, poring over a Talmudic text.

sooner had the ink dried on the Oslo agreements than a bevy of prominent rabbis – the most illustrious of whom was Goren, who was by then in retirement – published a manifesto that categorically prohibited the surrender of Jewish dominion over any part of the Land of Israel. More threateningly, that document also called upon religious troops to refuse orders to participate in operations designed to dismantle a settlement or IDF base prior to its transfer to Palestinian jurisdiction (S. Cohen 1997: 129–31, Inbari 2012: 59–71). Two other milestones followed. First, in November 1995 Prime Minister Rabin was assassinated by an IDF reservist who had graduated from a *hesder* academy and who claimed to have acted under the inspiration of rabbinic instruction. Ten years later, the Prime Minister of the day, Ariel Sharon, announced Israel's decision to 'disengage' unilaterally from the Gaza Strip and to dismantle the Jewish settlements located there and in northern Samaria. Once again, there was a flurry of rabbinic denunciations and exhortations to disobey orders, which this time were accompanied by efforts to get national–religious reservists to sign proclamations warning that, in the last resort, they would obey their rabbis rather than their commanding officers.

Thus far, experience indicates that the fears thus generated, culminating in dire warnings of a religiously inspired revolt by the IDF rank and file, have been almost entirely unfounded (Bick 2007). As Chapter 7 shows (below pp. 109–126), even in 2005 the mountain of pamphlets calling on national–religious troops to refuse to participate in the disengagement from Gaza, produced a tiny molehill. Testifying to the *Knesset*'s Foreign Affairs and Defense Committee in September 2005, a month after completing the operation, the then Chief of the IDF General Staff, Lieutenant General Dan Chalutz, stated that just 63 soldiers had been placed on trial for refusing orders during the operation (50 conscripts – 24 of whom served in the framework of the *yeshivot hesder*, five petty officers, three other ranks in professional service, and five reservists). Literally tens of thousands of others, including numerous national–religious servicemen and women, had carried out their duties without flinching. Prophecies of doom, in other words, were proven mistaken. Although undoubtedly tormented by disengagement, the vast majority of national–religious rabbis had ultimately preached the priority of maintaining national unity. And although many of their students had clearly experienced serious misgivings, in the last analysis they too prioritized the national interest (that is, subordination to the civil authority) over religious inclination. As one influential rabbinic principal of a *hesder* academy informed his students on the eve of the disengagement operation:

> It is obligatory to obey military orders, even though the Land of Israel is our land, every inch of which it is a religious and Zionist duty to settle. It is obligatory to obey military orders, even if they mean destroying our own house or that of our kinsfolk. It is an obligation to do so because that is the backbone of our common existence. Any other course involves tearing society to shreds. It is an obligation to do so because a country in which there is no norm of orderly government and obedience to commands is in danger of extinction (Cherlow 2010: 108).

Common sense cautions against placing too much reliance on a repetition of that precedent. There exists no guarantee that national–religious troops would display a similar rate of compliance should an Israeli government ever decide to implement a withdrawal from all or part of the West Bank. The latter, after all, encompasses Judea and Samaria, regions that lie in the very heart of the Holy Land and that therefore exercise a hold on Jewish attachments far greater than Gaza ever did. Not incidentally, they are also home to a significant number of middle rank national–religious officers, whose growing numbers will in any case make it increasingly difficult for the IDF to juggle the units involved in settlement evacuation (as it reportedly did in 2005) and thereby minimize the number of potentially disaffected soldiers involved in the 'inner circle' of dismantlement operations. Even so, as matters stand, warnings that national–religious soldiers might en masse refuse to take part in future territorial withdrawals remain entirely speculative. Only isolated handfuls have declared their intention to do so.[5] Hence, absent concrete evidence to the contrary, there is still no reason to consider national–religious soldiers any more prone to political disaffection than other segments of the IDF's complement. Senior echelons in the IDF certainly do not seem to think so, which is why the religious identity of soldiers and officers has in no way influenced decisions concerning their promotions.

Operational Behavior

Fears that the changing demographics of the IDF might be affecting its operational behavior must also be placed in perspective.

First, there is the historical background. In conformity with military chaplaincies throughout history, the IDF rabbinate has always considered one of its principal tasks to be the maintenance of troop morale at moments of mortal danger. From the very beginning of his tenure as chief military chaplain, R. Goren consequently sought to provide spiritual encouragement to soldiers in the field and instill them with faith in eventual victory. For the most part, his efforts were confined to inserting a message of encouragement in the flyleaf of the copies of the Bible that every new recruit received on induction and to giving occasional pep talks at individual bases. As Chapter 5 shows, however (below p. 76), far more dramatic was the address that he delivered on national radio during the tense first hours of the Six Days War of 1967, which resonated with citations from Deuteronomy Chapter 20, Judges Chapter 7, and Psalms.

In this sphere, too, Goren's successors have taken matters several institutional steps further. Hence, instead of being a sporadic phenomenon, rabbinic exhortations to show courage have become persistent features of the military timetable. In part, that message is conveyed during the course of informal talks that teachers in the *yeshivot* and *mekhinot* are invited to give when they visit their students on service, itself a common occurrence. More widely, the same message is conveyed through

---

5   For one such demonstration, in December 2009, see below p. 120.

the activities arranged by the military rabbinate's 'Combat Values Branch' and its successor, the 'Jewish Awareness Department'.

At one level, these developments have produced nothing more serious than intra-IDF turf wars, prompting complaints by senior officers in the Education Corps that the military rabbinate is infringing on areas of activity that lie four-square within their domain.[6] Far more fundamental, however, have been the concerns expressed, amongst others by a CO of the IDF's Manpower Directorate on the eve of his retirement, to the effect that the Force might soon have to confront a religious 'takeover' (Zamir 2011; see also Gal 2012).

Some secularists in the Israel general public have added a further dimension to that warning. Protesting that the military rabbinate is using its influence to inject a religious dimension into Israel's strategic outlook and behavior, they have accused recent incumbents of the post of Chief IDF chaplain of exacerbating tensions between Israeli and Palestinians by depicting the relationship in terms of a confrontation between rival faiths. Those charges became especially rife during and immediately after Operation Cast Lead in 2009 – so much so that they became items of international media interest. Thus, a lengthy article entitled 'A Religious War in Israel's Army', published in *The New York Times* on March 21 2009, quoted one soldier as saying that in Gaza:

> the rabbinate brought in a lot of booklets and articles and their message was very clear: We are the Jewish people, we came to this land by a miracle, God brought us back to this land and now we need to fight to expel the non-Jews who are interfering with our conquest of this holy land. This was the main message, and the whole sense many soldiers had in this operation was of a religious war.

Testimony such as this has created an atmosphere in which it has been possible to infer that heightened rabbinical influences over troop behavior, together with the new sociology of the IDF, might have unleashed the trigger-happy 'proclivities' of some soldiers in their confrontations with Palestinians (Levy 2008). As far as national–religious troops are concerned, however, that argument carries little conviction. There exists no empirical evidence proving that units with an exceptionally high proportion of national–religious soldiers and officers (such as the infantry brigades) are responsible for more Palestinian casualties than others (such as the air force and artillery). Moreover, studies of the content of current rabbinical teachings on warfare indicate that – contrary to much caricature – the messages imparted by the second generation of national–religious spiritual leaders are no more bellicose than those of their predecessors, and in some cases significantly less so (Lubitch 2009). All that has changed, perhaps, is that the discourse now attracts considerably more publicity than was the case in the past.

------

6   These complaints were investigated, and in large measure verified, by the State Comptroller and Ombudsman 2012: 1599–1626.

Troop Cohesion

Whereas fears that the growing prominence of national–religious troops might be undermining both the IDF's political neutrality and its record of operational ethics thus appear to be highly exaggerated, the same cannot be said of charges that the IDF's changing demographics are adversely affecting interpersonal relations within the military.

This is a new departure. After all, for many years, analyses of the role of religion in Israeli military service depicted its social impact in terms that conveyed an overall impression of harmony. Common service was said to mitigate the stresses otherwise generated by intra-Jewish dissension in Israel, enabling both observant and non-observant segments of society to sublimate their separate interests within a military setting that tightened their communal bonds (Rolbant 1970: 154). A more updated review, however, necessitates significant qualifications. One obvious reason is that altogether recent years have witnessed the steady demise of the old 'consociational' spirit, a process itself brought about by the different ways in which traditional and non-traditional Israelis have responded to the cultural climates of recent decades. To this must be added the more specific influence exerted by the territorial conquests of 1967. By the 1980s it was already apparent that the drive to settle the new areas had injected an element of messianic purposefulness into the consciousness of many national–religious Israelis, which growing proportions of their secular fellow citizens found discomfiting (Ash. Cohen and Susser 2010).

In a far more specific sense, however, the current level of secular–religious dissonance in the IDF reflects growing differences in the educational frameworks attended by the two segments of the complement prior to their enlistment (Lieberman 2004). Thus, whereas in the non-religious community the mixed gender day school still predominates, the national–religious world has witnessed the proliferation of single sex schools, many of the most highly regarded of which (*yeshivot tichoniyot* [for boys] and *ulpanot* [for girls]) are also residential. Furthermore, national–religious schoolchildren participate in a thriving network of their own youth movements (*B'nei Akivah*, *Ezra*, Religious Scouts), most of which also maintain gender segregation.

Attendance at this multilayered system of exclusively orthodox educational frameworks produces a cocoon-like effect. This, it transpires, may not be the best preparation for coping with the societal challenges posed by military service, since it accustoms national–religious teenagers, of both sexes, to patterns of behavior (gender relationships, language, dress and entertainment) that are peculiarly their own. Not until enlistment will they have any meaningful contact with secular contemporaries raised in a vastly different milieu.

Reactions vary. Almost a quarter of the graduates of national–religious high school graduates welcome the opportunity to break out of the mold, and become non-observant during the course of their military service. But many more undergo a process of retrenchment. A study of the communications that pass back and forth between religious conscripts and their spiritual mentors (many of which are posted on web sites) reveals an almost obsessive concern with the preservation of a way of life to which military service seems to present a threat. That explains why most of the communications focus on questions of personal conduct, amongst the most popular of which are: the conditions required for prayer services; the preservation of the traditional code of inter-gender relationships in the cramped conditions of military vehicles; and even forms of everyday speech. In each of these areas, what principally worries the troops (and, it must be added, their parents) is the corrosive danger that contact with the secular world might exert on their traditional mores. As Chapter 8 (below pp. 127–142) demonstrates, one of the mechanisms that they develop in order to avoid that danger is to articulate their distinctiveness and to insist on it being acknowledged. Within that context, size certainly matters. The higher the numbers of national–religious personnel in a unit, the more likely they are to be recognized as constituting a segmented section of the complement.

True, the IDF has always sought to mitigate the most blatant of such schismatic influences by fostering frameworks that might accommodate troops of very different shades of religiosity. Most regularly, even non-observant servicemen and women are exposed to orthodox Jewish rituals and practices, such as attendance at a festive meal welcoming the advent of the sabbath on Friday nights. But the overall impact of such measures seems to be only marginal. Whatever feelings of affinity might be attained through the sharing of rituals seem to be transitory and limited almost entirely to the time spent in uniform. In the terms coined by MacCoun (1993), the distinction between 'task cohesion' and 'social cohesion' thus becomes especially stark. Religious and secular troops in a single unit certainly share what he calls a commitment 'to achieving a goal that requires the collective efforts of the group' and are motivated 'to coordinate their efforts as a team to achieve that goal [task cohesion]'. But they do not necessarily 'like each other, prefer to spend their social time together, enjoy each other's company, and feel emotionally close to one another [social cohesion]'. On the contrary, observation indicates that once religious and non-religious personnel leave the military framework, they revert to their separate lifestyles.

One further fissiparous circumstances warrants attention. Since the early 1990s over 1,000,000 immigrants from the former Soviet Union have arrived in Israel. Contrary to most previous waves of immigrants, newcomers from the FSU have actively resisted the 'melting pot' ethos. Instead, and by means of Russian language theaters, newspapers and social clubs, they actively seek to retain and perpetuate their cultural traditions. And whilst the majority seeks classification as 'Jewish' in terms of ethnic affiliation, a significant minority does not. Indeed, several thousand members of the FSU community in Israel proudly proclaim themselves to be Christians.

Thanks to conscription, those preferences have affected the sociological composition of the IDF. Ever since the late 1990s, FSU immigrants and their offspring have comprised at least 10 percent of every annual cohort of new recruits (sometimes more) thus adding yet another distinctive hue to the mosaic of which the Force is composed (Eiskovits 2006). Indeed, every year about 200 new inductees of FSU origin declare themselves to be adherents of the Russian Orthodox Church, and hence insist on swearing the Oath of Allegiance to the IDF on the New Testament (copies of which it is the duty of the Military Rabbinate to supply). Even though their dispersal amongst various units prevents members of this segment from becoming a distinctive element in the Force, it is surely only a matter of time before they too will require that the IDF provides them with their own religious facilities.

A more opaque 'religious' boundary results from the fact that roughly one third of the 5–6,000 FSU immigrants who enlist in the IDF every year, are known to be sons and daughters of gentile mothers. As such, even if they do not declare themselves to be Christian, they are not recognized as Jews by traditional Jewish law [*halakhah*]. Instead, they seem condemned to go through their military lives in a state of uncomfortable liminality. By virtue of their performance of military duty, they can claim to have undertaken what they and many members of the general Israeli public regard as the most significant rite of passage to identification with the Jewish state and all it represents in terms of Jewish identity and survival. Yet, because they are still officially 'non-Jewish', they are not recognized as fully integrated members of the Jewish–Israeli collectivity. One consequence is that the official rabbinate, which by law possesses an exclusive right to register and conduct Jewish marriages, will refuse to do so for these persons as long as their status remains unchanged. Another, which affects considerably fewer individuals but possesses symbolic overtones that are even more pertinent to the subject of the present chapter, is that – even if killed in action – their right to be buried in cemeteries reserved for Jewish IDF soldiers will be questioned (Shaviv 1994).

Recognizing the abnormality of that situation, and indeed its immorality, General Elazar Stern, then CO of the IDF Manpower Directorate and himself an observant Jew, in the late 1990s established a framework (named *Nativ* ['path']) that would enable men and women in service to undertake, during the course of their conscript terms, a program of instruction that would culminate in their conversion to Judaism by an orthodox rabbinic tribunal (Stern 2009). But notwithstanding the considerable efforts and funds invested in putting together the program and negotiating its approval by the military hierarchy, the results have not (yet) reached expectations, and only a fraction of the potential target audience has in fact followed the course through to its conclusion.[7] In part, the dropout rate can be attributed to the severity of the demands that the *Nativ* program imposes on participants, who are expected to display an exceptional degree of perseverance

---

7   As late as the autumn of 2010, and notwithstanding over a decade of generously funded activity, the sum total of conversions to Judaism resulting from the *Nativ* program had barely scaled the 3,000 mark, which is only a fraction of the potential during that period. Of the 3,000 troops who registered for initial Nativ courses (out of an estimated cohort of roughly 7,000 possible candidates), only 800 (most of whom were women) completed the entire 7-month cycle and went on to convert. Interview with the director of the *Nativ* program, Mr. Amichai Eitam, February 15 2011.

and commitment. But equally influential, surely, is the deterrent effect exerted by periodic announcements issued by prominent civilian Israeli rabbis to the effect that they will not recognize the conversion certificates issued to persons who do complete the IDF course. Leaders of the *Yisrael Beteinu* party, which claims to represent FSU immigrant interests, have tabled a bill that, if passed, would enshrine IDF conversions in law. But until such time as this legislation is improved (and coalition arithmetic casts doubts on the matter), the military service of FSU immigrants born to non-Jewish mothers, instead of diluting religiously-based differences in Israel, will continue to demonstrate just how wide they are.

The chapters that follow do not purport to offer solutions to the challenges and dilemmas that have here been outlined. Their purpose, rather, is to analyze the manifestations of the relevant phenomena in somewhat greater detail and to itemize the stages in which they have risen to prominence. Only the 'epilogue' will attempt, tentatively, to gaze into the crystal ball by weighing the possible outcomes of current attempts to unravel the several knots – political, legal and ethical – in which Israel has tied itself by exempting so many ultra-orthodox (*haredi*) male Jews from military duty. The repercussions, it will argue, need not be limited to the introspective *haredi* world. On the contrary, they could transform the entire IDF, perhaps even hastening its reconfiguration as an all-volunteer force. If that happens, a new library of studies will be required in order to analyze the further alterations in the nexus between military service and religion that will undoubtedly emerge.

PART I
The Legacy of Ambivalence

Chapter 2

Reversing the Tide of Jewish History: Culture and the Creation of Israel's 'People's Army'[1]

Ever since its establishment in 1948 the Israel Defense Force (IDF) has prided itself on its character as a 'people's army'. Of the several justifications for that depiction, undoubtedly the most obtrusive is Israel's persistent adherence to a system of military service based on the nominally universal conscription of all 18 year-old youngsters (women as well as men) for draft terms of two to three years and on compulsory reserve duty (principally for males) until middle age.

Over the years, the consequences of Israel's military service system, operational as well as societal, have been the subjects of several critiques and counter-critiques, each of which has generated intense debate.[2] By contrast, the circumstances that explain the original decision to institute conscription and mandatory reserve duty appear to be matters of broad scholarly consensus. Indeed, for some years now it has been assumed that all that needs to be known about the origins of the IDF's force structure has been said, most definitively by Drs. Zahavah Ostfeld (1994) and Yitzchak Greenberg (2001).

Thanks to the prodigious and exhaustive archival research conducted by both scholars, there is no doubt about the pivotal influence exerted on IDF force planners during the initial, crucial months of Israel's existence by two essentially material considerations. One was the need to raise an army large enough to engage and defeat the several Arab forces, regular and irregular, that had invaded the newly established State and thus threatened to throttle it at birth. The other was the equally essential requirement that the IDF's apparently insatiable demand for manpower be balanced with the treasury's insistence on financial parsimony and the retention of a large industrial workforce. Combined, these constraints negated the possibility that the

---

1   The original version of this chapter appeared in: Stuart A. Cohen (ed.), *The New Citizen Armies: Israel in Comparative Perspective* (Routledge: London, 2010), pp. 56–74.

2   Two clusters of subjects have generated particularly intense controversies. One cluster focuses on the strategic-operational corollaries of Israel's reliance on reservists, and examines its possible influence on the IDF's traditional predilection for short wars and pre-emptive strikes. The other cluster emphasizes the societal impact of Israel's draft, and in particular its contribution to the military–civilian symbiosis that is widely recognized to be a hallmark of the country's domestic landscape. See Horowitz and Lissak 1989, Lomsky-Feder and Ben-Ari 1999, Kimmerling 2001 and Maoz 2007.

IDF might simply become an extension of the *Haganah* [the principal pre-State underground militia] and hence be constituted as an all-volunteer army. At the same time, however, they also precluded the copycat adoption of the Swiss model of a militia force based on short conscription terms (which, although certainly cheaper than a professional force, could not guarantee the standards of military proficiency that Israel required). Hence, it was virtually by a process of elimination that Ben-Gurion, Israel's first Prime Minister and Minister of Defense, eventually hit upon a hybrid structure, which combined elements of both the professional and the militia models in an integrated tripartite system, consisting of conscripts, reservists and a core cadre of salaried professionals.

Why a 'People's Army'?

In immediate terms, the enlistment policies and practices thus adopted undoubtedly served their purpose. Even when due note is taken of recent revisionist history, which considerably modifies the view that Israeli forces in the War of Independence were massively outnumbered and outgunned by their enemies (Kadish 2004), the military utility of the draft during the crisis years of 1948–9 remains undeniable. What is not at all clear, by contrast, is whether the retention of conscription thereafter was quite as inevitable as is sometimes suggested. If anything, once the fighting had died down in 1949, almost precisely the same sets of considerations that had initially underscored the need to establish a mass-based army began to work in favor of its dismantlement.

For one thing, there were the economics. It has been calculated that at the height of the war roughly 30 percent of Israel's workforce was mobilized, with the result that GNP dropped by over 12 percent (Barkai 2004: 760–5). Ben-Gurion's attempt to solve this problem by dispatching 'labor battalions' to industry and agriculture (a device that he had picked up from Trotsky's initiative as early as the 1920s), proved to be a short-lived failure and collapsed in a bureaucratic shambles (Greenberg 2006). Ultimately, only massive demobilization in 1949 enabled the economy to rebound by some 20 percent, and even then the Treasury felt it necessary to impose a regime of strict austerity. Under those circumstances, the continued diversion of labor from industry and the farms to the barracks made necessary by conscription could only prolong and make more painful the road to anything resembling economic recovery.

No less compelling were the military arguments in favor of a reconsideration of the universal draft. Clearly, Israel had to maintain a high level of mobilization. As early as October 1949, Ben-Gurion was convinced that the Arab states were preparing for a 'second round', and hence insisted on the need to 'educate a fighting people, and prepare every man and woman, young and old, for self-defense in the hour of need' (Ben-Gurion 1955: 138–9). So self-evident was this imperative that the National Service Bill, which introduced conscription, was voted into law in 1949 by the *Knesset* (Israel's parliament), almost without demur. But the operational disadvantages of the service system thus established became apparent almost as soon as the procedure was put into effect. Between 1948 and 1953 Israel's Jewish population more than doubled, principally thanks to the arrival of almost 750,000 new immigrants, about half of whom were Holocaust survivors from Europe and the remainder mostly penniless and (by Western standards) educationally disadvantaged refugees from Arab countries. Neither background proved conducive to satisfactory absorption within the new Israeli military framework. On the contrary, in both cases conscription, rather than providing a military asset, soon proved to be a disadvantage.

One early indication of the extent of the problem was supplied in the spring of 1949 by the IDF's own fledging psychological research unit. Surveys showed that the low rates of morale found to be prevalent amongst the 20,000 Holocaust survivors who had been hastily drafted into IDF combat units was proving infectious, and hence impairing the fighting spirit of native *sabras* (Yablonka 1995: 562–5). Similar conclusions were subsequently drawn when immigrants from Oriental countries became the focus of attention, as was increasingly the case after 1951. Figures compiled by the IDF recruitment center in each of the following three years showed that almost 70 percent of all new recruits had been in the country less than four years before their draft, and only 22 percent were native born (Torgan 2008: 30–42). Many of the newcomers were not only barely literate (Peled 2000), but also appeared especially prone to indiscipline. A General Staff report compiled in 1953 (cited in Drori 2006: 426) found that petty theft and racketeering were particularly rife in infantry units, where new immigrants from Oriental countries, principally Morocco and the Yemen, comprised some three quarters of the complement. It also discovered that a version of Gresham's Law was taking effect. 'While good soldiers were squeezed out, soldiers with a record of disciplinary problems on their bases or at different facilities are placed in [combat] brigades'.

Under those circumstances, it is hardly surprising that IDF operational standards plummeted. During the early 1950s IDF infantry units repeatedly failed to accomplish their missions. Some could not locate the designated objective; others panicked at the first whiff of gunshot. Faced with this situation, Ben-Gurion bowed to pressure that the IDF's order of battle be revised. In 1955 he agreed that future reprisal operations would be entrusted to an unabashedly elite fighting force ('unit 101') comprised almost entirely of quintessential *sabras*, residents of *kibbutzim* (Sharon 1989: 90, Morris 1993: 236–9).

Given the power of the economic and operational currents thus working against the retention of the draft, why then did the IDF nevertheless remain welded to the format of a 'people's army'? The conventional answer to that question is that nothing short of universal conscription could possibly balance the fundamental demographic asymmetries between the IDF and its Arab foes, potential as well as present. Indeed, that argument was accorded axiomatic status in the two works that most authoritatively distil Israeli security thinking over time: *Masach Shel Chol* ('Curtain of Sand', 1960), by Yigal Alon, the most successful IDF general of the 1948–9 wars; and *Bitachon Le'umi* ('National Security', 1996) by Israel Tal, the renowned commander of the IDF armored corps in 1967 and deputy Chief of the General Staff in 1973. Although separated by almost four decades, where force structures are concerned both works make much the same argument. Condemned to a position of chronic material and quantitative inferiority against its potential foes, the IDF must maximize its use of manpower, most obviously by retaining the 'three-tier' service system initiated in 1948. Thus, Alon was insistent on the need for Israel to attain 'the full integration of the population in security tasks' (Alon 1960: 48). Tal succumbed to greater hyperbole, declaring that 'The reserve military is among the most important collective creations of the Jewish people' (Tal 2000: 67).

Though manpower needs thus appeared prominent in analytical retrospect, this chapter suggests that in the early years of statehood, especially, their influence over IDF force structures was complemented – and may even have been exceeded – by a cluster of considerations whose focus, like that of so many other subjects in this period of Israel's history, was essentially domestic. This is not to argue, as others have done, that Ben-Gurion's determination to establish and retain the universal draft responded to an essentially parochial assessment of the way in which conscription might diminish the influence of the left-wing *Mapam* party and, by contrast, serve the political interests of his own more moderately socialist *Mapai* party (Ben-Eliezer 1998: 155–68). Rather, a more appropriate context for an understanding of Ben-Gurion's assessment of the required IDF force structures is provided by what Stephen Rosen (1995) and Alastair Johnston (1995) have referred to as the 'cultural' dimension of strategic planning: the way in which perceptions that are essentially value related both shape understandings of supposedly realistic security challenges and, in turn, influence the steps that will be taken in order to deal with them (see also Katzenstein 1999). This prism appears especially important in the present context when it is recalled that, as far as Ben-Gurion was concerned, the armed forces were not merely designed to provide the new state with security. They were also supposed to carry out the even more difficult task of reconstructing the inner worlds of its Jewish citizens and – through mass conscription – of overthrowing an attitude of aversion to matters military that was widely considered to constitute an integral component of Jewry's collective culture.

Traditional Judaism and Military Thought

The enormity of that task can hardly be exaggerated. After all, the new citizenry that Ben-Gurion sought to mobilize almost entirely for war in and after 1948 had for almost two millennia deliberately avoided cultivating anything like a martial ethos. True, matters had not always been thus. The Biblical record of the tribes of Israel, beginning with the book of Exodus and ending with the last chapters of Chronicles, leaves no doubt that the earliest and most influential of Jewish traditions were formulated and transmitted against a backcloth of almost incessant military activity. Moreover, and as Ben-Gurion himself became fond of pointing out, the military service system that according to the Book of Numbers the Children of Israel adopted during their 40 years of wandering in the Sinai desert, certainly contains unmistakable militia elements (for example, Ben-Gurion 1955: 223–8). Quite apart from prescribing military duty for all able-bodied men (unless they happened to be members of the priestly caste) between the ages of 20 and 60, the text also assigns draftees to formations, whose order of battle reflects the pecking order of the tribes that supply their membership. (De Vaux 1961). Nevertheless, such Biblical threads of continuity were not at all self-evident in 1948. On the contrary, they had largely to be reinvented.

Principally, this was because of the hiatus in Jewish history and memory brought about by Rome's obliteration of the last vestiges of Judea's independence in 70ce and her even more savage suppression of the rebellion that erupted in the province six decades later under the leadership of Bar-Kochba, a figure to whom many contemporaries attributed messianic attributes. With the loss of sovereignty –'the defining political event in the life of the Jewish people' (Wisse 2007: 4) – Jewry's links with its martial past seemed to have been irrevocably broken. To all intents and purposes, the Jews thereafter became a non-combative people, exhibiting what Luz (1987: 53) terms, 'an aversion to bloodshed'. Indeed, for both oriental and European communities soldiering was, throughout the medieval and pre-modern periods, strictly off limits.

Deviations from that norm were sporadic. We can identify a handful of Jews who fought under either the Cross or the Crescent in the great confrontations between Christians and Moors in medieval Spain and know of one, Ismail ibn Nagrela (993–1055/6; in Jewish sources named *Shemuel ha-Nagid*), a Hebrew poet and scholar of considerable talent, who had the unique distinction of commanding a Muslim army on behalf of the ruler of Grenada. Many more, termed 'cantonists', were during the nineteenth century forcibly conscripted into the ranks of the Imperial Russian army as young children, and condemned to perform military service on behalf of the Tsar for periods lasting as long as 25 years. Elsewhere, the enactment of Emancipation also wrought some change. A handful of Jews eager to take advantage of the opportunity to become fully accepted citizens in their countries of residence began to enlist voluntarily in the emerging national armies of The Netherlands (as early as the seventeenth century, see Wiznitzer 1956) of the United States (in the eighteenth century), in the National Guard established in Revolutionary France in 1789, and in one or another of the assorted fighting units that made fleeting appearances during the doomed heyday of the Polish national revival that flourished between 1794 and 1863 (Bartal 1997). These examples were soon imitated elsewhere in western and central Europe. Indeed, the quantity of Jews in uniform in Britain, France, Germany, the Hapsburg Empire and Italy rose steadily during the second half of the nineteenth century, even before the imposition of conscription.

All of those instances certainly possess intrinsic interest, not least for what they have to say about the receptivity of the host armies to Jewish service.[3] Nevertheless, they do not obscure the overall picture. For the vast majority of Jews worldwide, as a profession of choice, even after Emancipation soldiering remained marginal. Tellingly, the high rates of Jewish enlistment recorded in all the belligerent armies of World War I and in the Allied forces during World War II were not sustained once the draft was repealed. Thereafter, the Jewish soldier reverted to being an exception. As had always been the case, the proportion of Jews who earned their livelihood by serving in the armed forces persistently lagged far behind that of the gentile average, and never comprised more than a fraction of the total Jewish population (Baron 1977).

Overwhelmingly, traditional Jewish thought underscored the non-belligerency thus prevalent in traditional Jewish practice. By the sixth century ce, at the latest, 'war' had become an allegorical concept, denoting not armed combat but an intellectual confrontation over the correct interpretation of Scriptures: '*milkhamtah shel torah*' (Chamitovsky 2007). In the same vein, the Bible was itself subjected to a process of reinterpretation, whereby its tales of martial valor and heroism were deliberately divested of their plain meanings. Thus, thanks to the alchemy of rabbinic exegesis, King David, for instance, was transformed from a warrior into a scholar; his band of champions underwent a similar metamorphosis from fierce soldiers to pious students (Edrei 2006: 194–5). Simeon Bar-Kochba, the fabled leader of the last gasp Jewish revolt against Rome in the second century ce, suffered an even more extreme form of literary transmutation. Medieval narratives successively dispossessed Bar-Kochba of the quasi-mystical aura preserved in the older tales of his physical prowess and political charisma. Instead, they emphasized the orgy of destruction that resulted from the failure of his revolt, during the course of which some 500,000 Jews were slaughtered and vast portions of Judea turned into wasteland. In so doing, they transformed what had once been a great myth of national heroism into a discourse on the price of national folly (Marks 1994: 224).

There are indications that the handful of Jewish Bible commentators and Talmudic exegetes who somehow rose to positions of influence in diaspora lands could not avoid devoting some thought to what would today be termed grand strategy. As Inbar (1987) discovered, scattered references indicate that those with personal experience of high politics in fact readily acknowledged warfare's utility as a tool of statesmanship in an inherently anarchical world. Others, however, were noticeably reluctant to develop that theme, even as a topic of purely speculative and abstract analysis. Overwhelmingly, the great minds of pre-modern Jewry seem to have been far too sensitive to the precariousness of their people's existence to

---

3   According to Penslar 208: 314–5, in 1883 the active officer corps in the French army 'featured nine colonels, nine lieutenant colonels, 45 majors, 90 captains and 89 lieutenants. (In Jewish collective memory, the experience of one of those captains, Alfred Dreyfus, is seen as proof of widespread antisemitism in the French military, but in fact this institution was highly receptive to Jewish participation)'.

risk the accusations of incitement to rebellion that might result from evidence that they were indulging in systematic analyses of warfare and its pursuit. With discretion imposing its own rules of silence they consequently shied away from any discussion of the use of armed force. As a result, military activity and thought constitutes one of the very few spheres of universal human endeavor to which Jews made no significant contribution whatsoever after ancient times.

The titanic exception to all such rules is, of course, Rabbi Moses ben Maimon (1135–204), better known in Jewish tradition as the *Rambam* and to the wider world of letters as Maimonides, the most authoritative and influential Jewish philosopher and codifier of all times. A personal physician to the ruler of Egypt, Maimonides was undoubtedly sensitive to Jewry's lack of coercive power. Indeed, he explicitly broke with the convention of discretion maintained by his co-religionists when committing to writing his assessment of the dire consequences that had flowed from the decay of ancient Israel's martial ethos ('The reason that we lost our kingdom and that our temple was destroyed [in 70ce] ... was that they [the nation's spiritual leaders of the time] did not concern themselves with studying war or with foreign conquests, which they imagined would be of no use' [cited in Blidstein 1983: 219]). More noticeably, he incorporated teachings and religious instructions relating to war within his magisterial and all-embracing code of Jewish law, which he unabashedly named the *Mishneh Torah* ('Supplementary *Torah*'). The fourteenth volume of that work, entitled 'Laws of Kings and their Wars', contains an exceptionally detailed review of the available sources, presenting both a summary of the uses and misuses of military force and a benchmark Jewish classification of conflict situations, distinguishing wars that are 'commanded' (*mitzvah*) from those that are 'permitted' (*reshut*) (Walzer 2006).

A review of the fate of the Maimonidean enterprise, however, merely underscores the singularity of its author's treatment. In other areas covered by Maimonides' great Code, his rulings and opinions came to serve as a base for towering pyramids of subsequent addenda, criticisms, commentaries and supra-commentaries. Each a triumph of cerebral skill and forensic enterprise, these later works dissected every word of *Mishneh Torah*, and sometimes individual letters. Heaping one commentary upon another, they teased meanings out of Maimonides' dicta with respect to both arcane points of observance and the minutiae of private and public law. By comparison, however, only the most assiduous of the great master's students glossed his comments on the various ritual and ethical problems that warfare could pose. Where this subject was concerned, most scholars neither challenged nor confirmed Maimonides' rulings; for the most part, they were simply not discussed (German 2003: 313–64).

A similar conclusion emerges from the epistolary communications network between individual Jews and their rabbinic teachers, known to scholars as the 'responsa literature'. Military matters are almost entirely absent from this vast storehouse of correspondence, which spans continents, and which ever since the early Middle Ages has constituted a principal medium of instruction on every other imaginable aspect of Jewish law. The only significant exceptions, almost all of which begin to appear only in late eighteenth-century Europe, merely prove two rules. First, that enlistment was generally regarded as an anathema; and second that, as one particularly influential rabbi put it, 'Regarding this, silence is better than our speech' (Rabbi Moses Sofer, Hungary mid-nineteenth century, cited in Bleich 2007: 421).

The Era of Zionism

The advent of political Zionism late in the nineteenth century did not immediately bring about a reversal of the traditional Jewish attitude of reticence towards warfare. Although in many other respects the Zionists deliberately set out to reverse past Jewish practices, where the exercise of military force was concerned the lines of continuity predominated. Delegates to the first Zionist Congress held in Basle in 1897, who took the momentous step of resolving to secure 'the establishment of a Jewish homeland openly recognized, legally secured', made no provisions for the raising of a militia. When Theodore Herzl, the movement's founder, spoke and wrote of the Jews' State, he did not envision its attainment by military conquest, but by purchase and diplomacy. This scheme of things demanded neither universal conscription nor even the nurturing of a popular martial ethos – 'Just a professional army, equipped, of course, with every requisite of modern warfare, to preserve order internally and externally' (Herzl 1946: 147).

Virtually all of Zionism's precursors and early practitioners shared this naively utopian view. Soldiers are noticeably absent from all of the four early Zionist models of 'new Jews' analyzed by Anita Shapira (1997: 155–74). Only Zvi Hirsch Kalischer (1795–1894), a rabbi from the backwaters of western Poland, was prescient enough to foresee that Jewish settlers in Palestine might have to defend themselves from native marauders, a need to which he devoted an entire paragraph in his path breaking *Derishat Ziyyon* ('Seeking Zion'), first published in 1862. This explains why such military provisions as were initially made, of which the most famous was the *Ha-Shomer* ('The Guard') organization, founded in the lower Galilee in 1909, owed far more to local initiatives than to any centralized planning. Until as late as the outbreak of World War I, the official Zionist leadership ignored unmistakable signs of how vulnerable to occasional Arab assault were the small scale Jewish settlements established during the first and second waves of immigration (*aliyot*; 1881–1904 and 1904–1914). Instead, it continued to adhere to the conviction that the process of colonization would proceed peacefully. 'Conquest (*kibbush*) of the land', the term used to describe settlement, was thus deliberately emptied of military connotations.

> The war for which we are being prepared is very simple, not dangerous in the least. What we desire is to engage in patient labor, work devoid of any bloodshed, work that is only civilized colonization. Diligent labor is our sword and bow. In the end, no one will oppose us in enmity (Max Emmanuel Mandelstamm, cited in An. Shapira 1992: 41).

This attitude persisted during World War I, when it was further buttressed by fear that any hint of armed action on the part of Jews would provoke the Ottomans to even harsher action against the pioneers. Hence, even as late as the winter of 1917–1918, most of the new *Yishuv* looked askance at the suggestion that they join the specifically Jewish fighting forces that Jabotinsky had after much effort persuaded the British to recruit for service in the Middle Eastern theater. After much debate (Malkhin 2007: 162–82), only 7,000 men – not all of whom were committed Zionists – did in fact enlist in the three Jewish battalions eventually established (Watts 2004). Within a year, most of those had become disillusioned with the notion of a Jewish army and were instead reverting to the classic Zionist belief that labor and settlement promised to produce more results than did 'blood and fire' (An. Shapira 1992: 95–7). Similarly illustrative of how deeply ingrained the attitude of disdain towards the very idea of Jewish soldiering continued to be in the new *Yishuv* was the treatment that its members accorded to the Jewish legionnaires who participated in Allenby's successful campaign against the Ottoman forces in Palestine in 1917 and 1918. Instead of being welcomed with open arms by their co-religionists, as they had obviously expected, the soldiers in the 38th battalion (which was mainly comprised of new Jewish immigrants from Eastern Europe to England) reported that they were made to feel like stepsons, who were engaged in a task that the vast majority of local pioneers found inherently distasteful. The attitude of the local women was especially cutting: 'How lacking to those who had come to save the honor of the country was the soft and pleasant hand of the sisters of *Eretz Israel* [the land of Israel]' (Gogol 1919).

As both Anita Shapira (1994: 97–124) and Martin Van Creveld (1998) have shown, the period of the British Mandate certainly did witness a perceptible shift of both tone and organization where military matters were concerned. Specifically, the pre-World War I network of *Ha-Shomer* constabularies was welded into a larger clandestine organization, the *Haganah*, in 1920, which in turn was supplemented by more highly trained forces: the *Fosh* (*pelugot sadeh*: 'field squads', founded in 1937) and the *Palmach* (*pelugot machatz*: 'shock troops', founded in 1941). By the latter date, indeed, a deep transformation of cultural values seemed to have taken place, especially amongst the younger generation of *sabras*, men such as Yigal Alon, Moshe Dayan and Yitzchak Rabin (to cite only those who were later to become household names the world over) who had received an education deliberately designed to release them from the psychological ballast of non-bellicosity that still burdened most of their elders.

Indeed, they imbibed and disseminated an entire canon of new military-related myths. Theirs was the generation that first turned Masada, the desert crag that had been the site of the Jewish fighters' last stand against Rome in 70ce, into a place of pilgrimage during the 1930s (Ben-Yehuda 1995). It was they, too, who attached similarly mythological proportions to more recent armed skirmishes, such as the heroically unsuccessful defense of the Galilean Jewish outpost at Tel-Hai in 1920 (Zerubavel 1991). Members of the right-wing Revisionist movement, which had established the *Etzel* (*Irgun Tzevai Le'umi*: 'National Military Organization') as early as 1931, tended to be more explicit. At the 1938 convention of *Beitar* (the Revisionist youth movement) held in Poland, Menachem Begin, then a rising firebrand, convinced delegates to revise the wording of the oath that had been drafted just four years previously by the movement's founder, Ze'ev Jabotinsky. As before, Clause 4 was to commence: 'I will train to fight in the defense of my people', but the original continuation ('and I will only use my strength for defense') was replaced with a more bellicose undertaking 'to conquer the homeland' (Shindler 2006: 207).

Establishing the Draft: The War of Independence

But the practical result of all declaratory activity should not be exaggerated. Central though the use of force increasingly became to official Zionist thinking by 1948, it would clearly be mistaken to exaggerate the extent to which the *Yishuv* as a whole was prepared to undertake the martial commitment that should have been the logical corollary of the new mood. There are certainly no grounds for depicting the Jewish community of mandatory Palestine as anything like a nation in arms. Even during years of acute danger, military activity remained a minority activity. Thus in 1940–41, by which time the *Yishuv* numbered slightly over 400,000 persons, all of whose lives were imperiled by Rommel's advances in northern Africa, the *Haganah* could muster only 7,000 troops (1,000 of whom were members of the *Palmach* founded in 1940) and the *Etzel* – even by its own account (itself probably exaggerated) barely 3,000 (Eilam 1979: 82, 86). True, a further 30,000, including almost 4,000 women, volunteered in the next few years to fight against Nazi Germany in various branches of the British armed forces, including the Jewish Brigade established in 1944 (Gelber 1984: 299–303; Granit-Hakohen 2011). But impressive though that figure might at first glance seem – especially when compared to the fact that only 9,000 members of the far larger Arab population of Palestine took the same route – it hardly warrants depiction as evidence of a communal readiness to experience total mobilization.[4] Significantly,

---

4   Gelber 1984: 234 calculates that 6 percent of the Yishuv enlisted during World War II. This figure, he shows, compares favorably with those available for several Anglo-Saxon countries (as presented in a source published in 1980), such as the United States (5.6 percent) and white South Africa (5.5 percent), and falls only marginally short of Canada (6.1 percent), and Britain (8 percent). Only New Zealand (8.12 percent) and Australia (10.2 percent) recorded significantly higher rates, but there of course, enlistment was compulsory. Van Creveld 1998: 49 likewise estimates that: 'Numerically speaking and relative to its size, the Yishuv's contribution was … as great as that of any other country at the time'.

That argument is difficult to sustain. For one thing, it takes no account of the age structure of the Yishuv population, in which the proportion of men and women of service age was relatively high. Secondly, it ignores the situation in several countries where enlistment rates were significantly higher (Germany and the USSR). Thirdly, it omits consideration of the proportions of the population who in all industrialized countries (the USA, Britain, Germany, the USSR, Japan and even Italy) had to sustain production in

the *Yishuv*'s own political leadership had hoped for much larger figures (especially once news of the European Holocaust began to filter into public consciousness) and could barely conceal their disappointment when the successive recruitment drives that they launched failed to meet their expected targets (Eilam 1979: 132–3, 140, 165, 180, 253, 265–6; Brenner 1979: 174).

A significant rise in the proportion of Jews prepared to take up arms was not in fact registered until late in 1947, when the *Yishuv*'s official leadership at long last decided to establish the machinery required for a draft (Guvrin 1976). Only then was a concerted effort made to tap the resources made available by a total Jewish population of circa 630,000 persons, of whom 94,400 men and 92,000 women were aged 18–35 (the figures for ages 18–25 were 39,000 and 36,000 respectively). The results were almost instantaneous (Barkai 2004: 761). Whereas in November 1947 there were still only 21,775 members of the *Yishuv* under arms, by July 1948 the IDF already possessed a complement of 63,586. Six months later it had grown to just under 100,000, almost 30 percent of whom were new immigrants who had arrived in the country after 15 May 1948 and who had been drafted almost the moment they stepped off the boat (Markovizky 1995). Even then, however, the IDF was far from embracing the entirety of the newly emergent nation. As late as early 1949 it was clear that some 14 to 15 percent of the potential 'pool' of long-term Jewish residents of mandatory Palestine of draft age had in fact never put on an IDF uniform (Pail 1983: 127–8).

Writing almost 30 years after the event, Pinchas Guvrin – who had been responsible for coordinating the enlistment process in 1948 – insisted that by far the majority of the non-enlistees of the War of Independence received official discharges and that the incidence of draft dodging (*hishtamtut*) was low (Guvrin 1976: 50–92). However, he then spoils his own case by providing details of the quantity of the courts established to try suspects and of the facilities in which convicted offenders were imprisoned. Had motivation to service indeed been as persistently high as he claims, surely there would have been no need for so elaborate an apparatus, or for the successively shrill 'directives' issued by the 'Center for National Service', which published no less than 31 enlistment announcements between December 1947 and June 1948.

Just as significant as the fairly widespread phenomenon of non-enlistment was the sociological distribution of those who did serve. Contrary to the 'people's army' notion that was to become so essential to the IDF's identity, the pre-State generation of soldiers was not at all drawn from a cross section of the population at large. Rather, it was very much a product of the new *Yishuv*'s self-styled elite, whose opposition to anything like a popular militia was both deeply ingrained and widely spread. Indeed, one of the criticisms that Labor Zionists voiced against Jabotinsky's handling of the Jewish Legion in World War I was that 'he did not demand human elation, he did not care who was serving [in the Legion], while

---

mines and factories, and were hence deliberately not drafted into the armed forces. See Harrison 2000.

we demanded idealism, and the pick and salt of our Movement' (Rahel Yanait ben Zevi, cited in Schechtman 1986: 306).[5]

This sense of elitism was carried over into the 1930s and 1940s. It now transpires that the *sabras* who trekked to Masada and sat around the campfires with Yitzchak Sadeh (the founder of the *Palmach*) were not representative of their generation. Oz Almog, who has studied this cohort with particular care, estimates that – even though they stamped their imprint on the entire era – they in fact comprised little more than 10 percent of the population (Almog 2000: 23–72). For the most part, they were residents of small agricultural settlements, most of which were non-religious and some intensely opposed to the Jewish traditions of the Diaspora. They had been reared in a hot house atmosphere deliberately designed to produce a new *avant guard* of an entirely different breed of men and women. Confident in their ability to fulfill the national mission thus thrust upon them, they assumed the designated role of Jewry's new elite with almost religious enthusiasm. For them, certainly, military service in defense of the *Yishuv* was an integral part of their Zionist ideology, best expressed through the agency of precisely the type of militia force that the *Palmach* always aimed to be (Ben-Eliezer 1984). It was this background that injected such intensity into the debate that raged within the *kibbutz* movement during World War II as to whether its members ought to volunteer for service in the British army or stay put in the *Haganah/Palmach*. In part, at issue was the need to retain *in situ* formations that could guarantee the continued defense of the *kibbutzim* and supply the workforce without which they would wither. But another strand in the debate was the desire to preserve intact the group identity of what had already become a self-styled chosen core (Brenner 1979: 169–75).

For large sections of the Jewish inhabitants of the far more populous urban concentrations of Tel-Aviv (where almost 50 percent of the entire *Yishuv* lived in 1948) and Haifa, these were non-issues. Altogether, the bourgeoisie tradesmen and day laborers in the *Yishuv*'s bustling urban centers inhabited an almost entirely different world than that of the pastoral *kibbutzim* and *moshavim*. Even when they read the same newspapers and voted for the same parties, they had vastly different views of what Zionist commitment entailed. Especially was this so where enlistment for military service was concerned. Urban membership of the *Haganah* had always been proportionately low, and urban responses to the call to arms in 1939, in 1942 and even in 1947 were never enthusiastic. Tel-Aviv,

---

5   The implied charge, that Jabotinsky was prepared to accept anyone and everyone into a prospective Jewish army, is however also misplaced. Although persistently in favor of the establishment of a Jewish fighting force, what Jabotinsky had in mind was not a mass-based militia but a standing, professional force. See his letters on this subject to Weizmann on 12 March 1920, 7 October 1920, and 18 March 1921, published in Karpi 1997: 122–4, 149–50, and 190–1, and – especially – the various versions of his essay 'Defense Problems in Palestine' (October 1929), originally published in Hebrew in *Doar Ha-Yom*. In general, Shavit 1988: 96–8, 192–3.

especially, became a byword for draft dodging. 'When I came to Tel-Aviv on my weekly leave', wrote one new recruit to the British army in 1942:

> I felt very uncomfortable walking along the street. I thought people were laughing at me. I had the feeling they considered me wretched for wearing a uniform, that they regarded me as insane and miserable. Why should this be? Because this is the Yishuv's attitude towards enlistment. Because it kept aloof, joked about it (Cited in Ben-Eliezer 1998: 42).

These impressions died hard. *Kibbutz* members were known to have flocked to the colors during the War of Independence in vastly disproportionate numbers, and although comprising barely 2 percent of the population eventually accounted for some 15 percent of battlefield deaths (Sivan 1991: 243). By contrast, Tel-Aviv throughout retained its stigma as a locus of café-dwelling draft dodgers. So much was this so that the city was the scene of two massive Israeli man hunts for deserters: one in the first week of May 1948 (Guvrin 1976: 63–6); and another, much larger, in late August of that year, when the newly established IDF placed the entire area under curfew for five full days.[6]

The 'People's Army'

Once the war was over and the fighting had died down, Ben-Gurion seems to have feared that the majority of the *Yishuv* would revert to type. Personally, he was convinced that he was living through a period that he did not hesitate to designate as a 'messianic era' – a time of fulfillment that had been foretold in the prophecies of Isaiah, Amos and Ezekiel, all of whom he now regularly cited (Ohana 2003). But how many of his compatriots shared that conviction? And what could be done to ensure that even those who did so would sustain the levels of intense emotional tension that they had scaled in the heady days of 1947 and 1948? Rhetoric, certainly, was one possible mechanism – and one that Ben-Gurion undoubtedly exploited to the best of his not inconsiderable ability. As has often been noted, after 1948, his references to the state of Israel and its institutions as a 'chariot of the Messiah' increased markedly. Even more noticeable, and deliberate, was the growth in the quantity of the Biblical allusions with which he now enlivened his speeches on the virtues of *mamlakhtiyut* ('state consciousness'), the noun that Ben-Gurion coined in order to describe the revolution that Israel's foundation had wrought in the Jewish political condition (An. Shapira 1997b, Kedar 2002). But

---

6   After-action reports showed that 'Operation Betzer', as it was code-named, had in fact been entirely superfluous. The draft rate in Tel-Aviv was actually much higher than the national average and only a handful of genuine draft dodgers and deserters were netted (Feierberg 2004). Nevertheless, and as Bar-On (2006) points out, what remains significant is that the stigma should have been so prominent in the first place.

rhetoric alone could not suffice. What was also needed was a focus of affection that was at once both more tangible and at the same time enveloped in an aura of almost mystical veneration.

A 'people's army' promised to fulfill precisely that requirement. This was not simply because of the importance of its functions as the ultimate guarantor of state survival. To Ben-Gurion's mind, two other aspects of the IDF were still more relevant.

- First, an armed force nominally based on universal conscription promised to be an excellent tool of social engineering. Ben-Gurion had for many years been looking for precisely such an instrument, and indeed as early as 1922 had proposed that the *Histadrut* (Labor Federation) be constituted as 'the labor army' (*tzavah ha'avodah*), a framework that would serve as a homogenizing focus of identity and control for all workers in the *Yishuv* (Ohana 2003: 41–2). By 1948–9 the need for a state-centered agency that might fulfill that function on an ever larger canvass had clearly become more acute, principally because of the sudden arrival of so large a number of new immigrants from a wide variety of locations and backgrounds. Ben-Gurion now became convinced that only the common experience of military service could possibly weld all the new arrivals, not just into a new nation but – more importantly – into a new *Jewish* nation. As he informed a cadre of newly commissioned officers early in 1949:

  > While the first mission of the IDF … is the security of the State, that is not its only task. The Army must also serve as a pioneering educational force for Israeli youth, both native born and immigrants. The IDF must educate a pioneering generation, healthy in body and spirit, brave and faithful, which will heal tribal and Diaspora divisions and implement the historic missions of the State of Israel through a process of self-fulfillment (Ben-Gurion 1971: 81).

- Secondly, the effects of the educational process thus generated by military service did not have to be felt solely by persons in uniform. The 'people's army' would also – indeed, more effectively – earn its designation by virtue of the role that it would also play in the lives of the non-enlisted mass of citizens. Thus, the IDF could provide a magnet of societal affections through the medium of pageant – such as the military parades that became a central rite of Independence Day celebrations as early as 1949 (Azaryahu 1999: 89–106). But on a more quotidian basis, it could also act as a nation-binder by providing civilians with specific services. In this respect, too, Ben-Gurion was explicit. New conscripts, he insisted, were not to be shut up for the duration of their conscript terms in their barracks. On the contrary, the National Service Law of 1949 explicitly required them to devote one of their two years of compulsory service to agricultural work. Likewise, the IDF as a whole was – from the first – directed to undertake a wide range of essentially civilian tasks: establishing and maintaining agricultural settlements in areas of the country considered particularly inhospitable and/or dangerous; providing supplementary educational services to schoolchildren in under privileged regions; and constructing the transit camps in which large numbers of the new immigrants were housed during their first, difficult years in the country (Drori 2005).

In all these areas, the material and substantive dimensions of the assistance provided by the military were overshadowed by their symbolic importance. Together, they were to overturn centuries of ingrained Jewish attitudes, not just towards military service but with respect to all matters military. In this new atmosphere, Jewish soldiers would no longer be regarded as almost extraterrestrial beings, 'Different People' in the title of Yehudit Hendel's short story of the period that captures the awe in which new immigrants held their *sabra* officers (Hendel 1950). Rather, they would be looked upon as benign and integral constituents of the public realm. As Chief of Staff Yigael Yadin (who in this respect was of one mind with Ben-Gurion) put it in 1950: 'We are … called upon to show the immigrants, who were used to seeing the army in their native country as the enemy and oppressor, that the army of the State of Israel is their protector and helper' (Yadin 1950).

What made that vision of cultural transformation especially remarkable was the hold that it swiftly exerted on the national imagination. Indeed, as a mechanism for societal change Ben-Gurion's 'people's army' enjoyed a degree of success that not even he had dared to predict. Within less than a decade after the establishment of the IDF, the overwhelming majority of articulate Jewish–Israeli society had clearly come to accept Israel's armed forces and all they symbolized as far more than just an agency of national security. The military services were also widely considered to be integral components of what has been termed the country's civil religion – that capacious mosaic of symbols, themes, myths and associations that together fostered and conveyed feelings of national affinity and reciprocity (Liebman and Don-Yehiya 1983). Jewish history, in this sense, turned full circle, and the people that had for centuries made a virtue out of possessing no army at all now became the very epitome of a nation in arms.

The New Religious Outlook

Certainly, the process whereby traditional preferences for non-bellicosity were thus reversed was considerably assisted by martial success, especially in the campaigns waged by the IDF in 1956 and 1967. Yet, the emergence of a new attitude to matters military cannot be attributed entirely to events on the battlefield. Also at work was a more fundamental shift in cultural values under whose influence military symbols and rites assumed many of the integrative attributes that Jewish traditions had thereto bestowed on religious festivals and rituals. *Tzahal* (the acronym for the IDF that became as much a term of endearment as a designation) was now enveloped in an aura of reverence and devotion that previous generations of Jewry had reserved exclusively for subjects of religious faith (Hadari-Ramage 1995: 355–74). This, as much as a simplistic appeal to the instincts of survival, helps to explain why the incidence of draft dodging had by the mid-1950s dropped to almost negligible proportions while levels of propensity to service (referred to as 'motivation' and measured by the number of volunteers for assignment to combat duty) scaled heights unequalled elsewhere in the Western world.

This transformation of attitudes was especially evident in orthodox Jewish circles. Only the ultra-orthodox (*haredi*) community, whose influence on mainstream life remained marginal until the mid-1970s, kept faith with the time-honored teachings that decried the this-worldly properties of military activity and emphasized, instead, the protective and redemptive power of study of the Holy Texts and commentaries (Ravitzky 1988). By contrast, adherents to the more mainstream brand of religious Zionism (designated, with deliberate hyphenation, 'national–religious' Zionists) followed a very different course. True, their first steps in a new direction were somewhat hesitant. The initial reaction of their leaders to the introduction of the universal draft was to lobby Ben-Gurion to follow the segregationist policies adopted by the pre-State *Haganah* and allow religious soldiers to serve in their own homogenous military formations. But when Ben-Gurion flatly rejected any such idea on the severely practical grounds that 'the creation of religious units will result in the creation of anti-religious units' (Mo. Friedman 2005: 109–112), they shifted ground and instead demanded that the entire military framework conform to the basic precepts of traditional Jewish law.

Once assured that such would indeed be the case, national–religious Jewry underwent a transformation. Self-consciously jettisoning two millennia of anti-belligerent Jewish orthodox teachings, rabbis now endowed military service on behalf of Israel's defense with the status of an article of faith, a message that they passed on to ever-growing cohorts of young students in the educational establishments set up with the express purpose of providing prospective recruits with spiritual 'fortification'. No less practically, the new genre of rabbis (the most prominent of whom was Shlomo Goren, the IDF's first and most influential chief military chaplain [*rav tzeva'i rashi*]) also set about the mammoth task of formulating an entirely new codex of religious regulations with regard to military life, an area that to previous generations had been altogether considered *terra incognita* (Edrei 2006, S. Cohen 2007). Taken together, these developments indicated that Jewish history had indeed come full circle.

The Resilience of a Conception

Until comparatively recently, it might have been possible thus to end this chapter on an entirely affirmative note. In that spirit, its peroration would have needed to do no more than reiterate the benefits – societal as well as operational – that Israel's 'people's army' has bestowed on the nation that it is designed to defend.

But new times have fostered alternative perspectives. For several years now observers have been suggesting that the IDF might need to follow in the footsteps of other western armies and examine the option of becoming an all-volunteer force (for references, see S. Cohen 2008: 171–2). Clearly, several material hurdles have to be overcome before any such move can be implemented. To judge from the present state of the debate, however, considerations that are essentially cultural in nature may in the last analysis present even more serious obstacles. The arguments most commonly adduced against the restructuring of the IDF as an all-volunteer force is that the dismantlement of the 'people's army' would deprive Israel of the institution that has done more than any other to shape her character as a post-Exilic nation. Counter-arguments, to the effect that it is high time that civil society and its organs assume all such burdens, are invariably dismissed with references to the unmatched prominence of the military in Israeli life, public as well as private.

Set in the context of that debate, the process set in motion by Ben-Gurion during the crucial years 1948–1956 might be said to have come full circle. Once a source of dynamic change, his vision of the IDF as an instrument of cultural reconstruction has now become a force for rigidity, principally because it holds Israeli imagination in thrall. History may yet judge him to have been, if anything, too successful.

Chapter 3

Between the Transcendental and the Temporal: Security and the Religious Jewish Community in Israel[1]

The search for an appropriate equilibrium between the supernatural and physical dimensions of national security has traditionally constituted a continuous theme in Jewish religious thought. That quest finds modern expression in debates over territorial and other strategic issues within the contemporary Israeli orthodox community. Indeed, all such discussions reverberate with themes and motifs rooted in Judaism's religious heritage. Many are also framed in distinctly theological terms. This chapter identifies the principal issues of those discussions. After delineating the principal theological divide between the ultra-orthodox (*haredi*) and religious Zionist communities, it then focuses attention on the ideological differences over territorial compromise that emerged within the latter in the three decades following the 1967 Six Days War. It argues that this formative period witnessed the enunciation of positions that continue to influence national–religious positions on questions of national security.

The Religious Parameters of National Security in Judaism

Religious Jews necessarily believe Divine Providence to be a fundamental ingredient of Israel's collective national security. That article of faith rests on a bedrock of traditions that identify the Almighty as, among all else, a 'God of Hosts' and hence the arbiter of His chosen people's martial destinies. Divine active participation in the military endeavors of the ancient Hebrews constitutes a persistent theme throughout the Bible.

It supplies an equally emphatic motif in the long stream of formative rabbinic teachings that orthodox Jews regard as similarly sacred components of their literary canon. As portrayed in both sources, neither victory nor defeat results from exclusively human exertions. Rather, they manifest – respectively – God's grace and displeasure. The ultimate goal of all strategy must therefore be a concerted effort to sway His will.

---

1   The original version of this chapter appeared in: *Security Concerns: Insights from the Israeli Experience* (ed. D. Bar-Tal, D. Jacobson and A. Klieman: JAI Press: CT, 1998), pp. 371–393.

One paradigmatic illustration of that teaching is contained in an early rabbinic commentary on the Bible's depiction of the first military operation ever conduction by the Children of Israel: the war against the Amalakites. Exodus 17:11 itself intimates that Moses determined the fortunes of battle by raising and lowering his arms to heaven. The code known as *Mishnah* (compiled in the third century ce) elaborates on this theme.

> Now could Moses' hands make war or stop it? But the purpose [of the Biblical verse] is to say to you: So long as the Israelites [following Moses' hands] would set their eyes upward and submit their hearts to their Father in heaven, they would grow stronger. And if not, they failed (Tractate *Rosh ha-Shanah* 3:8).

Pursuant to that teaching, Jewish political traditions have always posited the need to harmonize what are here termed temporal and transcendental components of national security, harnessing both within a unified affirmation of religious faith. In practice, however, the implementation of such doctrines has throughout been an uneven process, marked by several discontinuities. Of these, undoubtedly the most significant was the experience of Exile and Dispersion, conventionally reported to have commenced with Rome's destruction of Jerusalem in 70ce. Thereafter deprived of territorial independence and fragmented into disparate communities, Jewry entered an extended period of 'powerlessness' (Biale 1996). As a result, diplomacy became the only available human means of ensuring material survival and welfare; even as a topic of purely abstract or speculative analysis, the notion of a collective resort to armed force was deliberately – and doubtless prudently – expunged from the agenda of Jewish political discourse. To the extent that a conception of this-worldly security at all existed, its parameters could only be defined in terms entirely dominated by the unfathomable depths of God's will. Human attempts to force the pace of history by secular means ('to hasten the [messianic] end') came to be regarded as intrinsically sinful. True faith demanded strict submission to the message of the prophetic injunction: 'Not by might nor by power but by My spirit, saith the Lord of hosts' (Zechariah 4:6).

The need to re-evaluate and reinterpret such concepts is not the least of the many challenges which the success of modern political Zionism presents to contemporary Jewish religious thought. Basically, this is because the protracted situation of armed conflict in which the state of Israel finds itself has once again brought to the surface tensions between the transcendental and temporal components of Jewish security, which had for almost two millennia laid dormant. Baldly summarized, the dilemmas generated by that circumstance can be presented as a series of interlocking questions.

- Now that a sovereign Jewish state exists, how might threats to the physical survival of its inhabitants best be met?
- Does orthodox religious doctrine still devaluate a resort to the military agencies and instruments conventionally employed by other polities?

- Or does Jewry's new circumstance itself signify God's will that Israel's long period of martial quiescence has at long last been terminated, and that there exists a religious duty actively to participate in the repossession of what is indubitably 'the promised Land' and its defense?

Despite wrestling with such questions for over half a century, Jewish religious thought in Israel has yet to offer unequivocal answers. Instead, the debate to which they give rise continues to generate a wide spectrum of opinions, each of which claims to rest on Divinely inspired tenets of belief.

The *Haredi* Emphasis on Transcendental Forces

One school of thought maintains that Israel's security remains absolutely dependent upon God's will, and hence entirely contingent upon the transcendental forces over which He alone exercises sway. This view finds most explicit contemporary expression among *haredi* ('ultra-orthodox') Jews, who now comprise some 11 percent of Israel's total population. Altogether conservative in their lifestyles, *haredim* seek to insulate themselves as far as possible from what they consider to be the contaminating influences of modernity. Consequently, they set deliberate limits on their participation in Israeli civic life. Quite apart from maintaining an extensive network of 'independent' (albeit largely state-funded) educational institutions and welfare agencies, *haredim* have also persistently insisted that their sons and daughters be excused from the obligations of military conscription legally incumbent on every other young (Jewish) adult. As Chapter 1 (above pp. 1–21) demonstrated, Israeli governments have ever since the late 1970s proven increasingly responsive to the latter demand, with the result that *haredi* non-service is now one of the most conspicuous phenomena in Israeli society.

Facile analyses of *haredi* non-service, especially when packaged for blatantly political purposes, often depict *haredim* as parasites who dodge the draft for entirely selfish motives.[2] But blanket imputations of that sort fail to do justice to what the spiritual guides of ultra-orthodox Jewry claim to be their primary concerns. Taken on their own terms, *haredi* demands for draft exemptions – far from demonstrating an insular disregard for Israel's security requirements – in fact encapsulate a breathtaking cosmic formulation of their substance. They are grounded, first and foremost, in a very clear conception of Jewry's unique mission. As a divinely designated 'holy nation', the *haredim* insist, the house of Israel is specifically charged with a sacred duty to preserve the way of life dictated by the word of God as revealed in the sacred texts generically designated *Torah*. Over the long haul of history the scrutiny of that corpus has contributed far more than any other single activity to Jewry's national security. In the present, too, its diligent

---

2   S. Cohen (1993: 89–92), provides a representative sample of these opinions, especially as expressed by left-of-center secular political parties in Israel.

study constitutes Israel's primary lifeline, as much to physical protection on earth as to spiritual salvation in heaven. By comparison, all conventional agencies of protection must be deemed totally irrelevant. In the words of one late twentieth-century formulation:

> The *Torah* was given to Israel in the wilderness ... and Abraham our father of blessed memory possessed the *Torah* in Haran (i.e. before entering the Holy Land) ... We became an everlasting people before we had the 'land of Israel' or 'territories' ... . Other than the *Torah* we have no security; neither soldiers nor the IDF will help us.[3]

There is much more to this attitude that a quasi-Platonic affirmation of the inherent supremacy of a contemplative way of life. Based upon passages of rabbinic exegesis whose pedigree stretches back for almost 2,000 years, haredi religious concepts of security articulate a belief in the protective properties of scholarship. In this view, *Torah* study, quite apart from being a spiritual ritual of intrinsic worth, also provides the community as a whole with the defensive amour required for physical security. Students of *Torah* not only preserve the faith. By pursuing their vocation they contribute as much (if not more) than do soldiers to national survival. It follows, therefore that the release of *haredi* males from military service in order to pursue that transcendental vocation, and of *haredi* females to create the domestic conditions which might facilitate its accomplishment, constitute supreme national priorities. 'If the government knew how much [*Torah*] students protect the state's well-being through their study, it would put guards in the schools, making sure that *Torah* study is never interrupted' (cited in Selengut 1994: 245).

'National–Religious' Israelis and National Security

Thus articulated, the arguments which underpin an entirely transcendental concept of Israeli national security have always appealed almost exclusively to the introspective world of the *haridim* themselves. They have been (and still are) are rejected with particular vigor by 'national–religious' Israelis who espouse religious Zionism and who, therefore, insist that the reconstitution of Jewish independence in the Holy Land does indeed mark a crucial stage in the theological progress toward messianic redemption. Moreover, since religious Zionists believe that the State of Israel possesses qualities inherently Divine, they maintain that all Jews possess a religious obligation to take whatever measures may be necessary in order to ensure the integrity of its borders and the safety of its citizens.

During the first two decades of Israel's independence (that is, prior to 1967), such teachings supplied an intellectual matrix within which religious Zionists were able to invest the concept of national security with a compound meaning. Study of

---

3   Rabbi Eliezer Shach (1898–2001; one of the most revered leaders of *haredi* Jewry), speech delivered in 1985, quoted in Doron 1988: 504.

the *Torah*, although obviously still vital to the maintenance of Israel's unique links to the Almighty, could therefore no longer be considered the only ingredient of overall national security. It had to be supplemented by more overtly muscular activity. As Rabbi Abraham Isaac Kook (1865–1935), undoubtedly the most innovative and influential of all religious Zionist thinkers, had put it as early as the mid-1920s:

> We require a healthy body. We have greatly occupied ourselves with the soul and have forsaken the holiness of the body. We have neglected health and physical prowess, forgetting that our flesh is as sacred as our spirit … . Our return will only succeed if it will be marked, along with its spiritual glory, by a physical return which will create healthy flesh and blood, strong and well-formed bodies, and a fiery spirit encased in powerful muscles (Kook 1993: 80).

In this formulation, the metaphysical and the tangible criteria for Israel's survival became inextricably fused. Indeed, those two constituents defied depiction as binary or even distinctly compartmentalized properties, which could only be actualized by separate modes of action. Instead, they were so complementary that they formed a single whole, neither segmented nor even hyphenated. *Ipso facto*, every activity undertaken in defense of the state and in its name became holy, and would be effective precisely because it was thus endowed. Especially was this true of operations conducted by Israel's Defense Forces (the IDF). Not even the predominantly secular complexion of the military complement could rob that institution, in its corporate capacity, of intrinsic sanctity. As 'the army of Israel that will liberate the Land of Israel' the IDF had been touched by the Divine. Hence, and as the elder Kook's son and most authoritative interpreter (Rabbi Zvi Yehudah Kook [1881–1982]) proclaimed in a famous address delivered to his students in May 1967, on the 19th anniversary of Israel's declaration of independence: 'Everything connected with the army, all the various items of ordnance, whether produced by us or by gentiles … . All is sacred' (*Psalm XIX to the State of Israel*, reprinted Kook 1969).

Set against that background, military service, especially, had from the first attained among national–religious Israeli Jews a value far in excess of its nominal status as a civic obligation. Whereas *haredim* regarded conscription as, at best, a distraction from the spiritual calling which Jews were placed on earth to follow, for religious Zionists it immediately attained the status of a spiritual privilege. Indeed, even before the IDF was officially established, authoritative exponents of national–religious thought defined service in the ranks of Israel's emerging army to be a *mitzvah*, a term which literally translates as 'commandment' but which in Jewish traditions carries the more meaningful connotation of a Divinely-mandated duty. As such, it provided a model for the manner whereby the temporal and transcendental components of national security could be harmonized and integrated within a single act of individual commitment.[4]

---

4   National–religious service in the underground Jewish fighting organizations established during the mandate period is now covered in Mordechai Friedman 2005.

When juxtaposed with so broad an interpretation, even the threat that military duty might expose religious youth to the perils of secularization (although never far from the surface of most practical minds) paled in importance. So, too, did fears that the demands of the draft might conflict with the need to advance the boundaries of *Torah* scholarship. All such supposed conflicts of interest were subsumed within an ecumenical concept of national security, which stressed overriding importance of sharing the obligations imposed by Israel's defense burdens among orthodox and secular communities alike.

Religious Zionist leaders therefore saw little need – or justification – to solicit anything like the scale of sectorial concessions tabled by their *haredi* counterparts. Prior to 1967 virtually the only substantive demand which they made of Israel's security apparatus was for the establishment of a military chaplaincy (*rabbanut zevayit*), whose principal duties were to ensure the IDF's conformity with orthodox requirements with respect to dietary regulations and sabbath observance (Michaelson 1982).

The Influence of the Six Days War

The Six Days War of 1967 wrought a change of seismic proportions. Regarded throughout Israeli society as an event of near-miraculous proportions, in the national–religious community it assumed an unabashedly apocalyptic meaning. The entry of IDF forces into the old city of Jerusalem, from which Jews had been summarily and ignominiously expelled in 1948, was invested with particular importance. In the words written soon after the war by one of the younger Kook's most articulate disciples:

> With the taking of the Temple Mount, we were suddenly thrust forward by a gigantic hand that propelled us out of the everyday and petty reality in which we had been submerged. At the same time, it seemed to us that we could not possibly absorb all the divine and spiritual force that cascaded onto us from heaven (Yoel Bin-Nun, cited in Aran 1986: 128).

For religious Zionists the scale of Israel's spectacular martial triumph over her enemies not only bore testimony to Divine protection; the achievement also heralded the imminent advent of the millennial End of Days foretold by the prophets. Exhilarated by that prospect, and determined not to forego the messianic opportunity for fulfillment thus provided, mainstream religious Zionist thought embarked on an entirely new course, defined by a determination to make up for lost time by accelerating still further the progress of 'the wheels of the Chariot of Redemption'. In this atmosphere the elder Kook's militant brand of religiously inspired nationalism was embraced with enthusiasm. What until 1967 had been an esoteric set of teachings, composed in an elliptical idiom intelligible only to the initiated few, thereafter became an outward looking and missionary ideology, exuberantly proclaimed by a growing number of Kook's disciples to be of immediate relevance to the entire nation (Aran 1997).

The energy thus released found several outlets. Of these, the most zealously publicized was a program of massive Jewish settlement in the newly conquered territories of Judea and Samaria, expressly designed to ensure the retention of Jewish sovereignty over what was now designated *Erez Yisrael ha-Shelemah* ('The Greater Land of Israel'; Gorenberg 2006: 268–315). Since many of the settlements initially constituted paramilitary outposts, they were justified as major contributions to Israel's overall security. From its inception, national–religious Jews played a vastly disproportionate role in the settlement campaign. They also figured prominently in *Gush Emunim* (the 'Bloc of the Faithful'), the extra-parliamentary lobby which spearheaded that enterprise, established in 1974 for the purpose of thereby facilitating the salvation of Jewry – and, for that matter, of humanity at large. *Gush Emunim's* first statement of intent blatantly announced that its aim 'is to bring about a large movement of re-awakening among the Jewish people for the fulfillment of the Zionist vision in its fullest scope, with the recognition that the source of the vision is Jewish tradition and its roots, and its ultimate objective is the full redemption of the Jewish people and the entire world' (Shafat 1995: 28–32).[5]

Even before it was thus formulated, the doctrine of 'the Greater Land of Israel' had revolutionized most national–religious definitions of the necessary conditions for Israel's security. Prior to 1967 religious Zionists has invariably aligned themselves with the more pragmatic currents of national security opinion, advocating that Jewry's spiritual aspiration to repossess the entire Holy Land might have to be postponed in order to satisfy more urgent exigencies. In 1903, for instance, religious ('Mizrachi') delegates to the sixth Zionist Congress held at Basel, Switzerland, had acknowledged the physical need for a territorial 'refuge', wherever located, and therefore voted to accept Uganda as a possible alternative to a Jewish homeland in Palestine (Vital 1986). Largely on the same grounds, they had in 1937 similarly (albeit more grudgingly) been prepared to accept the Palestine partition proposal momentarily submitted by the British government. Even when that offer was withdrawn, national religious spokesmen acquiesced in the policy of military 'restraint' (*havlagah*) adopted between 1936 and 1939 by the majority of the Zionist *Yishuv* (Wahrhaftig 1988; Don-Yehiya 1993). Overwhelmingly, religious Zionists had followed a similar course throughout the first two decades of Israel's statehood. Focusing their attention on such immediate concerns as the autonomy of the religious educational system and rabbinic courts, they had preferred to consign the hope for a restoration of Jewish sovereignty over the entire Holy Land to a time of God's own choosing.

But in the halcyon atmosphere generated in 1967 by the 'liberation' of Jerusalem, Hebron, Nablus, and Jericho – cities which embrace the very cradle

---

5 *Gush Emunim's*ts impact on religious Zionist messianic theology is now most thoroughly covered in Aran 2013.

of Jewry's ancient homeland and house its most sacred shrines – the tradition of compromise set by all such precedents appeared obsolete. It was for the most part displaced by a far more radical credo, in which the retention of Greater Israel under sovereign Jewish control constituted an axiomatic feature.

That shift had several major ramifications. For one thing it transformed national–religious political affiliations. Once overwhelmingly allied with the moderate left of the Israeli political spectrum, the vast majority of the religious Zionist constituency after 1977 consistently positioned itself on the right. Largely in response to that development, the National-Religious Party (*Mafdal*) adopted increasingly hardline postures on security issues – uncharacteristically preferring to remain in opposition during the second Rabin government (1992–1996) rather than participate in a coalition committed to territorial compromise. Even so, national–religious voters supported still more extreme *Knesset* factions in disproportionate numbers.

Second and largely in consequence, that shift helped to redefine the contours of wider domestic debates on national security. After 1967 these were conducted in terms and, often, in a language, which frequently reflected the nuances now stressed by religious Zionism and were often dominated by its postulates. Even though the transcendentalism associated with the doctrine of the 'Greater Land of Israel' never entirely superseded more temporal strategic imperatives in the overall roster of defense-related priorities, it did nevertheless frame much of the discussion on Israel's national security. In some accounts the definitive fault line in Israeli politics thereby created, marked a crucial state in the erosion of the public consensus on security affairs. Indeed, it opened up an apparently unbridgeable chasm between rival security concepts, based on what Kimmerling (1985b) termed the 'primordial' and 'civil' definitions of the collective identity. This, in turn, affected the possibilities of coalition formation, limiting the flexibility of political parties which in earlier periods had conventionally pursued more pragmatic policies. Issues of war and peace, once debated in a spirit of fundamental empiricism, and with a wide measure of agreement about basic national aims, thereafter had to bear the encumbrance of incompatible ideologies.[6]

Perhaps most profound of all, however, was the impact which the intrusion of the doctrine of a 'Greater Land of Israel' exerted on the intellectual inner world of religious Zionism. There it mandated a particularly rigorous examination of previous tenets of faith and, more specifically still, a fundamental reassessment of all past synthesis between the transcendental and temporal components in national religious security thought. Once again, the dilemmas posed amounted to a series of related queries.

- If, indeed, the Almighty had so clearly demonstrated His will to reestablish Jewish sovereignty over the entire Holy Land, then what right had the House of Israel to renounce its patrimony?

---

6 Changes in the conceptual maps adumbrated by national–religious Zionism (and, by way of comparison, by Labor Zionism and Revisionist Zionism, too) have recently been scrutinized by Shelef 2010.

- Quite apart from contradicting strategic logic (specifically, the need for 'strategic depth'), would not a voluntary withdrawal from all or part of Judea, Samaria and the Gaza Strip also constitute a sin, and thus run the risk of inviting Divine retribution?

- And if that is the case, then does not religious Jewry possess a national duty to take whatever steps may be needed to avert that peril to Israel's ultimate security? In short, does not physical possession of the Land transmute what had hitherto been a long-term aspiration into a tangible and immediate imperative?

On a purely theoretical level such questions were raised almost as soon as the 1967 War came to its speedy end (see Shaviv 1977, pp. 119–120, 130). But the need to grapple with them as concrete issues did not become compelling until after the 1973 Yom Kippur War,[7] which set in motion a train of events whose protracted effects rippled on for several decades. One scenario that attained practical form thereafter was Israeli territorial withdrawal from areas that had been settled after 1967, as was the case with Yamit as early as 1982 and the entire Gaza Strip in 2005. Another was the resort to violence on the part of Jewish vigilantes opposed to those withdrawals (or indeed to the prospect of any compromise with the Palestinians), a specter that first became tangible with the discovery in April 1984 of a militant 'Jewish underground', consisting of some 20 national–religious settlers (Lustick 1988; Weisburd 1989) and that convulsed all Israeli politics in November 1995, when Prime Minister Rabin was assassinated by a national–religious graduate of a *hesder yeshivah*. And behind these incidents lay the even greater drama being played out in the hearts and minds of Israelis whose mood oscillated with increasing tempo after 1987, when spasms of Israeli–Palestinian violence (the first and second *intifadas*) were interspersed with moments of Israeli–Palestinian agreement (notably the first and second Oslo accords of 1993–1995).

National–Religious Reactions

Analyses of Israeli public opinion leave no doubt that by the mid-1990s, when Rabin was assassinated, religious Jews in Israel were altogether evincing a significantly greater propensity to uses of military forces than other segments of the population. In the words of one contemporary study:

> Religiosity ... . accounts for the strongest variations in the figures regarding the use of force, with religious people favoring its use more than secular and

---

7   For an example of the degree to which the trauma of the 1973 war intensified national–religious militant fervor see the analysis of the thought of Rabbi Yehudah Amital (1924–2010), a principal of a leading *yeshiva hesder*, in Inbari 2012: 72–80. The example is especially interesting in view of the subject's subsequent record. After 1982 R. Amital became the most prominent of Israel's national–religious 'doves'.

> observant people ... . According to our data, it is the religious sector that
> displays the highest level of perception of threat (in particular from Syria and
> the Palestinians in the territories), and this is a central factor in the calculus of
> the utility of force exertion (Barzilai and Inbar 1996: 66–67).

Polled over an extended period (1988–1994), and with regard to a wide spectrum of force options against various opponents, religious respondents emerged as the most consistent supporters of what the analysts defined as a 'hawkish stance'. Almost 20 percent supported war initiation against all possible threats to Israel's security (as opposed to an average of under 14 percent in the secular sector); less than 4 percent favored outright territorial withdrawal (as opposed to an average double that figure in the secular community). What is more, the differentials thus apparent tended to become more pronounced over the period of the study.

Equally informative, albeit less precise, are statistics which compare the conformity of religious Zionists and secular Israelis with the demands of the annual military draft. As from the 1990s, 'motivation to service' among national–religious youth (particularly as registered by willingness to volunteer for service in combat units) began to rise markedly. The available data not only sharpened still further the contrast between national–religious and *haredi* interpretations of security; it also highlighted differences between religious Zionists and their secular counterparts. Reports released by the IDF in 1996 admitted that affirmative attitudes toward military service, once considered a hallmark of Israel's status as a 'nation in arms', had since 1992 dipped at the alarming rate of some 2 percent per annum. That trend was particularly marked in the secular segment of the population – and still more so among secular *kibbutz* youngsters. By comparison, the overall drop in the national–religious community was virtually negligible (Cohen 2008: 125–30).

It would clearly be stretching matters too far to attribute these figures entirely to religious conviction. Then, as now, many young national–religious males, like their secular counterparts, enlisted in the IDF in order to prove their abilities to themselves and their peers, or in the hope of subsequently improving their career prospects in civilian life. Nevertheless, among the religious segment ideological motives do seem to have played an especially important role. Surveyed in 1994, almost 50 percent of national–religious high school students attributed their willingness to enlist to a wish 'to fight Israel's enemies' (a term which carries particularly resonant religious connotations); some 30 percent indicated that their choice had been influenced by the teachings of their religious mentors (Ezrachi and Gal 1995). The salience of the latter finding is reinforced by the fact that the national–religious community had during the last decades of the twentieth century also established the paramilitary frameworks of *yeshivot hesder* and *mekhinot kedam tzevayiot toraniyot* (see above pp. 11–13). In its own way, each of these establishments constitutes an agency for social cohesion. Many also act as vehicles for the transmission of a particularly intensive brand of religious Zionist security activism. The refrain to the anthem of the very first *mekhinah*, located in the west Bank settlement of Eli, which was sung, somewhat incongruously, to the tune of the 1960s Pat Boone hit record entitled 'Speedy Gonzales', made no bones about the message instilled: 'Yea, here is this land which I gave to you alone/Yea, here is the land which shall assuredly be yours'.

The Doctrinal Debate

The impression of doctrinal unanimity thus conveyed is misleading. Undoubtedly, the overwhelmingly affirmative attitude of national–religious youth toward enlistment in the IDF testifies to the continuing strength of that community's abiding commitment to undertake whatever physical actions might be required in order to defend the state of Israel. Nevertheless, military service does not – of itself – reflect unanimity with respect to the relative weights of the transcendental and temporal ingredients which (as noted above) any religious Zionist concept of national security must necessarily entail. On this fundamental issue national–religious opinion in fact remains deeply divided, and continues to equivocate between points of view which emphasize one or the other of those extremities and invest each with new meaning. This situation permits a wide spectrum of opinions, many of which represent gradations of persuasion, rather than sharply dichotomous points of view.

The remainder of this chapter traces the nuances of the various positions which emerged after the Six Days War and identifies their principal issues of concern.

Although political passion is perhaps the most obtrusive feature of national–religious debates on Israel's security affairs, that is not their defining characteristic. What distinguishes discourse in this particular community is the need to authenticate the validity of security policies in essentially theological terms and to assess security concepts in the light of dogmas distilled from canonical sources. Such obligations have not only dictated the idiosyncratic texture and terminology of debate. They also help to explain its diffuse nature. The relative paucity of traditional Jewish national security teachings has provided considerable room for intellectual maneuver, allowing rabbinic interpreters of Israel's strategic dilemmas to give full rein to their polemic skills.

Given the complexities thus injected into the situation, it is perhaps hardly surprising that no monolithic national–religious formulation of Israel's security desiderate emerged. Instead, opinions were by the mid-1970s already sharply (albeit unequally) divided. Whilst the overwhelming preponderance of religious Zionist security thought adhered to the principles enunciated by rabbinic supporters of 'the Greater Land of Israel' and hence insisted on the need to retain military control over the regions conquered in 1967, other voices also made themselves heard. Prominent among the latter were a small sprinkling of academics and rabbis, the vigor of whose pronouncements often belies the paucity of their number. Opposed to the program advocated by *Gush Emunim* on religious as well as practical grounds, many members of this circle became firm advocates of territorial compromise. Quite apart from forming themselves into several, often overlapping pressure groups for that purpose (*Netivot Shalom*, *Oz ve-Shalom*, and *Meimad*), they also produced a string of pamphlets that inspired (indeed invited) responses by spokesmen for alternative viewpoints and thus gave birth to a security-related discourse the likes of which had not taken place in orthodox Jewry for over two millennia.[8]

Many such works are couched in the intricate lingua franca of Jewish legalistic (*halakhic*) discourse, and hence appeal principally to small circles of cognoscenti. Nevertheless, once the various layers of scholasticism have been peeled away, several central foci of more popular dissension clearly emerge. Undoubtedly the most persistent concerns the strategic implications to be drawn from a recognition of the inherent sanctity of the Land of Israel – a portion of the globe which, since invested by God Himself with attributes of holiness, must therefore be cherished and defended with especial zeal. In the words of the peroration to one of the most popular handbooks of ritual instruction on military matters (most of which is devoted to a detailed discussion of the do's and don'ts of Sabbath observance in camp), published just a few years after the Six Days War and some time before the foundation of *Gush Emunim*:

> The justification for our actions in the land of Israel and for our right to impose our will on a hostile population, for our right to establish settlements everywhere throughout the land of Israel, for our right to kill terrorists and blow up their houses ... the justification for all these matters is not to be found in quotidian considerations. Our right to all this derives from an entirely different plain; from our right to exist as a people and from our right to the land of Israel (Min-Hahar 1971: 206).

Precisely how much self-sacrifice such postulates might require from individual servicemen constituted only one bone of theological contention. As a pivot of debate on national security affairs it was gradually overshadowed in salience by at least two other conundrums of similarly profound religious relevance. One is the degree to which Israel's continued military rule over a large Palestinian minority might, or might not be reconciled with those passages of the Bible which define the limits – and prerogatives – of Jewish territorial sovereignty in the Holy Land. (Compare, for instance, Deuteronomy 7:2: 'Thou shalt not make a treaty with them or spare them', with Exodus 22:21: 'Thou shalt not wrong an alien or be hard on him'). The other is the equally hallowed recognition of the categorical need to avoid any action which might be classified as *pikuah nefesh* (a danger to [Jewish] life).

Although analytically distinct, and indeed treated entirely separately in the capacious compendia of rabbinic instruction which orthodox Jews consider binding, both tenets intruded with increasing force into the religious Zionist quest for a comprehensive security equation. In so doing, they created yet another layer

---

8   All previous surveys of this literature are superseded by Naor 2001.

of intersecting dilemmas which have yet to be resolved. Thus, to date there exists no uniformly accepted rabbinic guideline defining Israel's relationships with the Palestinians. Indeed, since the latter are variously categorized as either the present-day descendants of 'Amalek' (whom the Bible commands to be annihilated: Deuteronomy 25:19) or 'alien sojourners' (*gerim toshavim*; whose rights have to be respected; Leviticus 25:47ff), it is not at all clear whether peaceful coexistence between Israelis and Palestinians might, in religious terms, not only be politically attainable but also theologically defensible.

Neither has religious Zionist thought yet charted a unanimous course through the thicket of *pikuah nefesh*. Which scenario, it is asked, constitutes a greater infringement of the latter principle – an Israeli withdrawal from Judea and Samaria (which could immediately endanger the lives and property of local Jewish settlers there) or the retention of 'the territories' (which might ultimately provoke yet another costly war)? By the same token, which situation poses a greater threat to the moral fiber of the nation: rulership over a subject populace, or the dilution of societal belief in Jewry's right to repossess its God-given patrimony?

Even so bald a summary of the issues involved reveals the difficulties of attempting to align them on a unidimensional axis. Certainly, national–religious perspectives on security cannot be reduced to a matrix which might suggest a distinction between outlooks which are either 'pragmatic' or 'ideological'. In their pronouncements and writings proponents of all shades of religious Zionist national security thinking in fact deny the applicability of any such labels. In equal measure, all claim to base their positions on arguments firmly grounded in both empirical, physical ('temporal') considerations as well as in sublime, metaphysical ('transcendental') necessities. Where they differ is in their identification of the authorities best placed to determine the appropriate equilibrium between those components and thereby define whatever meaning the term 'national security' is meant to convey. At issue, therefore, is less the religious legitimacy of any particular act of security policy than the ultimate locus of the authority rightfully empowered to determine its course and implementation.

At this level of analysis, the variant positions – although cutting across the conventional 'hawk–dove' divide – did in other respects become increasingly dichotomous. One school of opinion argued that all religious definitions of national security must be commensurate with whatever determinants might be delineated by the professional military authorities and by the elected government to which they are responsible. It advocated, in other words, an attempt to accommodate (and, in extreme versions, even subject) inwardly determined formulations of the required balance between transcendental and temporal concerns to the external constraints imposed by governmental decisions, themselves arrived at on non-theological grounds and taken by non-rabbinic councils. Whether those decisions favor or reject territorial compromise is, in this view, subordinate to the procedures by which they are reached.

By contrast, a second body of opinion adopted what purported to be a far more intransigent stance and firmly placed the boot on the other foot. Specifically, it required the harmonization of political and military definitions of national security policies with an agenda set by theological priorities which, the last analysis, can be properly interpreted only by accredited 'masters of the [Jewish] law', and hence by religious Jewry's own spiritual guides.

Although sporadically articulated ever since the end of the Six Days War, the accomodationist school of national–religious security thought for long thereafter remained a marginal current of opinion. That situation changed dramatically in 1990, with the publication of an essay entitled 'Ceding Territory of the Land of Israel in Order to Save Lives' (translated in Yosef 1990). Interestingly, this pronouncement did not emanate from a source conventionally associated with the national–religious community. Its author was Rabbi Ovadya Yosef (born 1921), a former Sephardi Chief Rabbi of Israel who soon after his enforced retirement from that office in 1982 became the founder and spiritual leader of the Sephardi *haredi* party, *Shas*. Despite these anomalies, 'Ceding Territory' nevertheless immediately earned recognition as an authoritative exposition whose influence extended to laymen and scholars alike. In part, that reputation reflects the towering prestige of Rabbi Ovadyah Yosef (commonly, '*Harav* [Rabbi] *Ovadyah*'), who is widely regarded as among the most pre-eminent of all living *halakhic* authorities (*poskei halakhah*).[9] But it is also justified by virtue of the clarity of its content. For both reasons, it warrants analysis in some detail.

In the very first sentence of his essay, R. Ovadyah disclaims any intention of delivering 'a *halakhic* ruling whether the government of Israel should return territories of the Land of Israel or not'. What he presents, instead, is a rabbinic commission, which authorizes the government to reach its own decision, quite independently of religious pressure one way or another. Coming from a rabbi, that is a radical position, but one that (so he claims) traditional rabbinic methodology can comfortably accommodate. After all, for centuries rabbis have deferred to doctors – including, R. Ovadyah adds, non-Jewish doctors – when deciding whether or not a sick person may eat or drink on the Day of Atonement, which under any other circumstances, is a mortal sin. In so doing, they have not divested themselves of their own authority to decide which path to follow. On the contrary, they have given the full force of *halakhic* backing to medical advice. Precisely the same procedure must be followed when deciding on matters of national security. Here, too, *halakhah* does not relinquish all responsibility. Instead, it explicitly requires that non-*halakhic* 'expert opinion' has the last word.

In this view, the appropriate point of departure is neither the inherent sanctity of the Land of Israel nor even the deterrent value which might result from a governmental decision to retain control over the West Bank if the *halakhah* accepts both propositions (R. Ovadya himself emphatically concurs with the first but questions the second), its exponents cannot adduce either as a basis for deciding where Israel's security interests lie. The only acceptable touchstone of judgment is the principle of *pikuah nefesh*, which is here interpreted to mean the degree

---

9   R. Ovadya's *halakhic* philosophy has been extensively examined in Lau 2005.

to which a particular course of action promises to save, or endanger the greatest number of human lives. That is something which only military experts can decide, and their decision (like that of a doctor's) must be considered *halakhic*ally binding. 'If the commanders of the army, together with the political experts, determine that retaining the territories entails *pikuah nefesh*, we rely on their judgment and permit the cession of territory' (p. 18).

The alternative school of national–religious security opinion not only posited opposite conclusions.[10] More significantly, it started from an entirely dissimilar premise. Basic to its view is the axiomatic conviction that what God had granted, only He can possibly take away (Specifically: 'None of us owns the land of Israel. Hence, none of us has any right to relinquish any portion of the entire country' (Goren 1992)). One obvious conclusion was that any measure of voluntary Israeli withdrawal from the territories would constitute a mortal sin – by definition, the most tangible of all possible threats to national security. Another, still more explosive in its potential implications, was that any Israeli government which might decide to implement such a withdrawal must immediately forfeit whatever claims to legitimacy it might otherwise be entitled to possess. After all, no human agency enjoys a right to contravene Divine commandments. On the contrary, one of the most cardinal of all rules of Jewish constitutional thumb unequivocally maintains that 'should the king come to nullify the word of the Torah; he is not to be obeyed' (Code of Maimonides 3:9: 214).

There exists a certain symmetry in the fact that a principle proponent of the latter view, and certainly one of its most outspoken exponents, was R. Shlomo Goren (1917–1994). A one-time IDF chief chaplain (see above p. 10), R. Goren had shortly after his retirement been appointed Ashkenazi Chief Rabbi of Israel, an office which brought him into particularly close contact with R. Ovadya. Their views on the arbitration of security affairs nevertheless present sharp contrasts, as is illustrated by their polarized reaction to the news of the 1993 Oslo Accords. Whereas R. Ovadya saw no reason to alter one line of his earlier publication, R. Goren immediately rushed into print. Indeed, he issued a copiously footnoted *halakhic* ruling which not only categorically prohibited the surrender of Jewish dominion over any portion of Judea, Samaria and the Gaza Strip, but which also took that 'transcendental' position to its logical conclusion. Since it now seemed inevitable that IDF troops would be ordered to implement the transfer of sovereignty in 'the territories' to Palestinian jurisdiction, they must be prepared to disobey any such instruction on religious grounds. Specifically:

> It is clear that according to the *halakhah* a soldier who receives an order which contradicts the laws of the Torah must carry out the *halakhah* and not a secular instruction … *A fortiori* is it forbidden to obey a military order which contradicts the commandment of settling the land of Israel, which is equivalent to all the commandments of the *Torah* (Goren 1993).

---

10   For an English translation of one example, see Yisraeli 1990.

Where one of the recognized giants of national religious opinion thus chose to lead, others soon followed. Late in March 1994, a still more explicit call to 'conscientious objection' was published by an additional rabbinic triumvirate, comprised of some of national religious Jewry's most respected ideologues. Matters reached a still higher pitch in May 1995, when a group of 15 additional mentors (who termed themselves 'The Union of Rabbis on Behalf of the People of Israel and the Land of Israel') issued a manifesto couched in similar terms. Composed 'after analysis of the subject in all its aspects' and 'in response to enquiries from citizens and soldiers from all sectors of the public', the manifesto constituted an uncompromising attestation of the right of rabbinic authorities to exercise exclusive powers of adjudication – in national security matters as much as in all others. Hence, should transcendental push ever come to temporal shove, the latter had to give way.

> We determine that the *Torah* forbids the dismantlement of IDF bases and [their] transfer to gentile authorities … Hence, in response to the question, it is clear and simple that every Jew is forbidden to take part in any action which might facilitate the evacuation of a settlement [military] camp or installation (cited S. Cohen 1997: 131).

Implications

As subsequent chapters will show, echoes of the debate thus initiated were to rumble on well into the first decade of the twenty-first century. They became especially loud during the year that separated Mr. Ariel Sharon's initial announcement of his 'disengagement' plan in 2004 and its implementation in August 2005. Even then, no universally acceptable resolution of the issues involved was attained. Driven by the twin furies of transcendental aspirations and temporal necessities, religious Jewry in Israel still struggled to accommodate both within the bounds of a single equation.

PART II
Adaptations and their Price

Chapter 4

The *Hesder Yeshivot* in Israel:
A Church-state Military Arrangement[1]

Yeshivot ('seats [of learning]') is the Hebrew term for the academies in which Jewish males study their law and lore. Literary evidence for the existence of institutions bearing that name dates back two millennia, throughout which time they have enjoyed considerable reverence in Jewish tradition.

In part, the esteem which Jewish culture accords to *yeshivot* stems from the facilities that they provide for the study of texts regarded by orthodox Jews as sacred. But it must also be attributed to their inherent ambience. Like similar academies of learning in other cultures, *yeshivot* constitute agencies of socialization. By tradition, young men enroll in their chosen *yeshivah* when they are in their teens; thereafter they are expected to immerse themselves entirely in its way of life. Housed in dormitories and subjected to a rigorous timetable of study interrupted only by daily prayer, they are almost entirely secluded from extraneous influences. Pure scholarship is their aim; and the principals of the *yeshivah* are their role models and supreme authorities (under God).

Thus baldly described, *yeshivot* conform to characteristics which Lewis Coser attributed to 'greedy institutions':

> They seek exclusive and undivided loyalty and they attempt to reduce the claims
> of competing roles and status positions on those they wish to encompass within
> their boundaries. Their demands on the person are omnivorous (Coser 1974: 4).

Moreover, they thus manage to act with a remarkable degree of success. Even though very few of today's *yeshivot* are insulated from the pressures associated with modern, western society, most have nevertheless retained their essential exclusivity. Conforming to Coser's paradigm, they continue 'to exercise pressures on component individuals to weaken their ties, or not to form any ties, with other institutions or persons that might make claims that conflict with their own demands'.

Ironically, it is precisely in Israel, which was founded as an explicitly Jewish state, that *yeshivot* confront some of their most serious challenges. This is especially so since it is there that their students have to come to terms with the counter – demands on their loyalties imposed by another equally 'greedy' institution – the military. Israeli society has framed various solutions to the dilemmas which

---

1 The original version of this chapter appeared in *Journal of Church and State*, vol. 35 (1993), pp. 113–130.

ensue. This chapter will focus on one such solution (the '*hesder*' *yeshivah*) and investigate the specific tensions which it engenders.

As an institution, the Israel Defense Force is even 'greedier' than most other armies (Moskos and Wood 1988). Compelled to sustain the burdens of a protracted violent conflict, the IDF imposes heavy demands on the country's resources. Especially profound is the pervasiveness of the military impact on private lives (Kimmerling 1985). Conscription is mandatory for all citizens aged 18 (the present draft terms are three years for males and two for females); after demobilization, soldiers are also liable for annual reserve duty until middle age.

Even before conscription was formally enacted in 1948, principals of some prominent Israeli *yeshivot* petitioned that their students be exempted from its provisions. In the main, their case was based on the need to compensate for the mass destruction of the main European agencies of Jewish culture during the Holocaust. They also stressed the corrosive effect on their students' spiritual welfare bound to be produced by extended army service in a necessarily non-religious environment. On both counts, they asked that accredited *yeshivah* students might pursue their vocation without interruption (Me. Friedman 1990).

Military Responses to the Challenge of the *Yeshivot*

Repeated with varying degrees of intensity ever since 1948, that request has elicited three separate and contradictory responses from Israel's military authorities: confrontation, retreat, and accommodation.

Confrontation

Insistent on Israel's need for all available manpower, the IDF has refused to release *yeshivah* students from the call to arms. Individually, therefore, they are treated as are all other (non-Arab) citizens. Prior to a citizen's 18th birthday, each is summoned to an army induction center for medical and psychometric tests. Only if one fails those examinations is one formally excused from service.

Retreat

An alternative response has been to allow full-time *yeshivah* students to defer their army service until they complete their studies. This arrangement was sanctioned as early as 1947 by David Ben-Gurion, Israel's first premier and minister of defense. In response to the above-mentioned petition by the *yeshivot*, he allowed extended deferments of service for all males who could show that 'the study of *torah* [Jewish sacred texts] was their profession'. As a result, persons in that category were in effect exempted from all military duty.

Initially restricted to just a few hundred males, the scale of releases thus granted has in recent years increased considerably. Successive coalition agreements have of late virtually enshrined the blanket deferment of military service by *yeshivah* students. Official sources now report that the sum total of such releases now exceeds 50,000 (see above pp. 5–6).

Accommodation

By and large, deferments from military service by *yeshivah* students are sought by the ultra-orthodox (generally designated *haredi* [lit. 'zealous']) wings of Israel's Jewish population, of which they comprise some 11 percent. By contrast, that option has not been favored by the country's somewhat more moderate 'national–religious' sectors, which now make up some 12 to 15 percent of the total Jewish population. True, the latter's spokesmen and rabbinical guides were always just as committed as the ultra-orthodox to the maintenance of traditional scholarship – and equally concerned to protect their youth from the secularization which prolonged army duty might induce. However, they persistently declared military service in defense of the state to be a religious injunction no less obligatory than even the pursuit of learning. Hence, they acknowledged throughout the IDF's right to draft *yeshivah* students along with all other citizens. Nevertheless, they did not in consequence abandon all claims to special consideration for their own needs. Rather, they sought various compromises that might accommodate their hyphenated obligations to both religion and state (Liebman and Don-Yehiya 1984).

Hesder (lit. 'arrangement') *yeshivot* constitute striking examples of that sort of compromise. Briefly stated, institutions thus designated seek to provide a framework within which IDF male conscripts might simultaneously satisfy the requirements of both their civic duty and their religious vocation.[2] To revert to Coser's terminology, they thus attempt to moderate the conflicting demands of two essentially 'greedy' bodies.

Three aspects of that accommodation are particularly striking: length of service, locus of service, and conditions of service.

Length of Service

Unlike all other IDF conscripts, who are drafted for three years of consecutive service, entrants into the *hesder* program contract for a five-year term. Throughout that period, they are formally subjected to several restrictions (such as requiring written army permission to leave the country). However, they are not continuously under a direct military regimen. Rather, they alternate spells of *yeshivah* study

---

2   Traditional Judaism considered study of the holy texts to be an entirely male preserve. Hence, no institutions equivalent to *yeshivot* were ever made available to women. In 'modern orthodox' circles, both in the United States and in Israel, that situation has recently begun to change (T. Cohen 2004). One result has been the foundation, in the years since this chapter was originally published, of several *hesder* – type institutions for women, termed *midrashot* ('places of study'). See Rossman-Stollman 2005.

with army duty, and in total actually spend less time within a military framework than do conventional three-year conscripts.[3]

Locus of Service

As a rule, the IDF's Manpower Directorate (*AKA*) adheres to strict rules of placement. After evaluation, conscripts are assigned to army units in accordance with the IDF's current needs. Although draftees are encouraged to state their unit preference, the IDF is not obliged to comply with individual wishes. Indeed, Israel's Supreme Court has confirmed the military's autonomy over manpower placements even in the case of conscripts whom the IDF had itself permitted to attain a secular university education prior to their regular conscript service.

Hesder conscripts constitute one of the few exceptions to that norm. Once accepted by *yeshivot* into the *hesder* program, they are thereafter eligible for a restricted span of units. Basically, this is because they can only be assigned to military sectors whose training schedules are compatible with the *hesder* timetable. Initially, therefore, most *hesder* conscripts were placed in the tank corps. Over the past decade, the range has been expanded somewhat, and now includes some infantry brigades. Nevertheless, the extent of the IDF's autonomous control over *hesder* placements still remains comparatively limited.[4]

Conditions of Service

Ever since its establishment, the IDF has attempted to act as Israel's 'melting pot', primarily by bonding citizens from different backgrounds within a single framework. Accordingly, the composition of its units is deliberately designed to reflect the diverse origins and cultures of the Jewish population of Israel as a whole. There exist no special formations for conscripts from a particular region or

---

3   At present, the 60-month term of hesder service is generally divided up as follows: first ten months on the yeshivah campus; next eight to nine months on an army base where conscripts are given basic training and instruction in their particular military profession (in some units this period also includes two months of active duty); next 12 months in the yeshivah; next seven to eight months in their army units; remaining 20 to 21 months in the yeshivah, during which time they are also liable for reserve duty in their army units, if necessary. This timetable emerged after the commitment demanded of hesder conscripts was in 1976 extended from four years to five. Periodic changes in the timetable are now updated in the IDF website, which includes a portal dedicated to informing prospective recruits about their conditions of service <https://www.aka.idf.il/Main/giyus/general.aspx?catId=61323&docId=74383>, last accessed September 19, 2012.

4   On the one hand the minority of *hesder* conscripts considered physically unsuitable for either the infantry or armored brigades are usually assigned to such service units as the medical or intelligence corps. On the other hand, however, even suitably qualified *hesder* conscripts are disbarred by the needs of their program from service in a wider range of IDF branches (such as the computer programming unit).

ethnic group. No special provisions are made for draftees from common religious backgrounds to serve together, and although there did once exist a specifically Druze unit, this has now been disbanded (Ben-Dor 1973, Frisch 1993).

In this respect, too, *hesder* conscripts are exceptional. Unlike most other IDF troops, they do not enlist individually. Instead, they complete their basic training (at least) in their own homogeneous battalion formations. Moreover, they are not formally enlisted until after they have already spent several months together in the quasi-cloistered atmosphere of a *yeshivah*, by which time they know each other very well.

The conditions of service thus established are subsequently reinforced. *Hesder* conscripts, unlike others, are not insulated from the non-military institutions with which they were previously affiliated. Instead, their ties to their individual *yeshivot* are maintained by the receipt of periodic leaflets containing a short talmudic discourse as well as local *yeshivah* gossip. Only marginally less frequent are visits by *yeshivah* teachers to their students in base. Moreover, many such activities are coordinated by the umbrella council of the *yeshivot hesder*, whose staff liaisons with a small army unit especially mandated to deal with all matters pertaining to the *hesder* conscripts' conditions of service.

The Origins and Growth of the 'Arrangement'

Thus outlined, the *hesder* program is akin to parallel arrangements between the IDF and Israel's kibbutz movements. As early as 1948, the latter – representing yet another of the country's 'greedy institutions'– promoted the establishment of the *Nachal* [Youth Pioneering] corps. This allows young men and women to enlist as 'nuclei' (*garinim*). It also permits them to alternate spells of military service – usually in an infantry or parachute brigade – with agricultural labor in a kibbutz environment during their conscript terms (Lutwak and Horowitz 1975: 421–3).

Hesder was a subsequent development. Not until 1963 did representatives of 'national–religious' *yeshivot* persuade the IDF to expand and adapt the *Nachal* framework to suit the particular needs of their own student constituency (Bar-Lev 1989). Precisely how the case was presented is still obscure; but its attractions to the respective parties are readily apparent. To the military authorities, it presumably offered a method of stemming the potential loss of several religious recruits (Azarya 1983). The motives of the 'national–religious' *yeshivot* were probably more complicated. Besides promising to fulfill their ideological principles, *hesder* also provided a possible means of preventing the desertion of putative students to rival, *haredi* institutions of learning.

Although the majority of 'national religious' youth still enlist as regular conscripts, the *hesder* program has become increasingly popular. The number of accredited *yeshivot hesder* grew from just one (with under 30 students) in 1965 to 16 (with a combined annual intake of almost 1,000) in 1991. Equally striking has been the recognition won by the system. No longer under the nominal aegis of the *Nachal* corps, *hesder* troops are now integral members of the brigades to which they belong. Within the national–religious community, '*hesdernicks*' (as they are affectionately termed) are lauded as personifications of that sector's commitment to both the traditions of Orthodox Jewry and to the State of Israel. Other sectors of Israeli society, although somewhat less effusive, are equally congratulatory. In 1991 the *hesder yeshivot* were collectively awarded the prestigious Israel Prize for their unique contribution to the texture of national life (see above p. 12).

Hesder Yeshivot and the IDF: Sources of Possible Tension

Deserved though such accolades undoubtedly are, observation suggests that the *hesder* program is not without flaws. Like several other attempts to frame hybrid accommodations between competing 'greedy' institutions, in some respects it creates tensions of its own. Hence, the program has already undergone several modifications. As will be argued below, further adjustments might yet be required.

Of the several areas of tension generated by the *hesder* program, three are particularly obtrusive. They may be designated as social, professional, and personal.

Social

Interviews with IDF service personnel of various ranks leave no doubt that unit cohesion in *hesder* military formations is usually very high.[5] Basically, this is because such formations are comprised of like-minded individuals whose ties of comradeship have been forged in the closed atmosphere of the *yeshivah* (if not earlier, by virtue of their membership of the same youth movement; Bar-Lev 1988).

From a military standpoint, this situation has several advantages. First, it markedly moderates tendencies toward friction in the highly pressured and stressful atmosphere which strenuous military training frequently induces. Thus, within *hesder* units, incidences of personal theft and 'ragging' in boot-camp are unusually rare phenomena. (Presumably, they are in any case discouraged, if not altogether precluded, by the religious standards to which *yeshivah* students usually aspire). Doubtless for the same combination of reasons, *hesder* conscripts commonly display understanding towards those of their comrades-in-arms who experience difficulties in adjusting to the rigors of army life.

Analysis has long emphasized the relevance of such support systems to combat motivation. Noting the importance of the 'buddy' syndrome in fighting forces, the literature has endowed the principle of unit cohesion with virtually axiomatic status. Indeed, it is widely regarded as an essential prerequisite of effective military performance under fire (Henderson 1985). Judged by those standards, the *hesder* program would appear to be eminently satisfactory. This is especially so since the *hesder* troops themselves are in any case generally regarded as highly

---

5   See also Rossman-Stollman 2005.

motivated soldiers. Nevertheless, there exists a danger that the very homogeneity of the *hesder* unit might itself prove to be a double-edged sword.

Fears to that effect have been voiced by a former head of the IDF Education Corps, General Nehemiah Dagan, whom I interviewed in 1991. He regards the establishment of *hesder* units as incompatible with the army's integrative function. Principally, this is because their composition deprives conscripts from religious and non-religious backgrounds of almost the only opportunity they will ever have for day-to-day contact. As such, the 'arrangement' threatens to add a further dimension to the divisions between those two communities which, since they pervade so many areas of public life, are in any case undermining the unitary fabric of Israeli society.

To this must be added the more painful effects which might be exerted on the 'national–religious' sector itself – should *hesder* units ever suffer a high rate of casualties in battle. In such a circumstance, the homogeneity of the *hesder* units' composition is likely to increase the vulnerability to distress of the specific community from which they are drawn. This kind of vulnerability became painfully apparent during the 1982 Lebanon War, when a tank unit of *hesder* troops sustained particularly heavy losses in an engagement with Syrian forces near Sultan Yakub (10–11 June 1982). The consequences were not randomly distributed throughout the entire nation, but were concentrated within the 'national–religious' segment – and, indeed, within specific *yeshivot* (Schiff and Ya'ari 1984: 173–9; Gabriel 1984: 104).

One way of reducing both dangers is to distribute *hesdernicks* among other battalion formations within the brigades. Indeed, in light of the 1982 experience, the tank corps often disbands organic *hesder* once the conscripts conclude their initial six to seven months of basic and advanced training. Thereafter, the troops are attached on an individual basis to other battalions for whatever duties are required.

But such procedures merely create alternative problems. The constraints of their timetable do not permit the *hesder* troops thus disbursed to become fully integrated members of their new units. Rather, they are virtually 'in transit'. Quite apart from impeding the development of close interpersonal relations between the *hesdernicks* and their comrades, that situation undermines unit cohesion by generating numerous areas of petty friction. Perhaps latently resentful of the fact that the *hesder* additions to their complement are 'here today and off to the *yeshivah* tomorrow', other troops in the battalion are apt to assign them a disproportionate load of the menial tasks whose rotation occupies so large a part of all army life. *Hesdernicks*, indeed, frequently find themselves unevenly burdened with kitchen and latrine duties, or granted less leave. To protest against such inequalities is to invite the retort that they merely rectify distortions produced while the *hesder* nicks were comfortably ensconced in their *yeshivot*.

Professional

Although in origin the outgrowth of an underground fighting force, the IDF has always placed a premium on the acquisition and deployment of advanced weaponry. Indeed, its commanders have regularly maintained that only by maintaining a qualitative edge over her several foes might Israel compensate for her quantitative disadvantages. In recent years especially, the IDF's arsenal has accordingly become increasingly sophisticated.

The possible effects of that development on the IDF's battle doctrines lie beyond present concerns of this chapter. More immediately relevant are its implications for the type of military personnel required. Briefly stated, the introduction of 'high-tech' weapons has necessitated progressively specialized levels of troop training and exercises. The IDF still retains many of the characteristics of a 'people's army' (not the least obtrusive of which is mandatory annual reserve duty until middle age). Nevertheless, it is also becoming increasingly professional. This trend has long been evident in the air force, traditionally the most technologically advanced of the IDF's arms, where all trainee pilots contract for extensive periods of professional duty. The same trend is apparent in other services, some of which also provide pre-conscript instruction for new recruits (R. Goren 1989).

Within that context, the *hesder* program (very much like the *Nachal* arrangement on which it was modeled), appears to be something of a military anachronism.[6] As has been seen, the *hesder* conscript's alternating timetable *ab initio* restricts the span of units to which he can usefully be assigned. Even within those units, however, the same constraint also impedes the proficiency of a soldier's battle-readiness. Sedentary study, after all, can hardly be conducive to the maintenance of the conscript's physical fitness between his two spells of military duty. Moreover, the interruption of army service by *yeshivah* studies soon after the completion of initial training courses impedes the retention of the skills which modern weaponry demands.

Significantly, recent modifications in the standard *hesder* program have shown an awareness of that drawback, and have attempted to overcome it. A change introduced in 1991 now provides for what is termed the 'joining' of the fragmented segments of the *hesder* conscripts' service. Instead of spending two relative short spells in the army (in between roughly equally short terms in the *yeshivah*), many will now complete their conscript term in one longer tour of duty.

Even if accepted by all principals of the *hesder yeshivot*,[7] that arrangement – by itself – is unlikely to remove entirely all existing professional differentials between the *hesdernicks* and their peers. Indeed, if anything, the distinctions might thereby be accentuated. Since the *hesder* battalions are now likely to retain their homogeneity throughout the term of conscript service, their members might collectively be assigned the 'outsider' status hitherto attributed to them on an individual basis. As such, they are more likely to be treated as supplements to their parent brigade, rather than as one of its integral components. Indications of this likelihood are already apparent from a review of the rotation of constabulary

---

6   S. Cohen 2008: 95–6.

7   Two of the largest *hesder yeshivot* (Kerem be-Yavneh and Har-Etzion) long resisted the change, arguing that so extended a period of uninterrupted army service would dilute the students' scholastic commitment.

duties within one of the IDF's tank brigades in 'the territories' (as the regions conquered by Israel in 1967 are commonly known). *Hesder* battalions, it seems, are assigned a disproportionate share of that chore which, besides being inherently distasteful to many conscripts, is also one which lies beyond the arc of their distinctive military expertise. Their sense of relative inferiority is intensified by the fact that other (non-*hesder*) battalions in the brigade are meanwhile engaged in training exercises or line duty.

Even if such a practice does not become the norm, other problems will still have to be resolved. Primary among these are the inherent tensions created by the conflicting demands which the *yeshivah* and the military will continue to make on the individual conscript's talents. One prominent instance regularly occurs at the conclusion of the initial professional military courses, when gifted graduates are invited to join their corps' officers training program. Since most officers are expected to 'sign on' for an additional period of service, this is altogether a major personal commitment. But the burdens that it imposes on *hesdernicks* are particularly onerous, because their *yeshivot* require them to make up for their absence during the officers course by adding several months to their final period of study. Thus, by the time an officer *hesdernick* is discharged, the officer will have spent some 70 months within its framework and be over 24 years old. Furthermore, should the aspiring candidate still not be deterred by that daunting prospect, the candidate's 'parent' *yeshivah* retains what amounts to the power of a veto over the candidate's choice. Before registering for an officer's course, *hesder* students have to obtain the explicit permission of their *yeshivah* principals – by no means an automatic procedure.

Such academic intrusions into areas which standard military convention otherwise regards as the army's own autonomous sphere are not exceptional. Indeed, the *hesder* program is altogether riddled with similar anomalies. Unlike other conscripts, who are rigorously insulated from all sources of authority other than those which are strictly military in origin, *hesder* troops can regularly remind themselves of the existence of an alternative hierarchy. Even during basic training, they have access to various 'escape routes' from the normal military demands regimen which precludes all contact with non-military frameworks (Gal 1986: 162–80). At the very least, the IDF is obliged to satisfy *hesder* troops' religious requirements: for time to pray three times each day, or for reduced physical exertions on prescribed fast days. Although it is true that requirements of this sort are equally incumbent on non-*hesder* religious troops, from a military–organization perspective the two cases nevertheless differ. Because the *hesder* units are homogenous, such constraints have to be built into their collective timetable; whereas in other units, the individual religious soldier must find his own way of meeting his needs. Still more intrusive are the institutionally provided opportunities for non-military relief in *hesder* units. Summary intermissions in training – virtually unknown to other troops – are sometimes caused by visits of *yeshivah* teachers to the base, where they give their students impromptu discourses.

Precisely how the training staff reacts to such invasions of the usually secluded military domain must await further inquiry. Preliminary investigation leaves little doubt, however, of the professional strains to which it is prone. Neither the officers nor the NCOs assigned to train *hesder* units are required to be members of the *hesder* program. Many come from secular backgrounds and require – and are given – their own courses of instruction in basic Jewish religious rites prior to their assignment. Even thus prepared, however, they can hardly empathize with the *hesder* troops' special needs and demands. As a result, a latent potential for friction between them and what is in any case an exceptionally cohesive (and often highly articulate) cohort of trainees is constantly present. After all, the latter's conception of a chain of command is not limited to their sergeant on the parade ground. Rather, their horizon extends to their *yeshivah* principal and, in the last resort, to God.

Thus to indicate the *hesdernick*'s opportunities to escape his military environment is not to question the seriousness with which he otherwise takes his army duties but merely to point out the extent to which he cannot entirely compartmentalize the two segments of his world. Indeed, that phenomenon cuts both ways. When in the *yeshivah* he is similarly distracted – albeit this time by the imminence of military commitments. As a result, his academic standards are to some degree impaired.

Most interruptions in *yeshivah* studies are caused by technical circumstances such as the students' needs to make physical and administrative preparations for the shift to a new environment which they know to be forthcoming. Psychological adjustments, however, are also required. Much of their conversation towards the end of their first year in the *yeshivah* is devoted to anxious speculation about their forthcoming military service (the presence on the campus of senior students ensures an adequate supply of informants). Similarly tense is the parallel 'boundary' period immediately preceding the second stint of service. Lapses of concentration during such times are consequently fairly frequent, and individual absences from the *yeshivah* for several days (otherwise a rare occurrence) are not uncommon. Although the *yeshivah* authorities attempt to curb such behavior, their efforts are not always successful. The *hesder* student need not resort to guile to justify his absences.

Personal

From the standpoint of the individual conscript, enrollment in the *hesder* program seems to be motivated by two distinct impulses. One is his need for a social environment which might ease his adjustment to army life. By providing an assurance that the conscript will spend his initial months of military service (at least) in the close company of young men who share his educational background and religious lifestyle, *hesder* moderates many of the uncertainties which might otherwise make enlistment a threatening as well an uncomfortable experience.

A second impulse towards enrollment in the *hesder* program is ideological. This is an especially important consideration for the more intellectually sensitive conscript. It finds expression in his quest for a framework that can legitimize the way in which he spends his time. Equally committed to both the study of the *torah* and to service in the defense of the state, he trusts that the *hesder yeshivah* will enable him to fulfill both obligations, without forcing him to make an impossibly difficult choice between them.

By all accounts, the *hesder* program certainly satisfies the first of these two expectations. With regard to the second, however, the evidence is more equivocal. Notwithstanding the provisions made to enable *hesdernicks* to straddle the two worlds of the IDF and the *yeshivah*, not all manage to reconcile the conflicting demands of their twin responsibilities. In some cases (often the more interesting) the program instead generates personal discomfort, if not dislocation. Compelled to divide his energies and loyalties between two very different 'greedy' institutions, the conscript runs the risk of a sense of failure at his inability to satisfy the highest demands of either.

The feelings of frustration thus likely to be induced are not, of course, altogether unique. Similar burdens must presumably be borne by all persons who consciously resort to compromises. Potentially, moreover, they are in any case inherent in the world of 'modern Jewish orthodoxy', in which most prospective *hesdernicks* have grown up (Liebman and Don-Yehiya 1984: 100–18). Nevertheless, the *hesder* program, precisely because of its dual character, seems to accentuate the consequent tensions. This is evident from some of the literature produced by and for the *hesder* students. These writings evince a virtual obsession with a need to resolve the rival duties incumbent on Jewish males in terms which meet the rigorous standards of conventional rabbinic discourse. Clearly anxious to prove their credentials before the bar of traditional orthodox scholarship, they deploy much intellectual ingenuity (and erudition) in attempts to prove that the 'arrangement', because it is dictated by the nation's current security needs, is also consonant with Judaism's religious norms (for example, Lichtenstein 1981, Shaviv 1987).

Arguably, such theses were never likely to convince persons not already converted to the philosophy which *hesder* espouses. More intriguing a question is whether they can continue to appeal even to that audience. The national–religious community, like others in Israel, is not a static entity. Constantly buffeted by the march of events, it has recently been particularly affected by two concurrent (albeit different) developments. One is increased public sensitivity to the country's security predicament – of late especially aggravated by the *intifada*. The other is the perceptible rise in influence of the *haredi* communities. Not only have these communities grown in size and political prominence,[8] but fortified by the massive increase in their own *yeshivah-*

---

8   Prior to 1984, *haredi* interests were represented entirely by one or more parties based on *ashkenazi* ultra-orthodox constituencies. On average, they commanded six *Knesset* seats That situation was transformed in 1982 when R. Ovadya Yosef (see above p. 54) launched an

student population (itself largely an outgrowth of the system of military deferments), they have also put forward adamant claims to constitute the authentic repositories of Jewry's scholastic tradition (Me. Friedman 1991).

Personal interviews indicate that these two developments are diminishing the attractions of the *hesder* program in some sections of young adult national–religious opinion. Indeed, several potential *hesdernicks* have in recent years themselves begun to express dissatisfaction with the military-*yeshivah* compromise which the *hesder* program encapsulates. Soul-searching is occasioned by two common accusations. The first, based on a simple count of months spent in the field, suggests that the *hesdernick* is not shouldering as much of the country's security burden as are other (religious and non-religious) conscript of his age. The second accusation, based on a simple count of months spent in the academy, suggests that the *hesdernicks* arc likewise not making a substantial contribution to the furtherance of *Torah* scholarship. To persist in such half measures, many may feel, is to fall between two stools. Unable to serve fully in the IDF, graduates of the *hesder* program are also incapable of preventing the realm of *torah* study from falling almost entirely under the 'non-nationalist' auspices of the *haredi* community (much of which is explicitly anti-Zionist).

Significantly, two separate programs have recently been developed in apparent response to such sentiments. Although very different in content, both constitute deviations from the basic *hesder* norm. The first is the establishment of a one-year program of pre-military *yeshivah* studies. Known as the 'Eli' system (after the name of the *yeshivah* by which it was introduced) this follows the *hesder* routine in providing suitably qualified 18-year-old boys with an opportunity to 'fortify' their religious convictions and scholarship prior to conscription. On completion of their one-year course, however, graduates of that program place themselves entirely at the IDF's disposal for a full three-year term. Hence, they enlist on an individual basis without any further interruptions in their military service. To adopt Coser's terminology, under this system the 'greed' of the *yeshivah* is subordinated to that of the military.

The second alternative stresses the primacy of the *yeshivah*. This is particularly evident in the timetable adopted by students who enroll in the 'Merkaz Harav Kook' *Yeshivah* in Jerusalem. Conventionally considered to be one of the most prestigious of the 'Zionist' rabbinic academies and also, especially since the

---

additional *haredi* party, *Shas*, which blatantly appealed for support from traditional Jews of *sephardi* origin. The latter's representation grew from just four seats in 1984 to ten in 1996 and peaked at 17 in 1999. Although its fortunes have since declined (it gained 11 seats in both 2009 and 2013), the combined *haredi* representation in the *Knesset* still averages at 18 seats. By contrast, the party that traditionally represented national–religious interests (originally the *Mafdal* more recently *Ha-Bayit ha-leumi*) has experienced mixed fortunes. It representation, which had peaked at 12 seats in 1977, fell to five after the general elections held in 1999, to six in 2003 and to just three in 2006. It remains to be seen whether the rebound to 12 seats in 2013 – a result lower than expected by most pollsters – can be sustained.

early 1970s, one of the most fiercely nationalist, 'Merkaz' is clearly distinct from *haredi yeshivot* (Sprinzak 1992). But despite the deep ideological differences which therefore separate their respective complements, students in both types of institutions nevertheless make analogous demands of the IDF. Like his *haredi* counterpart, the 'Merkaz' student also claims scholarship to be his full-time occupation. Consequently, he too applies for an extensive deferment of military service (usually for between seven and ten years, after which many 'Merkaz' graduates do indeed enlist for an abbreviated span).

Thus far, neither the 'Eli' nor the 'Merkaz' programs have attained *hesder*'s popularity or prestige. Nevertheless, their emergence might itself indicate *hesder*'s apparent failure to satisfy all of the emergent and diverse demands of contemporary Israel's 'national–religious' youth. Without entirely breaking the mold of military-*yeshivah* accommodation embodied in the *hesder* system, both offer options which, because they are more sharply defined, might in the present national climate prove to be more attractive. On the one hand, 'Eli' promises to remove whatever stigma is attached to a truncated spell of military service; 'Merkaz', on the other hand, assures that the national–religious camp will possess an adequately trained cadre of *torah* scholars (the usually unspoken assumption being that the normal *hesder yeshivot* are incapable of satisfying that need, which would therefore have to be met from *haredi* sources). Because both of these programs are also more clear-cut than is the *hesder* system, they also present ways of avoiding some of the other inconveniences to which, as we have seen, *hesder* is prone. In their different ways, they neither threaten to affect overall unit cohesion in the IDF, nor to impede on its professional standards.

Conclusions

Although there is much to criticize in the *hesder* program, its drawbacks must not be allowed to obscure its advantages. As an experiment in accommodation between military and religious 'greedy' institutions, it is possibly unique but also typically Israeli. Both circumstances, coupled with *hesder*'s relative youth, require that judgment on the compromise which it represents must still be reserved. Since its inception in 1965 the arrangement, as has been noted, has already undergone several changes. In view of the tensions to which it gives rise, further modifications will probably be required. Besides reflecting shifts in the IDF's military needs, these could also foreshadow wider movements of opinion in Israel's religious community. In short, the *hesder* will continue to mirror the society from which its complement is drawn.

Chapter 5

'The Lord is a Man of War: The Lord is His Name' (Exodus 15:3).The Use of Religious Motifs in Contemporary Orthodox Jewish Perceptions of Military Activities in Israel[1]

Warfare and its conduct receive very little attention in the massive medieval library of philosophical and legal works that constitute the basis for normative Judaism. The authors of such texts were certainly aware that the Biblical God of the Hebrews had been regarded, in addition to all else, as 'a man of war' (Exodus 15:3). Moreover, they appreciated that, according to the Old Testament narrative, military activity played a crucial role in the formation of ancient Israel's national identity. But they also acknowledged the extent to which Jewry's national circumstances had been revolutionized by Rome's conquest of Jerusalem in 70ce. Exile and subjugation required that a discreet veil of silence now be drawn over Jewry's martial heritage. Indeed, throughout the medieval period, none of the great minds of Diaspora Jewry focused their talents on the elucidation of the religious and ethical problems to which warfare gives rise – let alone on such practicalities as operations and logistics. With the notable, but singular, exception of Maimonides (Rabbi Moses ben Maimon; Egypt, 1135–1204, a figure to whom we shall return), neither did any of the authoritative codifiers of Jewish law even summarize the random regulations relative to warfare and its correct conduct scattered in earlier sources.

Arguably, the absence of a specifically Jewish body of teachings with respect to warfare could be tolerated as long as very few Jews actually practiced soldiering. In the modern era, however, that has no longer been the case. Jews began to be conscripted into the mass armies of Europe as early as the nineteenth century, and participated in substantial numbers in the Allied forces that fought the two world wars of the twentieth century. Both experiences generated a demand for a much more articulate expression of the contribution that traditional Jewish teachings might make to military performance. Rabbis soon found that they were not merely required to provide practical advice on ritual matters. They were also expected to utilize their familiarity with the sacred texts in order to fortify the faith of Jewish

---

1   The original version of this chapter appeared in: 'Religie: godsdienst en geweld in de twintigste eeuw'. *Aarboek van het Nederlands Instituut voor Oorlogsdocumentatie*, 17, ed. Hans Blom (2006), 258–75.

soldiers and their families in Divine providence, and thereby to contribute to the maintenance of troop morale (for example, Hertz 1941, Yoshor 1943).

Such demands became even more pressing in 1948, with the establishment of Israel as a sovereign Jewish state. Born into war, and ever since almost continuously involved in military activity of one sort or another, Israel has throughout its history maintained a system of military service based on the draft and compulsory reserve duty. As a result, military service has become a mass phenomenon amongst Israeli Jews, female as well as male, and indeed one of the hallmarks of their citizenship. Inevitably, this situation has compelled a fundamental revision of the traditional dissociation of the Jewish religion from matters military. Only the ultra-orthodox (*haredi*) community continues to regard military service as incompatible with the observance of traditional Jewish beliefs and practices. Elsewhere, however, the dichotomies which traditional Jewish teachings posited between religious practice and martial duty have virtually disappeared. For members of the 'national–religious' (that is, modern orthodox) community, military service constitutes a sacred duty (*mitzvah*). Even secularists invest it with a ritualistic aura, expressive of its status as the most meaningful of all Israeli civic obligations.

The result of this circumstance is a hybrid situation. For one thing, rabbis – especially those affiliated with the national–religious community – no longer share the traditional attitude of Jewish reticence towards all matters military. On the contrary, they have launched a determined effort to rescue Jewry's Biblical martial heritage from the oblivion to which it was consigned for some two millennia. In so doing, they have transformed military matters from subjects of only peripheral rabbinic concern to central topics of theological discourse. At the same time, religious themes and motifs have also permeated military life. Although certainly the military arm of what is essentially a secular and liberal state, the Israel Defense Force (IDF) makes no attempt to confine religious themes to the domain of the army chaplain. Rather, traditional Jewish religious symbols and standards are deliberately introduced into multiple areas of military life.

The purpose of the present chapter is to illustrate both sides of that situation, and to analyze some of its contemporary manifestations. Specifically, it will illustrate three ways in which religious motifs and traditional texts appear in the modern IDF:

- as sources for inspiration in battle;
- as teachings that legitimize the resort to force in self-defense (*ius ad bellum*);
- as guidelines for a code of military ethics (*ius in bello*), especially in the 'fuzzy' circumstances characteristic of operations involving Palestinian non-combatants, as well as terrorists.

Religion as a Source of Military Inspiration

Since the IDF never publishes precise statistics about the sociological composition of its manpower, the exact proportion of orthodox Jews in the Force cannot be ascertained. It is estimated, however, that only some 15 to 20 percent of the total complement observes traditional Jewish ritual practices with any regularity. Nevertheless, religion does not constitute a segmented subculture in Israeli military fabric. Rather, it constitutes one of the IDF's integral components. Within the Force, traditional Jewish rites and symbols intrude on life in numerous spheres. Besides servicing the requirements of troops who profess orthodox Jewish beliefs, they also act as integrative referents for the IDF as a whole.

One measure of the symbiosis between religion and military service in Israel is provided by the scope of the activities of the IDF rabbinate (in Hebrew: *ha-rabbanut ha-tzeva'it*). When originally constituted in 1949, this was merely a skeleton body, tasked with only 'advising the Chief of Staff on religious affairs'. That is no longer the case. Commanded by the IDF's Chief Rabbi, who holds the rank of Brigadier General, the chaplaincy is now a full-blown military formation. It possesses its own distinctive unit emblem (the Ten Commandments upheld by a sword) and its own tradition of battlefield valor (supplied by the service performed under fire by those of its troops whose military mission is to identify fatal casualties and bring them to burial). According to the IDF Spokesman, the military rabbinate is now also:

> Fully integrated into the army down to the battalion level and represented in every unit by a religious affairs officer or a religious affairs coordinator who attend to the religious needs of the unit and its soldiers (Cited S. Cohen 1997: 82).

Many of the duties performed by this workforce are tailored to needs that only professing religious troops commonly require. That category includes: the provision of spiritual counsel; the upkeep of synagogues on military installations; and the distribution of the manifold ritual artifacts (phylacteries, prayer shawls, prayer books) used by practicing orthodox Jews on a regular basis. In fact, however, the *rabbanut ha-tzeva'it* effectively wields much wider influence. It also carries prime responsibility for infusing the entire force with the Jewish heritage – that capacious legacy of shared associations, collective myths and common means of expression that have for generations fostered the retention of a specifically Jewish national identity. In various ways, and for various reasons, these motifs strike responsive cords, not only amongst the Orthodox but also amongst the non-observant mass of military personnel, many of who define themselves as 'traditionalists' (Liebman and Katz 1997). As a result, they play a particularly crucial function in the process of welding the entire Force into a whole.

The *rabbanut ha-tzeva'it* has established various agencies for the dissemination of specifically religious cultural themes throughout the IDF. For instance, its 'religious tradition and knowledge branch' regularly conducts day-long seminars on Jewish values and Jewish history for conscript cohorts. It also provides new immigrants with occasional publications that summarize traditional teachings in simple terms. At a higher level, these are also transmitted in the IDF's Officer Training School, where 'The Army in Jewish Perspective' or 'What is Judaism'? constitute integral features of the curriculum. Still more extensive, to take another example, is the IDF Rabbinate's annual 'Awakening Campaign', conducted every autumn during the month preceding the Jewish New Year. Made into a regular fixture on the military calendar ever since 1959 (previously it had been left to the discretion of individual commanders), the Awakening Campaign provides the IDF rabbinate with an opportunity to introduce troops to both the major ritual practices of the period and to the spiritual messages that they convey.

Finally, and at moments of particularly high drama, the IDF Rabbinate also takes upon itself the task of instilling the troops with faith in eventual victory. It most memorably did so in the tense first hours of the Six Days War of 1967. Unabashedly assuming the task allotted to 'the Priest' in Deuteronomy 20:3–5, the then IDF Chief Rabbi, General Shlomo Goren (who held office from 1949 until 1971), broadcast to the troops a particularly stiff dose of spiritual encouragement, laced with a series of well chosen citations from Deuteronomy Chapter 20, Judges Chapter 7, and Psalms:

> Hear O Israel. Today you approach battle against your enemies. This is the great day for the people of Israel, as you march out towards the massive and decisive engagement for the deliverance of the people of Israel from its enemies, who have come to destroy and uproot us. The eyes of all Israel are on you.
>
> Dear soldiers! Let not your hearts be faint. Do not be afraid, do not tremble before them. For the Lord your God goes with you to fight on your behalf against your enemies and to save you. Today He will give us courage! Today He will make us great! Today our enemies shall be crushed beneath us! … Be strong and of good courage for the sake of our people and the cities of our Lord. And will the help of the God of Israel's battles you shall win a great victory over all of Israel's enemies … O Lord, save us! O Lord, send us success! (Cited Michaelson 1982: 103).

As has already been pointed out (see above pp. 1–2), traditional Jewish themes and motifs are more subtly woven into the texture of the IDF by a variety of supplementary mechanisms, the most notable of which are the pageants held at important points in the military life cycle. Although the ways in which religious themes are thus imparted are often subliminal, their intended function is absolutely clear. Their purpose is to infuse the IDF as a whole with a sense of shared identity, shared values and shared purpose. This aim is particularly transparent during the week that marks the Hebrew anniversary of the outbreak of the Yom Kippur War in October 1973. Ever since, the editors of *Ba-Machaneh* ('In Camp'), the IDF's most popular weekly newspaper, have emphasized the symbolism inherent in the fact that the most severe of modern Israel's military trials commenced on the date revered in Jewish tradition as 'The Day of Judgment'. Repeatedly stressed, accordingly, are such motifs as the common fate of Jewry and the function of faith as a stimulant to heroism under fire. Profusely illustrated, and produced in glossy format, each annual issue of *Ba-Machaneh* provides a striking demonstration of how the IDF transmits essentially religious themes to an overwhelmingly secular audience. Traditional religious associations, at this level, serve as a social coagulant, and thus as a vehicle for fostering the feelings of affinity and reciprocity that have always been recognized to constitute essential criteria for military cohesion and, ultimately, for effective battlefield performance.

Religion as a Source for the *Ius ad Bellum*

Thus to point out the extent to which religious themes are mobilized for military purposes in the IDF is by no means to imply that contemporary Israel's battles are portrayed as 'holy wars'. In this respect, the contrast between traditional Jewish sources and their parallels in the Islam is especially stark. As will be seen, the formative texts of Judaism – like those of Islam – certainly do grant some state-initiated military activities greater license than others. However, absent from the traditional Jewish discourse on 'just' and 'unjust' hostilities is the terminology of 'holy wars' that occurs so frequently in Islamic sources (Khaled 1999, Knapp 2003, Kelsay 2003). Most obviously is this demonstrated in the work known as *Mishneh Torah* ('Supplementary Torah'), widely recognized as the most comprehensive and authoritative of all codes of Jewish law, compiled in the twelfth century by Maimonides, who (as noted above) was one of the very few Jewish medieval authorities to relate to warfare at all. Significantly, Maimonides entirely avoided all discussion of military subjects in those sections of his Code that he devoted to matters of holiness, purity, or doctrine. Rather, he sites his summary of laws relating to the resort to organized force within the wider analysis of the rights and duties of kings. That schema clearly underscores the notion that only properly accredited governmental agencies can take decisions regarding the initiation of hostilities, and their cessation (S. Cohen 2005). But, in addition, it also invests all Jewish teachings on war with a political emphasis, which has been accurately described as 'quasi-Clausewitzian' in thrust (Inbar 1987).

The contemporary orthodox Jewish discourse in Israel on the validity of war initiation has deliberately adopted the Maimonidean paradigm, and even its terminology. Hence, when discussing the rights and wrongs of a particular conflict, that discourse eschews standards of judgment derived from universally applicable gauges of right intention. Instead, when identifying a *ius ad bellum* it resorts to the taxonomy that Maimonides had employed in his own Code. Indeed, ever since its inception, the contemporary *halakhic* discourse on the *ius ad bellum* has been characterized by strenuous intellectual efforts to adapt the Maimonidean template to contemporary conditions (for example, Ye. Amital 1987, Sherman 1995).

Summarizing previous rabbinic teachings that dated back to the third century ce (at the latest), Maimonides had identified two categories of armed conflict: one classified as *milkhemet mitzvah* (that is, 'mandatory' war), and the other classified as *milkhemet reshut* ('discretionary' war). Both constitute religiously valid forms of state-initiated military activities. Their difference lies in the source of their respective mandates. As defined by Maimonides, 'discretionary' wars respond to human impulses, of which the most generic, he says, is a monarch's desire 'to extend the borders of Israel and enhance his [own] greatness and prestige'. Since these are morally questionable justifications for the spilling of blood, wars of that nature can only take place when sanctioned by the nation's spiritual leadership (referred to by Maimonides as 'the court of 71 [sages]'). By contrast, 'mandatory' wars derive their license from a source that is transcendental, in the sense that it can be traced to an explicit Divine command. Hence, in these cases, neither the initiation of hostilities – nor even the imposition of compulsory military service – requires the sanction of any human agency whatsoever. To cite Maimonides once more:

> For a mandatory war, the king need not obtain the sanction of the court [of 71 sages]. He may at any time go forth of his own accord and compel the people to go with him (*Laws of Kings and their Wars* 5:2).

The three examples that he cites as illustrations of such wars are:

> [i] The war against the seven nations [i.e. the inhabitants of the land of Canaan prior to its conquest by Joshua in biblical times]; [ii] that against Amalek [the first tribe to attack the Israelites after the exodus from Egypt; Exodus 17:8–14 and Deuteronomy 25:17–19]; [iii] [a war] to deliver Israel from the enemy attacking him.

For over 60 years now, contemporary Jewish orthodox thought in Israel and elsewhere has wrestled with the task of applying the Maimonidean taxonomy to contemporary circumstances. It is generally agreed that there exists no religious basis whatsoever for the initiation of 'optional' campaigns, whose only motive is territorial aggrandizement and/or martial glory. Even if brought to the consideration of a body equivalent to 'the court of 71 sages' (the possibility of whose establishment is itself a moot point), they could not possibly be sanctioned – especially not at a time when enlightened international opinion opposes any such enterprise (Aryeh 2002).

'Mandatory' wars, however, present a more complex challenge. One school of thought tends to regard each of Maimonides' illustrations as examples of far broader instances of military activity, and hence as prototypes that lend themselves to subsequent expansion. This reading is especially favored by right-wing religious circles, who altogether emphasize the inherent sanctity of the Land of Israel and the everlasting nature of the Divine commandment (Deuteronomy 20:10–18) to destroy all of its non-Jewish inhabitants. In this reading, accordingly, Maimonides' reference to Joshua's 'war against the seven nations' could be (and has been) extended to any present or future campaign fought in order to dispossess whichever non-Jewish population might happen to reside in the Holy Land. Similarly, since 'Amalek' has entered traditional Jewish demonology as a generic personification of all evil (for sources see Sagi 1994, Eisen 2011: 105), the commandment 'to wage war against Amalek' could be – and, again, in some modern rabbinic teachings has been – extended to include any foe that might fit that depiction, and not least Palestinian terrorists (examples are cited in Rubinstein 1984, and Blau 2000). Other modern commentaries, however, adopt a more restrictive interpretation. In their view, the Palestinians are neither one of 'the seven nations', nor Amalek. Hence, contemporary Israel's military activities against them cannot be legitimated solely in terms of biblical instructions (Carmy 2007).

There does of course remain for modern-day application the third of Maimonides' instances of a 'commanded war': one fought 'to deliver Israel from the enemy attacking him'. Ostensibly, this phraseology seems clear enough and appears to set out fairly precise conditions as to when the *ius ad bellum* might exist and when not. It undoubtedly provides a general sanction for the use of force in national self-defense, such as is expressly permitted by Article 51 of the UN Charter. At the same time, albeit without actually saying so, the same formula seems also to outlaw unprovoked military operations, such as acts of blatant aggression against peaceful neighbors. It also appears to lay down other curbs on the license to bloodshed, such as the need for just cause and/or due authorization (Ravitzky 1996, S. Cohen 2005). With the *halakhic* boundaries of permissible and prohibited uses of force thus clearly defined, observers could be excused for assuming that the application of the category of mandatory wars to contemporary conditions presents few problems.

In fact, little could be further from the truth. Modern Israel's military practice has seldom conformed with the tidy categorizations of the rabbinic mind, and closer inspection reveals that the instances in which IDF operations can be said to meet traditional criteria are in fact few and far between. The principle of self-defense could most obviously, and most justifiably, be invoked as *ius ad bellum* when the Jewish State was attacked by her neighbors, as was the case in 1948 and in October 1973. But neither situation has been typical. For the most part, the circumstances compelling modern Israel to resort to military force have been far more complex, and her own responses also far more varied. Those situations do not necessarily invalidate the Maimonidean category of a mandatory war. They do, however, underscore the need for considerable interpretative maneuver in its application.

As part of that exercise, particular attention has been focused on the precise rules of engagement that rabbinic definitions of the *ius ad bellum* might allow. Here, however, the Maimonidean prooftext seems especially recalcitrant (J.D. Bleich 1983). At first glance, its sanction for wars waged 'to deliver Israel from the enemy attacking him' appears to cover only 'reactive–defensive' actions, initiated after the enemy offensive has actually commenced. Particularly is this so since the Hebrew term that Maimonides employs (*ve-ezrat*) more precisely translates as 'to assist', which itself implies a reactive response. But this bland ruling is self-evidently fuzzy at the edges. Does it imply that operations are 'mandatory' only when they take the form of a second strike? Or, to put matters another way, does the Maimonidean definition preclude the use of force at a prior stage, when military commanders might wish to nip a prospective danger in the bud by taking the offensive?

That these are not merely theoretical questions is illustrated by the specific contexts in which each is framed. How would Maimonides classify a 'pre-emptive' strike, designed to forestall immediately anticipated enemy aggression, such as was launched by the IDF against Egypt in June 1967? Could his taxonomy accommodate 'preventative' operations, such as the Sinai campaign of 1956 and Israel's air operation against Iraq's nuclear facility in 1981, both of which were initiated in order to destroy a putative predator's war making potential before the threat materialized?[2] And what would his ruling be in the case of 'offensive–defensive' actions, of the type exemplified by Israel's 'reprisal raids' of the 1950s or, on a larger scale, 'Operation Peace for the Galilee' in June 1982? Altogether, need applications of his taxonomy be restricted solely to conditions of conventional warfare, waged against organized armies? Or is it sufficiently flexible also to accommodate sub-conventional and asymmetric situations, such as Israel confronted during both the first *intifada* (1987–1993) and its even bloodier successor (2000–2007)?

Since many of the traditional sources lend themselves to various interpretations, rabbinic opinions on such issues have been divided. Nevertheless, by way of interim summary it can be said that the span of imponderables has definitely been narrowed over time. Gradually, but inexorably, the *ius ad bellum* intrinsic to Maimonides' 'mandatory' classification is being applied to Israeli force applications that are offensive as well as defensive in form, and to operations that are launched within 'low intensity' as well as 'high intensity' contexts. In both categories of conflict, the IDF's apparent predilection for pre-emptive deterrence, 'by denial', seems to be receiving as much rabbinic sanction as do the more traditional applications of deterrence reactively, 'by punishment' (Yaniv 1985; cf. Ushpizai 1983).

Undoubtedly, that tendency has been influenced by sensitivity to the specific theater of battle. For national–religious scholars, especially, the duty 'to deliver Israel from the enemy attacking him' carries particularly potent overtones in the Holy Land. After all, in their view this portion of the globe possesses an inherent sanctity, derived from its Divine designation as the eternal patrimony of the Jewish people. A minority of militants has taken that argument to extremes, contending that the duty to defend Jewish possession of the Land is incumbent upon each and every Jew when the homeland is in danger. A resort to arms for such purposes, they have suggested, hence requires no governmental authorization at all (Lustick 1988,

---

2 Precisely the same query would arise with respect to the *halakhic* legitimacy of an Israeli strike on Iran's nuclear facilities. In this case, however, matters would be further complicated by the argument that, by publicly threatening to carry out such an action, Israel's leaders might be providing Iran with an excuse to launch a pre-emptive attack of their own.

Sprinzak 1992). Few rabbinic authorities sanction the appeal to vigilantism implied in those doctrines. Many, however, concur with the basic premises thus being articulated. Certainly, they endorse the argument that the protection of Jewish sovereignty in the Land of Israel (*eretz Israel*) constitutes a religiously valid *ius ad bellum* in its own right (Aviner 2000: 34–5, 37–8). In so doing, they have harnessed traditional religious teachings to contemporary strategic doctrines, and thereby provide an evocative layer of justification for military action in what is categorized as Jewish self-defense.[3]

Religious Teachings as Guidelines for a Code of Military Ethics (*Ius in Bello*)

The third area in which traditional Jewish religious texts are studied in Israel as guidelines for military behavior concerns the *ius in bello*. Here the focus is on the measures that may (and may not) be taken during hostilities. For instance: to what extent does Judaism obligate troops to respect the dignity of human life, including that of an avowed enemy? Are IDF commanders required to endanger the lives of their own troops rather than risk shedding the blood of civilians, however hostile?

Although occasionally asked ever since 1948, such questions have become especially insistent since the 1980s. Two circumstances explain why that is so. The first is the profound change that has occurred in the character of Israeli military agenda. Whereas the IDF's operational record once consisted principally of 'high intensity' armored and air campaigns against neighboring armies (the Sinai Campaign of 1956, the Six Days War of 1967, the War of Attrition, 1969–1970 and the Yom Kippur War of 1973), ever since the 1980s Israeli troops have increasingly found themselves fighting 'asymmetric' conflicts against sub-conventional enemies (as during the occupation of southern Lebanon, 1985–2000, the first and second Palestinian *intifadas*, 1987–1993 and 2000–present, and the second Lebanon War of 2006).

Primarily because they blur conventional distinctions between combatants and non-combatants, 'asymmetric' conflicts present the armies of liberal, democratic societies with especially acute moral challenges. Hence, they have frequently necessitated reformulations of the *ius in bello* as laid down in military codes of ethics (Peters 1996). Such has also been the case in Israel, where the experience of the first *intifada* prompted the IDF in 1995 to disseminate (and subsequently revise) the ethical code that it entitled *Ruach Tzahal* ('The Spirit of the IDF'; Kasher 1996). Although the three 'basic principles' of moral conduct and ten additional 'values' itemized in that document are grounded in western, humanitarian teachings, the problems that they address necessarily generate Jewish theological interest as well. To what extent does Judaism too prioritize 'the defense of the state, its citizens and

---

3 Recent rabbinic debates in Israel over the obligation to wage war in order to conquer the Holy Land – and, indeed, disputes as to whether such an obligation 'trumps the *halakhic* rule which gives precedence to the preservation of life' – are analyzed in Newman 2012.

inhabitants', listed as the *The Spirit of the IDF*'s first 'basic principle'? In which way do its religious teachings seek to implement the notion of 'the purity of arms' (*tohar ha-neshek*), the sixth in that document's ten 'values'?

The pertinence of such enquiries has been vastly augmented by a second and simultaneous development: the substantial growth in the number of troops from a national–religious and 'modern Orthodox' Jewish background serving in IDF combat units. In many infantry brigades the quantity of such servicemen, once very small indeed, had by the mid-1990s risen to almost twice their proportion in the overall complement. Amongst the IDF's cadre of combat lieutenants and captains, the ranks at which officers are most likely to exert a direct influence on the conduct of troops under their command, the ratio between religious and secular servicemen is often two to one. More significantly still, by the turn of the twenty-first century as many as 30 percent of all national–religious troops were attending one of the institutions (*mekhinot kedam tzeva'iyot toraniot* [pre-conscription religious colleges] and *yeshivot hesder* ['arrangement' academies]), established in order to allow them to combine military service with a study of Jewish traditions and teachings.

The precise reasons for that development need not detain us here (see Chapter 4). More germane are its consequences. It has created a unique audience, a sizable body of orthodox Jewish military personnel who seek religious guidance in what has become a core area of their operational activity. That demand cannot apparently be satisfied by the appeal to the universal values stressed in *The Spirit of the IDF*, which is tailored to the sensitivities of a largely secular audience. Instead, there exists an urgent need for an exposition of specifically Jewish teachings with respect to a wide range of delicate moral issues.

Significantly, it is not the IDF Chief Rabbinate that spearheads the response to that challenge. In fact, official military chaplains play only a minor role in the discourse now taking place on the substance of Jewish military ethics. The lead is taken by wider circles of civilian rabbis, many of whom teach in one of the theological academies attended by a large proportion of Orthodox IDF troops. Several of these rabbis do possess a military service record, often at fairly senior rank. Nevertheless, their influence over the troops stems more from their academic positions than from their military status.

Contemporary discussions of Jewish military ethics by these persons take two principal forms. One consists of detailed examinations of Jewish texts and their applications to the morals of the contemporary battlefield. Some such works have found their way into print within the covers of collections specifically dedicated to the subject. Others appear as individual items in one of the many scholarly journals that specialize in the elucidation of modern Orthodox Jewish thought and practice in a variety of fields. In this respect, the tone was set as early as 1954. Following reports that over 60 Palestinian civilians had been killed in an IDF reprisal raid, *Ha-Torah ve-ha-Medinah*, a journal that specialized in presenting orthodox Jewish solutions to the challenges of political sovereignty, published an essay entitled 'The Qibya Incident in the Light of Jewish Law', a pioneering analysis of Jewish military ethics written by Rabbi Shaul Yisraeli, one of the most renowned rabbinic figures in the modern Jewish world of letters (Yisraeli 1954; see the analysis in Eisen 2012). Other milestone publications soon followed. Amongst the issues addressed in subsequent decades were: the morality of risking soldiers' lives in order to save those of civilians held hostage (as at Entebbe in 1976; Yosef 1977); religious views on the IDF's siege of Beirut in 1982 (Goren 1996); permissible action against Palestinian terrorists (Ariel 2003); and – most recently of all – the religious challenges posed by the conduct of military operations in areas of high civilian concentration (as in Jenin in 2002; Cherlow 2002).

The second forum for the contemporary discussion of Jewish military ethics consists of what is known as 'responsa': letters containing the replies that individual rabbis compose in response to specific queries addressed to them on matters of *halakhah* (Jewish law). This body of materials is especially interesting, since it reflects the issues that most concern the soldiers who compose the questions, and hence provides a window into their inner world. Indeed, once published (as many are) they constitute documents of almost unparalleled sociological value.

Ever since 1948, responsa have been widely used as a means of clarifying matters of military interest – so much so that there now exists an entire library of works specifically focused on providing solutions to the multiple ritual and ethical religious problems to which the modern experience of military service in the IDF has given rise. Recent years, however, have witnessed an especially interesting expansion of the genre. Young soldiers confronted with a moral dilemma no longer need to write laboriously long letters to their rabbis – and then wait weeks or even months for a reply. Instead, they can log in to one of the many web sites expressly devoted to the dissemination of rabbinic opinion on matters of current interest.[4] These enable virtually instantaneous communication between the soldier and his mentor, which can also be made available with equal speed to a much wider audience. Thanks to this technology, there now exists a vast storehouse of epistolary exchanges that provide troops with religious and moral instruction on day-to-day behavior.

Just as impressive as the quantity of electronic responsa that now discuss military ethics is the vast range of issues that they encompass. This reflects not only the sensitivity of the correspondents, but also the variety of situations to which they are exposed during the course of their military duties. The following is a random sample, which summarizes the questions asked within the course of just *one week* in October 2005 and posted on just *one* of the available websites (www.moreshet):

- Are soldiers permitted to eat fruit found in a Palestinian orchard, which would otherwise rot on the trees during the owner's enforced absence?
- What, if anything, do orthodox Jewish teachings have to say about the propriety of the IDF policy of 'targeted killings'?

---

4   The four main sites, all in Hebrew, are: <http://www.moreshet.co.il/web/shut/shut_result.asp?kodeshut=19000>; <http://www.kipa.co.il/ask/cat.asp?cat=10>; <http://www.moriya.org.il/shut/ShutArt.asp?CatList=102&SubList=262>; <http://www.yeshiva.org.il/ask/default.asp?category=7&page=1>.

- In view of the use that Palestinian insurgents are known to make of women and children as 'human shields', does the *halakhah* permit IDF soldiers to likewise parade Palestinian civilians in front of them when seeking out suspected terrorists?
- What are the points of agreement, and of dispute, between the *halakhah* and the IDF's Rules of Engagement where civilians are concerned?
- How can soldiers reconcile the need for maximum security at the roadblocks established in the West Bank with consideration for the feelings and property of the Palestinians whose persons and belongings are scrutinized in those locations?

A review of the responsa literature reveals that there exist no monolithic rabbinic answers to all such questions (S. Cohen 2007b). On many issues, and especially those that in moral terms are especially sensitive, responses very much vary – if not from individual rabbi to individual rabbi, then certainly from one 'school' of rabbinic thought to another. In one form or another all subscribe to the teaching that: 'It is most important that a person going out to war knows that he is not moving from a world with one scale of [moral] values to a world with another scale of values'.[5] Nevertheless, precisely what the content of those values might be often remains a matter of some dispute.

Conclusions

Thus to indicate that the quest for a cohesive and universally accepted body of Jewish military ethics is still incomplete is not, however, to belittle the advances that have been made in this area of rabbinic activity. The symbiosis between orthodox Judaism and military service is today very different from that prevalent just a few decades ago. As we have seen, in retrospect it is possible to identify three distinct phases of development. What began as a mobilization of religious themes and motifs in order to foster military cohesion, and then progressed to a more severe examination of the *ius ad bellum* in Jewish sources, has now become an intensive quest for religious guidance in the most sensitive areas of military operations. Only further research can ascertain how much (if at all) this activity might be influencing the behavior of IDF troops, and especially of those who, in increasing numbers, turn to rabbis for spiritual guidance. Even on its own terms, however, the phenomena outlined here deserve recognition as a significant chapter in the history of the intersection between religion and military violence in the modern State of Israel.

---

5   Rabbi Aron Lichtenstein (principal of the 'Har Etzion' academy), in a 'round table on war and ethics' (Hebrew), cited in S. Cohen 2007b.

Chapter 6:

The Re-Discovery of Orthodox Jewish Laws Relating to the Military and War (*dinei tzavah u-milkhamah*) in Contemporary Israel: Trends and Implications[1]

Warfare was noticeably marginalized in the vast library of pre-modern texts that transmit orthodox Judaism. By and large, rabbinic commentators limited their remarks on military matters to sporadic snatches of scriptural exegesis. With the notable – but singular – exception of Maimonides (Rabbi Moses ben Maimon; Egypt, 1135–1204), none of the medieval codifiers of traditional Jewish law (*halachah*) even summarized the random regulations respecting the application of armed force scattered in biblical and talmudic sources.

Contemporary rabbinic literature presents an entirely different picture. The ubiquity of military service and armed conflict in the modern Israeli experience has over the past 60 years stimulated intense interest in *dinei tzavah u-milkhamah* ('[religious] laws relating to the military and war'). Indeed, that segment of the Jewish legal corpus is now being elucidated in a swelling tide of detailed publications. As a result, an area that for two millennia constituted one of the great lacunae of rabbinic instruction is now a thriving field of halachic inquiry.

Hitherto, scholarly interest in the new Jewish discourse on warfare has been diffuse. The handful of studies that note its emergence generally confine themselves to either broad-brush surveys of contemporary Jewish thought or to specific analyses of individual developments (Blidstein 1996, 2002, Achituv 2002, Dorff 2002, Luz 2003).[2] Despite these contributions, however, still lacking is both an integrated survey of recent writings in the field, and a preliminary map of their authorship, content and means of dissemination. The present chapter attempts to repair such gaps and, in conclusion, to analyze the implications of the phenomena described.

---

1   The original version of this chapter appeared in *Israel Studies*, 12/2 (2007): 1–28. Reprinted by permission.

2   Amongst the important studies that appeared subsequent to the first publication of this chapter, especially valuable are: Rozenak 2007, Lubitch 2009, Eisen 2011, Newman 2012.

Precursors

Modern rabbinic interest in warfare and the problems that it poses for orthodox Jews dates to the introduction of conscription by some European governments during the late eighteenth and early nineteenth centuries (Kahana 1948). As early as 1789, the renowned Rabbi of Prague, R. Ezekiel Landau (1713–1793, the '*Noda Bi-Yehudah*') recognized the need to dispense practical religious advice to the first Jewish recruits drafted into the Austrian army, a duty that he reportedly fulfilled tearfully and in German (Wind 1961: 115–6). A century later, R. Yisrael Meir Ha-Kohen ([Kagan], 1838–1933, the '*Hafetz Hayim*') felt it necessary to devote an entire tract (*Sefer Mahaneh Yisrael* ['The Book of the Camp of Israel', 1881]) to an examination of the extent to which rabbinic sources might permit the Jewish soldiers of his time some leeway in the performance of various ritual commandments. Mass conscription during the two world wars intensified the demand for similar works. In 1944, for instance, the committee on Jewish Law appointed by the Rabbinical Assembly of the American conservative movement reported that: 'By far the most important questions we had to deal with pertained to the religious dilemma of the large numbers of recruits in the training camps of the United States Army'. (Rabbinical Assembly 1944: 34–5).

But it was in the newly established State of Israel that war-related issues most prominently thrust themselves to the forefront of rabbinic attention. The reconstruction of an independent Jewish polity in 1948, together with the necessity to defend that action by force of arms, revolutionized the entire rabbinic agenda. Rabbinic discussion in this area could not now be limited (as was the case in the diaspora and even in the *Yishuv* [Jewish community in mandatory Palestine]; Holzer 2002) to the resolution of the tensions generated at the level of the individual soldier by the conflicting pressures of ritual injunctions and military commands. Responses now also had to be framed to macro-level issues, pertaining to citizenship responsibility and government accountability in matters affecting national security. What, if anything, did the canonical sources have to say about the justice of warfare in general and about the ethics of specific applications of force in particular? Under which circumstances do the dictates of national security override the generally paramount religious commandment to avoid both endangering one's own life and taking that of another? Do military instructions to the general public, when declared to be 'emergency decrees', possess any standing in Jewish law?

In Israel, especially, the scope and number of such enquiries has very much increased over time. In part, that development can be attributed to the pervasiveness of regular and reserve military service in the lives of so many Israeli citizens. But it also owes much to the variety of the military missions undertaken by the Israel Defense Force (IDF) since the early 1950s, which cover a span that includes 'reprisal raids', hostage rescue missions, sieges and constabulary actions – as well as full scale wars. Each category of operation has added a further layer to the halachic discourse generated by the overall phenomenon of autonomous Jewish military action. The cumulative effect has been to produce an entire library of works on topics once considered entirely beyond Judaism's purview.

The appearance of so extensive a body of new rabbinic literature raises three primary questions. Who are its authors? Where do they publish? What are they writing about? The pages that follow discuss these subjects sequentially.

Authorship

Understandably, the modern exploration of *hilchot tzavah u-milkhamah* is essentially an Israeli phenomenon. Nevertheless, it would be mistaken to ignore the contributions to this field also made over the past half century by several interpreters of Judaism based in the Diaspora, and especially in the United States. During the Vietnam era, for instance, American–Jewish scholars analyzed conscientious objection with intensity then considered unthinkable in Israeli circles, and in so doing pre-dated Israeli examinations of the issue by over three decades (Liebman 1968, Vorspan 1969, Kimelman 1968, 1970, Lamm 1978). Even today, the most informative discussions of Jewish approaches to the ethics of international military intervention or of nuclear warfare are to be found in English (Polak 1983, Bleich 1984, Artson 1988, Dorff 1991, 2002). In addition, it is to a long and distinguished line of American–Jewish scholars that we owe several analytical surveys of whatever earlier rabbinic materials exist with respect to the legitimacy of combat initiation and certain forms of military conduct (for example, Shapiro 1975, Kimelman 1991, Broyde 1996, Solomon 2006).

Just as remarkable as the range of war-related topics thus covered by contemporary Diaspora scholars is the spectrum of their denominational affiliation. Whilst several are members of Orthodox institutions and congregations, many others are leading figures in either Reform or Conservative communities. In Israel, by contrast, authorship of the new halachic literature on matters military is far less evenly spread. In fact, clearly demarcated boundaries of affiliation distinguish between those Israeli scholars who are eager to participate in this discourse, and those who evince a reluctance to do so. Overwhelmingly, persons in the former camp are associated with schools of thought generally associated with what is termed the 'national–religious' and/or 'religious–Zionist' community, a category roughly equivalent to Modern Orthodoxy in the Diaspora. By contrast, scholars and religious authorities associated with *haredi* ('ultra-orthodox') circles, both in Israel and abroad, by and large chose to play no more than a minor part in the contemporary Jewish discourse on topics related to war and its pursuit.[3]

---

3   For some outstanding exceptions, see Ehrenberg, 1998 2: 126 (on the command to leave the enemy an avenue of escape) and 5: 15 (on the release of terrorists in return for captive soldiers); and Halberstadt ('the rabbi of Tzantz') no. 148 (on the carrying of weapons on the sabbath). For an example of non-Israeli *haredi* rabbinic writings on these matters, see Schechter 1997: 205–20.

Two circumstances account for the comparative absence of *haredi* scholars from such discussions. One is the markedly low rate of *haredi* enlistment into the IDF. Since the 1980s, over 80 percent of each annual cohort of potential male *haredi* conscripts in Israel has taken advantage of an administrative concession that enables them to defer, and ultimately avoid, the draft whilst attending theological academies (*yeshivot gevohot*) [for statistics, see above pp. 7–9]. Hence, the majority of this community simply has no personal religious interest in matters of military relevance. But to that consideration must be added, secondly, the influence exerted by the deep ultra-Orthodox conviction that there is any case something inherently sacrilegious about a Jewish recourse to military force, certainly for the purpose of re-establishing Jewish sovereignty over the Holy Land. Exile from Zion, after all, had been a Divine punishment; hence, a return to the Almighty's grace is the necessary precondition for the promised Redemption. When it comes, national renewal will have to be Divinely inspired and await definitive signs from heaven that the House of Israel has indeed worked its passage home. In the absence of such omens, precipitate communal action of any sort – especially military action – rebels against God's plan. Instead of hastening the Messiah's coming, it threatens to postpone his arrival. In the meantime, devotion to the study of the sacred texts (*Torah*) is the only guarantee of true security

None of the spiritual leaders of Israel's 'national–religious' community could ever take that position. Indeed, central to their entire ideology is a rebellion against the traditionally resistant attitude towards this-worldly political action that *haredim* continue to espouse. Religious Zionism has always maintained that the reconstitution of Israel's independence in 1948 did not merely register a milestone in the mundane political chronology of the Jewish people. Far more fundamentally, it also defined a crucial stage in the teleological process of Redemption (Shimoni 1995: 127–64). One consequence of this essentially transcendental prism is the teaching that service in the IDF, the army entrusted with the mandate to defend Israel's sovereignty, constitutes a religious obligation. Another is that the elucidation of rabbinic opinion on all aspects of military conduct and army life is likewise a sacred enterprise.

In a very personal sense, many of national religious Jewry's contemporary rabbinic authorities are uniquely qualified to address this subject. Quite apart from demonstrating possession of the academic skills considered mandatory by traditional scholarship, pre-eminent amongst which remains mastery of the Talmud and its commentaries, many have also acquired first-hand knowledge of military life, thanks to their enlistment in the IDF. This dual experience of both 'the scroll' and 'the sword' not only distinguishes national–religious rabbis from most of their *haredi* counterparts. It also sets them apart from every other generation of spiritual leaders known to Jewish history.

Undoubtedly the most prominent early example of the new synthesis was Rabbi Shlomo Goren (1917–1994), a figure who still awaits his biographer. A man of perpetual motion and boundless energy, R. Goren was also blessed with organizational skills and an original mind. He exploited those gifts to the full during his long and distinguished military career as *rav tzeva'i rashi* (chief IDF chaplain), an office that he held from 1948 until 1971, by which time he had risen to the rank of Major General [*aluf*]). Virtually single handedly, R. Goren crafted the accommodation of traditional behavior with army life, and vice-versa. By means of a series of arrangements worked out with David Ben-Gurion, he also ensured that the ambience of the IDF as a whole would respect and reflect orthodox practice and thus make it possible for religiously observant conscripts to enlist alongside their secular comrades. His prolific stream of learned publications further demonstrated how traditional scholarship could combine with military experience to produce an entirely new type of rabbinical authority.

Most of R. Goren's writings on military-related *halachot* were originally composed whilst he was still in uniform and very much involved in their application. Many of the younger and more recent contributors to the rabbinic literature on *dinei tzavah u-milkhamah* have taken a different course. For one thing, several of the prominent figures in this field are not graduates of the IDF's rabbinate, but have served in field formations – sometimes at fairly senior rank.[4] Secondly, very few participate in the contemporary rabbinic discourse whilst still on active service. Rather, most postpone addressing military-related *halachah* until they have attained positions in the non-military world, either as communal rabbis or, more commonly, as principals and/or senior teachers at one of the several dozen academic institutions (*yeshivot hesder* ['Arrangement Academies', the first of which was established in 1964] and *mechinot kedam tzevaiyot toraniyot* ['Pre-Conscription Religious Colleges'], the first of which was established in 1988) that now enable thousands of national religious conscripts each year to combine military service with advanced Jewish studies (see above pp. 11–13). Thus brought into virtual daily contact with successive cohorts of soldier–pupils, the new generation of spiritual leaders is uniquely well placed, not just to conduct the quest for *dinei tzavah u-milkhamah*, but also to define the terms in accordance with which it is to be carried out.

Formats

Much of the contemporary religious discourse on military matters takes place orally. Indeed, entire areas within this field are developed and explored through the traditional Jewish academic medium of face-to-face dialogue. Especially since the late 1970s, however, many of the fruits of this research have also become available by means of written communications.

---

4   Thus, R. Avichai Rontski, the head of the *yeshivah* at Itamar who served as *rav tzeva'i rashi* 2006–2010), holds the rank of Lt. Col. in the combat reserves; R. Eyal Mosheh Krim, principal of the 'Ateret' pre-conscription college in Jerusalem is a former commander of an elite infantry formation, as was R. Yehoshua Hagar. R. Eliezer Shenwald, who heads the *Yeshivat Hesder* at Modi'in, is a deputy commander of a tank brigade in the reserves.

Two broad categories of publications warrant particular attention: (1) responsa (*shutim*; written replies to questions on specific points of Jewish law) and (2) books and essays of more discursive scholarly analysis.

Responsa

The first generation of modern Israeli rabbinic responsa on military matters follows the traditional format; the texts were transmitted to the public as part of the overall *ouvre* of the authority to whom the enquiry was originally addressed. Typical of this format is *Heichal Yitzchak* ('Chamber of Isaac'), the collected responsa penned by Rabbi Isaac Ha-Levi Herzog (1888–1959), whose tenure of office as Ashkenazi Chief Rabbi of Israel spanned the 1948–1949 War of Independence. R. Herzog's responsa include seminal examinations of such matters as the degree to which soldiers on active duty might be permitted to relax some traditional sabbath observances and the precise halachic definition of Israel's wars.[5] However, these discussions, which comprise only a fraction of the work as a whole, are not collated under a separate subheading of their own. Rather, R. Herzog's collection retains the time-honored structure of the genre, which dictates that individual responsa be categorized in accordance with the classificatory system of the 'Four Columns' (*Arba'ah Turim*) bequeathed to posterity by Rabbi Jacob ben Asher in the early fourteenth century. Since the latter (unlike Maimonides) did not allot to military matters a specific rubric within the overall framework of his code, neither does R. Herzog. Hence, his discussions of mixed gender military units, for example, or of the difficulties of religious observance in isolated bases, are tucked away within volumes dealing with (respectively) synagogue architecture and the sale of unleavened bread [*chametz*] on the eve of Passover).[6]

Several of the more recent authors of responsa follow R. Herzog's example. Two prominent instances are R. Ya'akov Ariel (Chief Rabbi of Ramat Gan) and R. Yisrael Meir Lau (a former Ashkenazi Chief Rabbi of Israel, and subsequently Chief Rabbi of Tel-Aviv). Although certainly sensitive to the contemporary demand for rabbinic guidance on matters of military relevance, neither figure has grouped his writings in this area under a separate heading, preferring to retain the more traditional rubrics (for example, Ariel 1998: 84–90 [conscientious objection on religious grounds], 2000: 172–5 [sabbath laws], Lau 2003: 260–2). Rabbinical heads of the Schechter Institute of Jewish Studies in Jerusalem, the Israeli 'branch'

---

5   See, especially, Newman 2012.

6   Herzog 1972, part '*Orach Chayyim*', nos. 37 and 39 (both dated spring 1948), pp. 96–99. For further examples of the same format in similarly authoritative works of responsa, see Waldenberg, 1972, vol. 12 no. 57 and vol. 13, no. 100, both of which discuss whether or not a soldier may endanger his own life in an effort to save that of a wounded comrade; and Frank, 1976, part '*Yoreh De'ah*' no. 109 (on utensils originally belonging to gentiles taken spoil by the IDF); and '*Orach Chayyim*' no. 146 (on how a soldier should treat his baggage when riding on horseback at the onset of the sabbath).

of the American Conservative movement, have adopted the same policy. Hence, on the Institute's website <http://www.responsafortoday.com>, responsa relating to the conscription of both women and students into the IDF are also incorporated within an overall framework that retains the structure of the *Arba'ah Turim*.

However, it is symptomatic of the recognition now being extended to *hilchot tzavah u-milkhamah* as an independent field of inquiry that other authors of responsa are increasingly opting for an alternative arrangement. Rather than scattering their replies to queries that focus on a military setting throughout the length and breadth of their overall oeuvre, they elect to gather them within a separate set of covers, whose title explicitly proclaims the specifically military slant of the subject matter.

Towering above all works of this type is R. Goren's *Meishiv Milkhamah*, three plump volumes of 'responsa relating to the army, war and security' (Jerusalem, 1983–1993) that summarize a life time of deep personal involvement in military matters both large and small. But these writings have been supplemented (and in some matters supplanted) by a string of subsequent works. R. Shlomo Aviner, communal rabbi of the Bet-El settlement, has been particularly prolific, and has over the past two decades published several collections of military-related responsa, prominent amongst which are *Me-Chayyil le-Chayyil* ('From Strength to Strength'; 2 vols, Bet-El, 1999); *Al Diglo* ('By His Pennant'; Bet-El, 2000). As their titles proclaim, similar volumes authored by senior faculty in several *hesder yeshivot* likewise address a wide gamut of the ritual and ethical issues, some practical others theoretical, raised by service in the IDF (for example, Rabinovitch 1994, Rontski 1996–2003, Rubin 1998, Krim 2001, Avidan 2006). Still more noteworthy, because more innovative, are those authors who have pioneered the adaptation of the traditional epistolary form of the responsum to the abbreviated and instantaneous style required by electronic mail and internet-based chat groups, the most popular of which likewise present military-related material within a dedicated portal.[7]

Thus to note the multiplicity of such works of a similar format is not to suggest, of course, that their content is altogether homogeneous. Although an individual author's ideological and/or political leanings seem only rarely to intrude into what are for the most part highly technical analyses and applications of tangentially-related classic rabbinic texts, each collection of responsa does nevertheless display distinct nuances, which seem to reflect individual interests and leanings. All discuss specific points of sabbath observance in a military environment, an area of traditional law that altogether dominates much of the contemporary literature in this field. Indeed, R. Avraham Avidan (who served for over 20 years in the IDF rabbinate and rose to the rank of deputy to the *Rav Tzeva'i Rashi*), devoted an entire volume to this subject: *Shabbat u-Moed be-Tzahal* ('Sabbath and the Festivals in the IDF'; B'nei Brak, 1994).

---

7   R. Yuval Cherlow, principal of the Yeshivat Hesder at Petach Tikva, is particularly prolific in this field. He regularly contributes to <http://www.moreshet.org.il>. Another such site, <http://www.yeshiva.org.il>, is dominated by the names of rabbis Zalman and Eliezer Melamed, whose responsa generally articulate more conservative (and right-wing) views.

But other authors specialize in very different areas of probable interest to the individual soldier on service. Relations between religious and secular troops in the IDF, for instance, receive particular attention in R. Nachum Rabinovitch's *Melumedie Milkhamah* ('Experts in War'; see especially pp. 29–77), as do liturgical and ritual matters in R. Rontski's *Ke-Chitzim be-Yad Gibor* ('Like Arrows in the Hands of a Warrior'; 4 vols. Itamar 1996–2003). Not even these works, however, can compete for specificity with *Sugyot be-Hilchot Tzavah U-Mishtarah* ('Studies in Laws Relating to the Army and Police'; Jerusalem, 2003) by R. Alexander Joshua Levinsohn, who has for many years served as chaplain to the Border Police (*Mishmar Ha-Gevul*). Given that background, it is not surprising to find that this collection of responsa and analyses includes sections devoted to such matters as the use of finger prints and of DNA in evidence, and the halachic issues that arise with respect to the identification of victims of terror attacks.

Notwithstanding its length, even this list of recent responsa literature covers only the tip of a much more extensive iceberg. In addition to the conventionally published works, note must also be taken of the literature produced in less formal style by the growing number of institutions that, as noted above, cater specifically to national–religious conscripts. There now exist 34 *yeshivot hesder* and 13 *mechinot*. Almost all these institutions maintain contact with those of their students who are on active military service by means of periodic newsletters. Although much of the content of such publications is devoted to items of local institutional gossip (which of the students is engaged to be married and/or has graduated from the IDF officers' training course?), they also often print the decision (*pesak*) issued by either the principal of the yeshivah or a senior faculty member in reply to a specific question posed by one or more of the students on active service. To the best of my knowledge, this corpus has never been fully collated – let alone adequately analyzed. Until such time as both tasks are accomplished, all assessments of the true extent and impact of the new branch of responsa literature under discussion must necessarily be considered incomplete.

Books and Essays of Scholarly Analysis

Although drawing heavily on the responsa literature, what are here defined as works of scholarship and/or analysis in the field of *dinei tzavah u-milkhamah* are designed to serve a different purpose. They do not purport to reproduce responses to actual inquiries addressed to the author by individual interlocutors. Rather, their point of departure is their author's wish to communicate the fruits of his researches into the origins, development and/or contemporary relevance of one or more aspects of the field as a whole.

The first generation of books of this type attempted to present panoramic reviews. As Achituv (2002) has pointed out, the results were occasionally very innovative indeed. Particularly worthy of attention is a work entitled *Mishpat Ha-Tzavah be-Yisrael* ('The [Religious] Law of the Army in Israel') published in Jerusalem as early as 1949 by Rabbi Alter David Regensburg, an otherwise obscure

American-born principal of one of the city's smaller *yeshivot*. Notwithstanding its outward adherence to the conventions of the traditional codex (that is, the division of the work into chapters and paragraphs, to each of which is appended a commentary that also cites sources), *Mishpat ha-Tzavah* broke entirely new ground. It constituted the very first known effort to intimate that 'the Torah' – a term that in this context necessarily referred more to biblical texts than to later rabbinic writings – had something to teach about every branch of military activity, including strategic decision-making and operational behavior. Indeed, R. Regensburg focused far more on macro-level issues associated with warfare than on the sort of micro-level matters that later constituted the staple diet of rabbinic fare in this field. Thus, he discusses even the problems respecting sabbath observance confronted by individual soldiers on active service only *en passant*. By contrast, he devotes entire chapters to force structures ('The Conduct of War', pp. 30–40) and topics of military policy ('Laws Respecting Captives', pp. 47–50).

Whereas R. Regensberg was virtually unknown to the wider rabbinic public, other early authors of works of halachic synthesis on war-related issues were virtually household names. One was R. Shlomo Yosef Zevin (1885–1978), editor-in-chief of the authoritative *Entzeklopedia Talmudit*, who in 1946 published *Le'Or Ha-halachah* ('By Light of the Halachah'; 2nd revised edition Tel-Aviv, 1957). A second was R. Eliezer Yehudah Waldenberg (1917–2006), a senior member of the Rabbinic Court of Law in Jerusalem, whose three volume *Hilchot Medinah* ('Laws Respecting the State') appeared in Jerusalem in 1957. The third was R. Shaul Yisraeli (1910–1995), one of the elder R. Kook's most prominent students and the editor of several publications devoted to *halachah* under conditions of statehood, who discusses war-related matters in two major volumes of essays: *Eretz Chemdah* ('Beloved Land'; 1st edition, Jerusalem 1957) and *Amud Ha-Yemini* ('The Pillar on the Right'; 1st edition, Tel-Aviv, 1966).

Significantly, none of these works was concerned exclusively with *dinei tzavah u-milkhamah*. This subject takes up only one (albeit lengthy) chapter in R. Zevin's *Le'Or Ha-Halachah* (pp. 9–84) and only one of the three volumes of R. Waldenberg's more extensive trilogy, most of which discusses other public domain matters appertaining to the reestablishment of independent Jewish statehood. R. Israeli's two books of collected essays evince a similar approach. In neither volume do his analyses of war-related issues stand in isolation. Rather, they form part of a panoramic discussion of matters raised by the uniqueness of Israel's location and God-given mission. In *Amud Ha-Yemini*, for instance, R. Yisraeli's ground breaking analysis of Jewish military ethics, entitled 'Military Operations in Defense of the State' (the first version of which was occasioned by the 1953 operation in which IDF troops killed over 60 innocent Palestinian residents of Qibya, see Eisen 2012), follows inquiries into such topics as the holiness of Jerusalem, the possible re-convention of a *Sanhedrin*, the authority of the state of Israel and its institutions, coalitions, the rights of gentiles in a Jewish commonwealth, and the census.

Equally noticeable, furthermore, is the retrospective attitude generally adopted by these authors. This characteristic is especially marked in the works by rabbis Zevin and Waldenberg. Principally concerned to present summaries of earlier halachic sources on war-related topics, both devote considerable space to such esoteric subjects as the traditional teachings that command a soldier to grant a divorce to his wife on the eve of battle (*get milkhamah*). By comparison, matters of more immediate relevance to contemporary servicemen (such as the military duties that they are and are not permitted to carry out on the sabbath) receive short shrift. That approach very much impairs the usefulness of both works. For all their stunning erudition, they essentially remain little more than academic enquiries.

The retrospective approach still finds some adherents, as is exemplified in R. Shemarayu Arieli's, *Mishmeret Ariel* ('Ariel's Watch'; Jerusalem, 2005, a second edition of a work that displays a mastery of obscure medieval materials, originally published in 1971 under the title *Mishpat Ha-Milkhamah* ['The Judgment of War']). But most recent works of synthesis fix their gaze firmly on the present, and aim to be far more practical. Such is certainly the case with respect to R. Yitzchak Kaufman's, *Ha-Tzavah Ka-Halachah: Hilchot Milkhamah ve-Tzavah* ('The Army in Accordance with the Halachah: Laws Respecting War and the Military'; Jerusalem, 1994). Reflecting the extent of advances made in the field over the previous 50 years, this work focuses almost entirely on the realities of everyday military life, especially as experienced by the very lowest ranks. True, in his 429 heavily footnoted pages of text and another 75 pages of appendices, the author does allot some space to such concerns as the traditional Jewish definition of the *ius ad bellum* and the importance in battle of moral fortitude and faith. For the most part, however, his concern is with the nitty gritty of army life: the form and substance of sabbath observance in specific military settings and situations (he concludes the book with an analysis of the procedures to followed in a military sickbay on the sabbath); interpersonal relations amongst troops; and problems confronted by the soldier with respect to the times of prayer. Each page of these discussions is informed by the personal experience of the author, who in the past held several senior posts in the military rabbinate. Indeed, in many respects, the book reads like a reconstruction of the problems to which he was expected to find solutions during his own military service.

As a work of reference, *Ha-Tzavah ke-Halachah* is truly encyclopedic in scope. Nevertheless, it can hardly be considered user-friendly for personnel on active service. Too expensive to be found in the libraries of any but the largest of military bases, which are usually those most distant from the front, it is also far too bulky to be carried around by soldiers in the field. Hence, it is superseded in popularity by several smaller digests of contemporary rabbinic decisions, most of which are expressly designed to fit into a soldier's shirt or trouser pocket. Prominent examples of this genre have been: R. Shlomo Min-Hahar, *Dinei Tzavah u-Milkhamah: Sefer Hachanah La-Mitgayes la-Tzahal* ('Laws of Army and War: A Guide for Prospective Conscripts'; Jerusalem, 1st edition, 1972, several subsequent editions); and R. Zechariah Ben-Shlomo, *Nohal Achid: Sefer Halachah be-Nosim Relevantiyim le-Chayalim* ('Common Practice: Laws Relevant to Soldiers';

Sha'albim, 1st edition, 1986, 3rd edition 2001). Both works are addressed specifically to young adults in the national–religious community. Both also seek to address halachic issues specific to individual military occupations (the medic, the intelligence officer, the communications operator, etcetera).[8]

Another genre of 'scholarly' writings on *dinei tzavah u-milkhamah* can be found in the articles published in learned journals concerned with contemporary Jewish practice. Individually, these necessarily cover much more restricted areas than do either the book length compendia or works of reference mentioned above. On the other hand, they possess the advantage of being able to analyze individual topics in greater depth. In many cases, moreover, because their choice of subject matter reflects current and/or very recent events, articles in learned journals also project a far more topical image.

Thus far, attempts to sustain a rabbinic journal dedicated specifically to military issues have not been successful. *Oz*, which translates as 'Strength', published by the *hesder* academy at Sha'albim, has so far made only one appearance (in 1994). *Machanayim*, issued under the aegis of the IDF rabbinate and billed as 'A synagogue journal for the soldier', did manage to last somewhat longer. But after appearing on an almost weekly basis during the 1950s and 1960s, it then dropped from view, and did not resurface, under the new title *Machaneichah* ('Your Camp') until 2006. As a result, a tradition was established whereby article length analyses of *dinei tzavah u-milkhamah* appear within the covers of journals whose mandates are not restricted to military matters but extend to all areas of contemporary *halachah* in the modern state of Israel.

This phenomenon dates back to the very first years of statehood, when the need for up-to-date opinions on military matters (as on others generated by the radically changed status of the Jewish population in the land of Israel) was first keenly felt. Several publications sought to fulfill that function: *Ha-Torah Ve-ha-Medinah* (13 issues, 1949–1962) and *Barkai* (six issues, 1983–1989), both edited by R. Shaul Yisraeli; *Noam*, founded and edited by R. Mosheh Shlomo Kasher (26 issues, 1958–1984); and *Torah She-be'Al Peh*, an annual that has since 1959 published the proceedings of the conference of leading rabbinical figures held every year in Jerusalem. All of these forums published articles on military issues almost

---

8   Both of the above cited works have now been superseded, in popularity and in relevance, by *Halakhah Mimkorah – Tzavah* (*'Halakhah* from its source – the army') published in 2010 by R. Yosef Tzvi Rimon, who teaches at the Har Etziyon *hesder* academy (Rimon 2010). This work originated in a series of printed instructions that R. Rimon issued to his students prior to their enlistment during the 1990s and which were originally collated in an single pocketbook format in 2007. The latest edition, consisting of two volumes, marks a significant upgrading of the genre. It is printed on high quality chrome paper; contains numerous charts and diagrams (some in color); provides an extensive bibliography and index; and discusses issues (such as interpersonal relations in a military unit), that previous works of this sort – all heavily focused on ritual matters – tended to relegate to the margins.

as a matter of course – albeit some more frequently than others.[9] Several indeed provided initial sounding boards for what were to become classics in the field. Thus, *Ha-Torah Ve-ha-Medinah* (volume 6 [1954]) first published R. Yisraeli's article on 'The Qibya Incident in the Light of Halachah' (see above p. 93), and in volume 19 of *Torah She-be'Al Peh* (1977) that R. Ovadya Yosef, who was at the time the Chief Rabbi (*Rishon Le-tziyyon*) of Israel's Sephardi community, first expounded his equally innovative analysis of the extent to which traditional sources permit troops to endanger their own lives in order to rescue hostages, under the title 'The Entebbe Operation in the Halachah'.

Of late, however, primary status as venues for essays of that type seems to have shifted to *Techumin*, a highly prestigious published annually by the Tzomet Institute in the West Bank settlement of Alon Shevut ever since 1980. True, *Techumin* too is not concerned exclusively with military-related issues, but seeks to cover the entire gamut of contemporary religious concerns. Nevertheless, essays on topics of specifically military relevance have from its inception constituted regular features of its contents. Moreover, the proportion of space allocated to such issues steadily grows. Analysis of the cumulative subject index published in 2000 (vol. 20, pp. 497–518) reveals that until that year less than 4 percent of the articles published in *Techumin* had been concerned with military matters. However, since the outbreak of the second *intifada* and the emergence of a new mode of warfare in the year 2000, the numbers have markedly risen. The zenith (thus far) was reached in vol. 23 (2003), eight of whose 60 essays were devoted to the section entitled 'Army and Security', which included analyses of such topical issues a: 'Theft from a gentile during war' (R. Yaakov Ariel); 'Combat in regions containing civilian population' (R. Dr. Nerya Gutal); 'Harvesting the olives of gentiles from trees located within the boundaries of a Jewish settlement' (R. Yaakov Ariel); 'The distribution of booty and loot in contemporary warfare' (R. Shlomo Rosenfeld); 'Acquisition (*kinyan*) by means of conquest' (R. Gad Eldad).

A similar development can be discerned in the case of *Tzohar*, a quarterly published by the association of younger Israeli national–religious rabbis and teachers of that name, which first began to appear in January 2000. Initially, *Tzohar* paid no particular attention to military matters. But that situation changed markedly with the publication in no. 11 (summer 2002, pp. 97–104) of 'Questions on Combat Ethics' by R. Yuval Cherlow, an article that was prompted by the fighting in Jenin earlier that year and that initiated a spirited exchange in subsequent issues.

Finally, note must be taken of the venue for article length studies on one aspect or another of the relationship between Judaism and warfare provided by the production of memorial volumes of essays, whose publication is sponsored by the family, friends and/or alma mater of soldiers killed on active combat duty. This

---

9   Thus, whereas I was able to identify 14 articles on military-related topics (out of a total of over 200) in the 13 issues of *Ha-Torah ve-Ha-Medinah*, and six (out of 180) in the six issues of *Barkai*, I could locate only three on such subjects in the 25 issues of *Noam*.

phenomenon, although not entirely recent,[10] has also become more pronounced since the 1990s. So too has the tendency for most such collections to make military topics (broadly defined) the very focus of their attention. One example is provided by *Kedushat Ha-Chayyim ve-Chiruf Nefesh* ('The Holiness of Life and Self-Sacrifice'; eds. Yeshayu Gafni and Aviezer Ravitzky, Jerusalem, 1992), a volume dedicated to the memory of Captain Amir Yekutiel. Another can be found in *Sefer Harel* ('The Harel Book'), subtitled 'Israeli Militarism through a Religious Prism', (637 pages, edited by R. Eliezer Shenwald, Chispin, 2002), which is dedicated to the memory of Lt. Harel Shram. Despite their differences in style and tone, both works contain several pioneering contributions to this field. The topics they cover range from 'the value of life in the Bible' to 'The Existential and Moral Dilemma of Armed Resistance in the Ghetto' (in *Kedushat ha-Chayyim)*, and (in *Sefer Harel)*, from 'The Conquest and Inheritance of the Land [of Israel]' to 'The Halachic Responsibility of the Military Commander'.

Subject Matter

The content of contemporary rabbinic writings on military themes and issues focuses on three principal areas. One is the observance of traditional commandments in a military setting; a second is the sanction for a resort to military force; the third is required conduct during military engagements. Although sometimes overlapping, each of these three themes warrants independent comment – not least because of the differences discernible in the tools of halachic assessment employed in their analysis.

The Observance of Traditional Commandments in a Broad Military Setting

In terms of sheer volume, this is by far the largest subject of concern in the contemporary literature on *dinei tzavah u-milkhamah*. It encompasses numerous attempts to reconcile the practicalities of modern military life with the stringent dictates of traditional Jewish practice in specific areas of behavior. Guidance in this field is particularly necessary during those long periods of military duty when servicemen and women are not engaged in actual combat, but – as is most commonly the case – involved in training exercises or employed on maintenance tasks.

Sabbath observance constitutes an especially prominent subject of concern. (For instance, it dominates 11 of the 45 chapters of R. Kaufman's *Ha-Tzavah Ke-Halachah*). But numerous other topics also cry out for attention. How is the

---

10   For a comparatively early example of the genre, see *Ner Le-Yechezkel* (Jerusalem 1971), a privately printed anthology of both articles on various halachic topics (some by leading national–religious rabbinic figures of the time) and memorial tributes to Yechezkel Ezra Bezalel, a young conscript in the IDF Rabbinate, who was killed on active service on the banks of the Suez Canal in April 1970.

restrictive nature of traditional Jewish attitudes towards inter-gender relationships (broadly categorized as rules of *tzeniyut* [lit: 'modesty']) to be squared with the increasing willingness of the IDF to integrate female soldiers into field units? (Ariel 2003) Is it possible to respect the demands of the orthodox male dress code (skullcap, fringed garments) and also observe the military requirement for camouflage? (Rontski 1996 1: 142–3, 1998 2: 105–6) Can orthodox troops signify their allegiance to the IDF by answering 'I swear' (*ani nishba*) to the standard oath of military induction, or should they restrict themselves to 'I affirm' (*ani matzhir*; Bruner 2002, Rimon 2002b)?

For the most part, contemporary rabbinic analysis treats the military setting in which such issues arise as an incidental circumstance. The underlying assumption is that, as far as the application of traditional rules of assessment is concerned, there is little that need be considered *sui generis* about the military context out of which the specific query arises. Hence, the determination of religiously permissible conduct ultimately depends upon the perceived applicability of rules and categories that the canonical texts originally applied to other, non-military, contexts.

The most obvious – and most common – examples of the application of this methodology concern issues considered amenable to categorization under the generic meta-rubric of *pikuach nefesh* (lit: 'regard for life', the rabbinical term applied to the religious duty to save an endangered human life, even when the attempt to do will necessitate transgressing other commandments). Military personnel are not of course the only group to whose activities the application of this consideration might apply. For centuries it has been analyzed in relation to doctors and midwives, particularly within the context of the circumstances that might permit some suspension in the normal rules of sabbath observance (Katz 1998). That being the case, all that the contemporary rabbinic authority needs to do is to determine how closely actions performed by soldiers on active service conform to the criteria for the saving of (Jewish) life already worked out for, say, members of the medical profession. Needless to say, this may be a highly specialized task. Nevertheless, by the standard of traditional enquiry, the mode of analysis thus adopted would ultimately be considered entirely conventional. Ingenious though the results of such analyses often are, they invariably involve little more than the extrapolation and application of accepted rabbinic categories, *ad hominem* and *ad rem*.

The Sanction for the Resort to Military Force

Different analytical paradigms are employed when attention shifts to the contemporary conditions under which the use of armed force might receive religious sanction. This branch of *dinei tzavah u-milkhamah* covers topics traditionally addressed by western political theorists under the rubric of the *ius ad bellum*. As such, it addresses the circumstances that license state-organized and state-directed violence and examines the extent to which they oblige citizens to respond to the call to arms.

Without exception, all contemporary participants in this portion of the rabbinic discourse manifestly recognize the singularity of the military experience. What is more, they work within the framework of rabbinic categories explicitly formulated for the purpose of its analysis. Specifically, they employ the talmudic taxonomy of *milkhemet mitzvah* and *milkhemet reshut* (translated, respectively, as 'mandatory' and 'discretionary' wars) adopted by Maimonides in the opening to the fifth chapter of his 'Laws of Kings and their Wars' (Walzer 2006: 149–68; and above pp. 78–9). With that template to hand, initial national–religious opinion overwhelmingly granted IDF military operations the umbrella sanction peculiar to 'mandatory' wars, dictated by the need – as Maimonides puts it – 'to deliver Israel from an oppressor attacking them'. Implicitly rejected, albeit not always explicitly so, was the suggestion that modern Israel's use of force might reflect nothing higher than the mundane impulses ('to expand Israel's borders' or to increase the ruler's personal 'power and reputation') that Maimonides ascribes to 'discretionary' wars (Aryeh 2002).

Time has shown this neat categorization to be far less serviceable than was once thought. On examination, the key phrase in the Maimonidean proof text relating to 'mandatory wars ('to deliver Israel from an oppressor attacking them') has stubbornly resisted precise application to every item in the kaleidoscope of modern Israel's force menu. Hence, it can hardly be said to provide blanket authorization for all actions. Certainly, the IDF could be said to be acting 'to deliver Israel from an oppressor' when launching 'reactive–defensive' operations in response to the Arab invasions of both May 1948 and October 1973. But whether or not the same phrase also covers deterrent activities seems far more problematical. Does it grant halachic *ius ad bellum* to a 'pre-emptive' strike, undertaken in order to forestall immediately anticipated enemy aggression, such as was launched by the IDF against Egypt in June 1967? (Eizental 2002) Does it incorporate 'preventative' operations, such as the Sinai campaign of 1956 or the Israeli air bombardment of Iraq's nuclear facility in 1981, both of which were initiated in order to destroy a putative predator's war making potential before the threat actually materialized? (Ushpizai 1983) And how does *halachah* classify an 'offensive–defensive' action, of the type exemplified by Israel's 'Operation Peace for the Galilee' of June 1982? (Bleich 1983) Or, for that matter, a 'targeted killing', aimed at a person suspected on being about to perpetrate an act of terror? (Avidan 2006)[11]

Far from being matters of theoretical interest, such questions raise several issues of severely practical import, of which undoubtedly the most salient is that of authorization. As portrayed by Maimonides, only in cases of a 'mandatory' war does the sovereign (translated in contemporary terms as Israel's government) possess the exclusive prerogative of war initiation. Likewise, only in cases of a 'mandatory' war is military serviceobligatory, and binding on all citizens, females as well as males (Akovi 2003). But if the precise determination of which operations do warrant the 'mandatory' categorization – and which do not – is to be left to rabbinic discretion,

---

11   See also above p. 80, note 2.

tensions over spheres of influence arc bound to arouse. Professor Aviezer Ravitzky long ago adduced evidence for a traditional Jewish conception of 'prohibited' wars (Ravitzky 1996), a rubric that necessarily implies a religious obligation to refuse summonses to military service that do not warrant rabbinic sanction.

Recent events in Israel have shown how that concept can be expanded much further, and broadened to encompass rabbinic instructions to individual soldiers to obey all military orders deemed to contravene *halachah*. Particularly significant, in this context, were rabbinic responses to government instructions that the IDF dismantle Jewish settlements in Yamit, in the Sinai, (1981) and in Gaza and northern Samaria (2005). At issue, on both occasions, was the halachic legality of the human sovereign's power to relinquish portions of land widely deemed to be Israel's God-given patrimony and, correspondingly, the rights of the individual soldier to refuse to participate in any such operation. A considerable body of rabbinic opinion insisted that *halachah* obliged national–religious troops, like all others, to obey whatever orders they were given (which, in fact, the vast majority did). But dissenting opinions were also voiced, arguing that this is precisely the sort of case in which military commands lack the validity required for religious authorization (see below p. 159).

Required Conduct During Violent Military Engagements

Musar ba-milkhamah (which translates as either 'ethics in war' or 'military ethics'.) has always constituted an integral part of the contemporary rabbinic discourse on *dinei tzavah u-milkhamah*. As already noted, R. Yisraeli addressed this subject at length in his pioneering essay on the 1953 Qibya operation; so too, even more extensively, did R. Goren, who devoted virtually the entire first volume of his collected responsa, *Meishiv Milkhamah*, to an extended examination of 'Combat Morality in War' (Edrei 2005). Nevertheless, and as Professor Ehud Luz points out, these were the exceptions rather than the rule. For many years, most expositions of contemporary military *halachah* simply passed over *ius in bello* concerns in silence (Luz 2003). Such, however, is no longer the case. Ever since the late 1980s, topics relating to military ethics have moved from the periphery of rabbinic attention to its very center (S. Cohen 2007b).

Of all the possible causes for that shift, undoubtedly the most salient has been the IDF's sustained experience of counter-insurgency operations during recent decades. Since Israel's 1982 invasion of the Lebanon, her troops have been virtuously continuously engaged in action against motley collections of armed gangs, guerillas, and terrorists. With the outbreak of the first *intifada* in 1987, and especially during the course of the even more violent second *intifada* that erupted in 2000, they were also called upon to take various forms of action against Palestinian civilians too. Like several other western armies, the IDF has discovered that the notoriously 'fuzzy' nature of such operations, with their tendency to blur distinctions between combatants and non-combatants, makes it particularly difficult for troops and their commanders to demarcate the boundaries between permissible and impermissible behavior in battle. Accordingly, the General Staff has issued (and revised) a 'Code of Ethics', entitled *Ruach Tzahal* ('The Spirit of the IDF') that specifies three 'basic values' and ten further 'values' of conduct (Kasher 1996). Sensitive to the same complex of pressures, rabbinic teachers have sought to compose a similar halachic guide to moral conduct.[12]

This has not at all been an easy task. True, the Bible does contain very explicit instructions with respect to booty and the spoils of war (Deuteronomy 20:1–20) and a more general injunction to moderate the corrosive atmosphere characteristic of military environments 'And your camp shall be holy' (Deuteronomy 23.15). And, indeed, these texts have ever since the 1970s been rigorously investigated with the explicit purpose of making them applicable to the experience of present-day IDF troops (for example, Horowitz 1972, Ben-Hamu 1982). Even so, the gaps remain glaring. On most other topics of contemporary *ius in bello* concern, the sources on which rabbis usually rely tend to be embarrassingly sparse. Biblical materials contain just one commandment to give the enemy a chance to make peace prior to launching an attack (Deuteronomy 20:10), an injunction that applies only in the case of a *milkhemet reshut* (Mandelkron 1994, N. Shapira 1998). Likewise, they have been found to contain just one instruction to leave him an avenue of escape – and even that might be motivated as much by tactical as by humanitarian considerations (Cherlow 2002). As J. David Bleich has noted, when discussion turns to 'collateral damage' and the (im)permissibility of certain types of weapons, two subjects that figure particularly prominently on the contemporary *ius in bello* agenda in the western world, the sources on which rabbis conventionally rely seem to have virtually nothing to say at all (Bleich 1983: 19).

Several efforts have been made to repair the resultant deficiencies in rabbinic instruction. The most conventional method has been to publish learned articles on various ethical themes, several of which now appear almost as a matter of course in such scholarly journals as *Techumin* and *Tzohar*. More innovative, however, has been the organization of seminars on 'military ethics and *halachah*' for prospective and current conscripts, whose purpose is to sensitize this population group to the need to maintain standards of ethical conduct – as much in combat situations as in any other (and, indeed, more so). Since the proceedings of such events are themselves also published, they are available to wider audiences, too. One particularly prominent example is provided by a volume entitled *Arachim Be-Mivchan ha-Milkhamah* ('Values in the Test of War: War Ethics in the Light of Judaism', 1984), based on a symposium organized that year by the 'Har Etzion' academy in memory of one of its pupils who had been killed in action in the

---

12 Even in the short time that has elapsed since this chapter was first published, several additional rounds of hostilities have broken out (notably, the second Lebanon War of 2006 and Operations 'Cast Lead' and 'Pillar of Cloud' in Gaza, 2008–9 and 2012). Each has posed new dilemmas, especially with respect to the difficulties of distinguishing between 'military' and 'civilian' targets. For one extensive rabbinic discussion, published – significantly – in the IDF Rabbinate's journal, see Lavie 2007.

Lebanon. This book deserves to be considered a landmark, not least because it pioneered the effort to take a comprehensive look at Jewish military ethics in the light of practical combat experience. Its 18 especially commissioned articles, some of which were written by non-rabbinic academics, laid down leads for a discourse on the subject that very much intensified in the wake of both the first and second *intifada*s (for example, Sherman 2002, Sharir 2005).

In many respects, all this effort has simply underscored the paucity of the sources available for the reconstruction of a specifically Jewish corpus of military ethics. If citations are anything to go by, the only available texts in this area are snatches of pre-modern scriptural exegesis – of which by far the most popular is a warning against the corrosive effects of military life contained in the commentary by Nachmanides (Rabbi Moses ben Nachman, Catalonia, 1194–1270) to Deuteronomy 23:10. In the hands of a master, such materials can support an entire edifice of correct conduct. ('It is most important that a person going out to war knows that he is not moving from a world with one scale of values to a world with another scale of values').[13] Even so, they remain very thin on the ground. The result is that in this area, especially, contemporary rabbis have very much been left to their own devices. Not surprisingly, therefore, the variety of their approaches to the religious legitimacy of IDF actions against Palestinian terrorists and their suspected supporters has been pronounced (Zoldan 2002: 284–303).

The fissiparous potential inherent in the absence of explicit traditional guidelines is exacerbated by the lack of agreement as to the appropriate tool of rabbinic analysis for military ethics. Some commentators have sought to go straight to primary sources, and read lessons into supposedly analogous biblical incidents, especially, Genesis Chapter 34, which recounts the action taken against the people of Shechem by Simeon and Levi in retaliation for the rape of their sister, Dinah (Shaviv 1994b). Others, however, have resorted to what might be termed a strategy of analytical transference, appropriating to the military context principles originally developed with non-military settings in mind. As Professor Gerald Blidstein shows, this methodology has enabled some especially militant observers to apply to the Palestinian population the category of *rodef*, the rabbinic term that defines the status of a person who endangers [lit. 'pursues'] the life of another, and who therefore himself constitutes a legitimate target of pre-emptive attack (Blidstein 1996).

Implications

The implications of the emergence of a branch of rabbinic discourse that focuses specifically on matters of military relevance are bifurcate. At the conceptual level, this development shapes intellectual constructs of the *halachah* and its application. In the operational realm, it can also influence the style of IDF troop behavior.

---

13   Rabbi Aaron Lichtenstein (Principal of the Har Etzion Academy) in round table on war and ethics cited in S. Cohen 2007b.

Conceptual

The recent explosion of rabbinic interest in *dinei tzavah u-milkhamah* has not merely created a whole library of new rabbinic texts. It has also stimulated declarations to the effect that warfare and its conduct constitute entirely self-contained areas of halachic 'space', whose uniqueness reflects the singularity of military conduct.

In its most basic version, that is not an altogether novel argument. For one thing, it seems firmly grounded in the license that the Bible itself gives in times of war to certain actions that are otherwise strictly forbidden. The spectrum ranges from placing one's own life in danger and killing another human being to theft, now categorized as booty, and sexual intercourse with gentiles (the '[captive] woman of beautiful countenance', see Deuteronomy 21:10–15; Rubinstein 1975). More specifically, it traces its intellectual origins to the view most famously advanced at the very beginning of the twentieth century by Rabbi Abraham Isaac Kook (1865–1935), the first Ashkenazi Chief Rabbi of mandatory Palestine, whose contention that *dinei milkhamah* comprise a self-contained category of *halachah* is generally recognized to be one of his most important contributions to modern rabbinic thought.[14] Nevertheless, a comprehensive exploration of that position had to await further analysis of its practical inferences.

Credit for initiating that enterprise belongs to Rabbi Goren. Convinced that war-related issues fully deserved to be considered a religious category of their own, he set about illustrating the validity of his position with characteristic verve. Hence, he deliberately applied his argument to the field of Sabbath observance, always a litmus test of rabbinic analysis. In publication after publication, and most famously in his magnum opus, *Meishiv Milkhamah*, R. Goren argued that soldiers had no call to base their permit to carry out military-related tasks on the sabbath on the traditional principle of *pikuach nefesh* (that is, the argument that they were involved in 'life-saving' duties). Rather, they could trace the duty (not 'permission') to carry out military-related activities on the sabbath to an entirely independent source. Specifically, Goren directed attention to one version of talmudic exegesis on Deuteronomy 20:20, which intimates that need for victory in war provides its own validity for sabbath violations (Goren 1983 1: 88–109).

Over the past decade, the position adumbrated in this somewhat complex reading has gained increasing support (see below pp. 152–3). A vital initial threshold was crossed when a group of younger scholars undertook a deliberately purposeful study of the relevant texts. By thus subjecting these materials to systematic analysis (as opposed to the more intuitive style usually favored by R. Goren), they sought to buttress the intellectual respectability of the thesis that war does indeed possess an autonomous station in *halachah* (for example,

---

14　Rabbi Kook projected this thesis in the course of four replies (dated 1916–17) to Rabbi S.Z. Pines of Zurich, which were later printed in R. Kook's responsa: *Mishpat Kohen*, nos. 142, 143, 144 and 148. For a thorough analysis see Rakover 2000.

Shenwald 2002). Equally significant, secondly, is the way in which the scope of that argument has been extended. Although sabbath observance continues to constitute its principal testing ground, the singularity of warfare has also been advanced as justification for the articulation of unique *halachot* in several other military-related areas too. The range extends from interpersonal relations on an army base to troop conduct vis-à-vis Palestinian civilians. In each case, the same reasoning is applied: war – not least when classified as a *milkhemet mitzvah* – is clearly *sui generis*. Hence, *halachah* cannot address it as no more than an extension of a non-military situation – not even one as fraught with the potential for violence as that of *rodef* (see above p. 102). Quite simply: 'It is inconceivable that the rules of warfare are no more than extensions of those of *rodef*. Rather, there exists a term 'war' that possesses independent status' (Amital 1994: 191; also Deichovski 2003: 156).

Military–Operational

In a pioneering study entitled 'War in Jewish Tradition', published in 1987, Efraim Inbar suggested that the development of a new corpus of *halachah* specifically relating to war might serve a political function, and grant 'religious legitimacy to the secular authorities of the state of Israel in pursuing warlike activities' (Inbar 1987). As matters stand, that prognosis hardly seems realistic. However much traditional Jewish themes might indeed influence some aspects of modern Israel's official attitude towards the external world, they hardly seem likely to override pragmatic considerations where ministerial decisions for war (and peace) are concerned.

Matters begin to look very different, however, once the search for the policy implications of the re-discovery of *dinei tzavah u-milkhamah* is broadened to include the citizen soldiers who form the vast bulk of Israel's armed forces. At this more extended societal level, the developments described in this chapter might have practical consequences, and in particular affect aspects of the IDF's operational behavior.

That hypothesis is supported by two related sociological trends, both already outlined in Chapter 1 (above pp. 1–21). One is the recent increase in the proportion of 'national–religious' troops in IDF combat formations, and especially amongst the cadres of junior officers who command them. The second is the growth in the numbers of national–religious servicemen (and, increasingly, women) who have begun to graduate from one or another of the various academies of advanced Jewish instruction in which the new rabbinic discourse on *dinei tzavah u-milkhamah* is being most intensively developed. Over 20 percent of the male graduates of national–religious high schools now attend one of the dozen pre-military academies (*mechinot kedam tzevaiyot*), whose students undergo a year of national and religious 'fortification' before embarking on their military careers. A further 18 percent enroll in one of the 30 institutions known as *yeshivot hesder*, where they pursue a five-year program in which periods of talmudic study and military service are interspersed. Although certainly not all cut of one cloth, these institutions have thus become the principal forums for dialogue between a new breed of Jewish spiritual mentors and the young soldiers who are most anxious to hear what their religion has to say about the specific military situations in which they now find themselves.

What makes those developments especially significant is their coincidence with the current emphasis in IDF military operations on counter-insurgency missions, to which reference has likewise already been made (above pp. 80–81). That shift has not only posed notoriously complex ethical challenges. It has also 'flattened' the command structure responsible for ensuring that troops behave in a morally acceptable manner. As the professional military literature points out, one of the defining characteristics of counter-insurgency operations is that they are invariably conducted by small and often isolated units whose deadly engagements with 'the enemy' (often no more than an individual sniper, or a seemingly harmless civilian who turns out to be a suicidal terrorist) flare up as suddenly as they thereafter die down. In such cases, officers of senior rank are rarely on hand. Instead, split second decisions on how to respond have to be taken by NCOs and/or junior officers (Dewar 1985: 177–8). The heavy representation in that cadre of a group that is particularly sensitive to the emergence of the new field of *dinei tzavah u-milkhamah,* in all its nuances, could well exert a profound influence on the tenor of IDF operations as a whole.

Conclusions

Focusing their attention on more conventional aspects of intellectual developments in Israel, even the most severe critics of the country's supposed tendency towards 'cultural militarism' have overlooked the emergence of an entire corpus of literature specifically devoted to *dinei tzavah u-milkhamah.* This chapter has attempted to redress the situation. Quite apart from delineating the scope of that literature and its principal formats, it has also drawn attention to its possible influences. These, we have suggested, could be much more profound than might initially be supposed. True, the frequently esoteric content of the relevant rabbinic literature often seems to indicate a conservative thrust, in content as well as methodology, an impression seemingly confirmed by the highly technical and traditional language in which it is usually composed. But beneath this surface appearance there lurk impulses whose import is little short of revolutionary and whose potential for further change is profound.

PART III
Tensions – and their Resolution?

Chapter 7

Tensions between Military Service and Jewish Orthodoxy in Israel: Implications Imagined and Real[1]

Of the several recent transformations in the sociological profile of the Israel Defense Force, arguably the most conspicuous is the growth in the number of male troops in field formations who adhere to Jewish orthodox practice and now wear a *kippah serugah* (knitted skullcap). Signs of that development, although evident for some time, have of late become especially obtrusive (see above, Chapter 1, pp. 11–12). Graduates of the religious state educational network, it seems, have altogether appropriated the mantle of extraordinary commitment to combat military service that once belonged to products of the secular *kibbutz* system.

The present chapter discusses some of the implications of that situation for societal–military relations in Israel. Its point of departure is that the *kippah serugah* constitutes a (male) symbol of affiliation; it serves as a widely recognized mark of attachment to what is termed the 'national–religious' (alternatively 'religious– Zionist') community. Admittedly, those designations beg serious questions: How 'national'? In what way 'religious'? They are also misleading, since they imply that the sectors thus defined are far more homogenous than is in fact the case (Sheleg 2000). *Kippot serugot* come in several sizes, colors and patterns, each favored by a separate shade of the 'national–religious' rainbow. Nevertheless, they remain generic badges of affiliation. A *kippah serugah* proclaims its wearer's commitment to a way of life that – broadly speaking –seeks to harmonize religion with Zionism, and that is therefore distinct from that of both the ultra-orthodox (*haredim*), on the one hand, and secularists, on the other. The *kippah* also declares fidelity to teachings that, to one degree or another, endow military service in the IDF with transcendent meanings (Sprinzak 1991: 30–5).

That is precisely why the prominence of national–religious soldiers amongst the IDF's combat complement sometimes generates undisguised dismay. Alarmists warn that members of the national–religious community who have attained senior ranks[2] might be in a position to impose a religiously-dictated straightjacket on

---

1   The original version of this chapter appeared in *Israel Studies*, 12/1, 2007, pp. 103–126. Reprinted with permission.

2   When this article was first published, in 2007, I counted over a dozen brigadier generals in field formations who wore a *kippah serugah*, and four members of the General Staff. In 2012, the respective figures were 14 and three.

the conduct of Israel's entire security policy (Ben-Eliezer 1998b, 2000). More sophisticated, but only slightly less ominous, is the argument that even the *suspicion* that so many troops and their officers might subordinate their professional military commitments to their ideological/religious preferences could confuse the chain of command and thereby spread dissension throughout the Force. At root, runs this argument, there will always exist a fear that the obedience of national–religious servicemen – of all ranks – to military commands will ultimately be dependent on their perception that the military institution's corporate behavior conforms to the religious Zionist understanding of security. Should the two ever collide, troops wearing a *kippah serugah* might refuse to obey orders or, in extreme circumstances, even rebel (Kasher 1997, Gal 2012).

The possibility that they could do so *en bloc* seems to be enhanced by the web of institutional networks through which much of national–religious youth in Israel passes. Besides a popular youth movement (*B'nei Akivah*), the range includes a countrywide system of gender segregated and residential national–religious high schools (*yeshivot tichoniyot* for boys and *ulpanot* for girls). Still more influential, it seems, are the post-high school frameworks that, with the sanction of the IDF, permit national–religious youth, females as well as males, to combine their military service with advanced theological studies. One such framework comprises the *yeshivot hesder* ('arrangement academies'), which offer a five-year program that allow students to intersperse their studies with an abbreviated conscript term, during much of which they serve in their own segregated companies. The other consists of the *mekhinot toraniyot kedam tzevaiyot* ('pre-military *Torah* colleges'), whose students undergo a year of spiritual and physical 'fortification' prior to their enlistment (see above pp. 11–13).

Both frameworks are suspected of fostering a system of dual control, which compels the IDF command to share authority with the *hesder* and *mekhinah* rabbis to whom, as we shall demonstrate below, national–religious troops frequently turn for guidance, even whilst on active service. This situation raises several questions: can those rabbis be trusted to resist the temptation to exercise – or threaten to exercise – their influence? Should they consider a military order to transgress a religious commandment, would they not feel obliged to instruct their pupils to express conscientious objection? And would not the very publication of such an edict dissuade national–religious troops from remaining obedient to the conventional military chain of command?

Such fears have been intermittently expressed ever since a reservist who had graduated from one of the most prestigious *yeshivot hesder* assassinated Prime Minister Rabin in November 1995. But they reached a crescendo a decade later, in the spring of 2005, when the IDF prepared to implement the disengagement from the Gaza Strip and northern Samaria, in accordance with the program that Prime Minister Ariel Sharon had announced in December 2003 and which, after considerable public debate, the *Knesset* eventually sanctioned by 67 votes to 45 in October 2004.

Far from putting an end to public controversy, the *Knesset* decision merely stimulated an even more intensive furor. Attention now shifted from the legitimacy/ illegitimacy of the measures used by Sharon to bulldoze his program through the parliamentary process to the steps that might be taken in order to sabotage its implementation. In this context, particular significance was attached to reports that several rabbis in the national–religious community were calling on those of their disciples who served in the IDF to refuse whatever orders they might receive to participate in disengagement operations. Led by Rabbi Abraham Shapira, an octogenarian former Chief Rabbi of Israel and long-time principal of one of the most prestigious religious Zionist academies (*Yeshivat Merkaz Harav Kook*) – and indeed virtually a cult figure in some religious Zionist circles – this group buttressed its exhortations with supposedly impeccable theological reasoning. The establishment of Jewish settlements up and down the country, and not least in the regions so miraculously 'liberated' in June 1967, had constituted an act of religious significance (*mitzvah*), making the settlers partners in the fulfillment of God's design. It followed that participation in the dismantlement of such settlements would signify a sinful absence of confidence in the Almighty's support. In the phrase used by Rabbi Shapira in a media interview: 'Heaven would never forgive' those who obeyed orders to do evict settlers from their homes (Av. Shapira 2004).

Throughout subsequent months, speculation that significant numbers of *kippot serugot*, in the ranks – reservists, regulars and conscripts alike – might declare their conscientious objection to disengagement attained obsessive proportions. The opposition to military disobedience voiced by senior non-rabbinic (and ex-military) figures in the national–religious world did nothing to quell anxieties,[3] principally because the influence of the rabbis was in this case deemed to be more relevant. What instructions were graduates of the *yeshivot hesder* and *mekhinot* receiving from their spiritual mentors in those institutions? How many would be likely to be thus persuaded to act in accordance with Rabbi Shapira's ruling (or dissuaded from doing so)? In the absence of precise data, various figures were bandied about. From time to time, opponents of disengagement claimed to have persuaded 'tens of thousands' of reservists to add their signatures to proclamations of intent to refuse service. Even supposedly hard-headed observers warned that feelings amongst national–religious troops were running high, especially since many were personally acquainted with – and related to – the settlers whom they would confront (Ben-Meir 2005). On the morning that the disengagement operation commenced (14 August 2005), a banner headline in one of the country's most popular newspapers pronounced that the possibility of widespread conscientious objection had brought the IDF face-to-face with 'an existential test' (Rappaport 2005).

---

3   For example by Brigadier General (res.) Effie Eitam, then chairman of the National Religious Party, reported in *Ha-Tzofeh* (Hebrew daily; organ of the National–Religious party), 7 January 2005, p. 1 and by Yisrael Harel (former chairman of the Settlers' Council), *Haaretz* 6 January 2005, B1.

In the event, such projections turned out to be widely off the mark. Testifying orally to the *Knesset*'s Foreign Affairs and Security Committee in September 2005, a month after completing disengagement, the Chief of the IDF General Staff, Lieutenant General Dan Chalutz, stated that just 63 soldiers had been placed on trial for refusing orders during the operation. (50 conscripts – 24 of whom served in the framework of the *yeshivot hesder;* five petty officers and three other ranks in professional service; and five reservists). Possibly, these figures do not tell the entire story. *Ba-Machaneh*, the IDF weekly, had on 23 August reported an additional 100 cases, including those in which male and female troops, a handful of whom were junior officers, either declared their intent to disobey military orders or refused to take part in some of the preliminary stand-offs between the IDF and the settlers. Arguably, allowances also have to be made for troops who came to private 'understandings' with their immediate commanding officers, and hence managed to detach themselves from units directly engaged in disengagement. Even so, the overall picture remains clear. En masse, the *kippot serugot* neither rebelled nor shirked their duties

The remainder of this chapter seeks to account for that outcome. I begin by presenting its two most obviously apparent causes: first, the measures taken by the IDF in order to minimize the possible incidence of conscientious objection; and second, the moderating effect exercised by divisions of opinion within the national–religious community's spiritual leadership over Rabbi Shapira's call for military disobedience. Thereafter, however, I draw attention to a third circumstance, whose influence seems to have been even more decisive. Specifically, the chapter will analyze evidence indicating that, contrary to most public perceptions, settlement dismantlement was not the sole source of anxiety to most national–religious troops. If anything, as an issue likely to generate their dissent, it was subordinate to other concerns. Failure to note that dimension of the subject, it will here be argued, not only inhibits an appropriate understanding of what occurred in the summer of 2005. More seriously, it also misrepresents the true nature of the elusive relationship between national–religious troops and the IDF, a relationship whose theoretical implications extend far beyond the confines of this particular segment of Israeli society.

The Steps Taken by the IDF

From the military–institutional perspective, 'disengagement' deserves to be considered an outstanding operational success. The IDF accomplished its mission swiftly, without any serious casualties, and with a minimum of internal turbulence.

What makes the ultimate result especially remarkable is the fact that it was by no means assured. After all, the Force had few reserves of relevant experience on which to draw for this type of operation. The only valid precedent was the evacuation in 1982 of the settlements that Israel had established in the Sinai after 1967 and whose dismantlement constituted part of the Israeli–Egyptian peace treaty signed by Prime Minister Begin and President Sadat in 1979. But the parallel was hardly precise. By the spring of 1982, most Sinai settlers had voluntarily left the region, and the IDF was only called upon to evacuate the township of Yamit, which then housed just a few hundred permanent residents (compared to almost 8,000 who remained in the Gaza Strip and northern Samaria in the summer of 2005). Besides, other than by a small faction of right-wing ideologues, the Sinai had not been invested with the sanctity attached to the 'historic' Land of Israel; in return for its evacuation, Israel had attained a peace agreement with the largest and most powerful of her neighbors; and the decision to withdraw (unlike disengagement) had been sanctioned by a clear majority of the Jewish citizenry (Kliot 2005). In addition, the Yamit experience had taken place long ago: before the settlement enterprise had taken deep root in the national consciousness and – most sensitive of all – before the settlers slated for eviction had paid a blood price for their residence in the area.[4] For all these reasons, the IDF clearly needed to invest extraordinary resources in preparing its personnel for the delicate challenges that disengagement would undoubtedly present.

That is precisely what was done. Despite his barely disguised suspicion that disengagement was a misguided policy, the Chief of Staff (Lieutenant General Moshe ['Bugie'] Ayalon) insisted on meticulous preparations for the operation, ultimately code-named *yad le-achim* (lit: 'a hand [stretched out] to brothers'). Moreover, the General Staff outline, which although not formally approved by the Defense Minister until February 2005 was to all intents and purposes ready as early as August 2004, made the parameters of IDF activity absolutely clear. Until complete, *yad le-achim* would take precedence over every other scheduled IDF mission. Fully 15,000 troops, male and female, were assigned to the task, and hence released from regular training exercises and courses of instruction.[5] At the same time, however, disengagement was to be viewed as a constabulary mission. This designation not only mandated full co-operation with the Police Force, but – above all – the adoption of an appropriate attitude towards the settlers. During disengagement, they were to be dealt with 'firmly but with sensitivity'. Hence, the soldiers most likely to come into contact with settlers were not to carry any weapons during the entire operation and would be supplied with special training as to how to maintain the prescribed 'rules of the game'.

---

4   According to statistics published by the Israel General Security Service, 57 percent of all Palestinian attacks on Israeli targets between September 2000 and July 2004 were directed at Jewish settlements and settlers in the Gaza Strip <http://www.shabak.gov.il/ SiteCollectionImages/תורייקס%20פוסרסומימ/terror-portal/docs/kreport090310_he.pdf> (accessed 19 September 2012).

5   IDF deployments for this operation are described in Ya'alon 2008. Ya'alon made no secret of his opposition to the disengagement proposal – a position that he thinks explains the Government's refusal to grant him another year of office when his term expired in June 2005, just three months before the disengagement was to take place. Nevertheless, he claims to have done all in his power to ensure that it would be carried out smoothly.

Ultimately, much of the latter burden devolved on the IDF's Education Branch and on psychologists serving in the Ground Forces Command and in the Behavioral Sciences Department, several of whom granted me personal interviews.[6] Together, these units prepared several 'kits', for use by the immediate commanders of the forces assigned to the operation. Consisting of videotapes, two CDs and 11 printed pamphlets on various aspects of the operation (free speech, the settlements; relations between the IDF and media), these were distributed throughout the early summer, and thereafter supplemented by several day-long seminars. With the approach of D-Day (set for 14 August 2005, corresponding to the morrow of the fast of the 9th Av in the Jewish calendar, commemorating the destruction of the second Temple in 70 ce), preparations moved into higher gear. The troops massed in the temporary military base near the Gaza Strip, especially constructed for the purposes of disengagement, received what to the rank and file seemed like an unending stream of talks from IDF psychologists, sociologists and senior commanders – all designed to inculcate the message that the settlers were by no means to be considered an 'enemy', and that the disengagement mission was as much a test of the individual soldier's civility as of his/her loyalty to the government whose orders they were carrying out.

Notwithstanding all this activity, there still remained the delicate issue of the *kippot serugot*. How could the IDF minimize the number of national–religious troops who might disobey orders to participate in the operation? Ultimately, two courses of action were adopted. On the one hand, senior commanders unambiguously warned that conscientious objectors would be heavily punished (Stern 2009). At the same time, however, some concessions were made to national–religious sensibilities. Thus, the Golani [infantry] Brigade, in which the concentration of *kippot serugot* was known to be particularly high, was kept outside the 'first circle' of troops assigned to eviction duties. Likewise, soldiers whose immediate families lived in settlements due to be dismantled were told that they could, if they so wished, ask to be excused from duties. Perhaps most subtly of all, all troops and policemen were instructed to wear caps throughout the operation (ostensibly to provide protection from the sun, but also in order to deny settlers the opportunity of easily identifying, and attempting to influence, the *kippot serugot* amongst the personnel concerned).

Noticeable by its absence from this matrix of activity was the IDF Chief Rabbinate, the military institution officially responsible for the maintenance of religious life in the IDF and, by extension, for ensuring the well-being of the orthodox soldier. Specifically, the Rabbinate neither sought, nor was it assigned, anything other than a marginal role in the containment of tendencies towards conscientious objection amongst national–religious troops. In part, that circumstance merely reflects the lowly status of the IDF rabbinate, which the *kippot serugot*, especially, have long ceased to regard as a source of authority (Gutel 1992). But it also owed

---

6   For subsequent written accounts see, for example, Shushan and Peltz 2007, Amitai and Minka-Brand 2010.

much to the personal dilemma faced by Brigadier General Yisrael Weiss, the IDF senior chaplain. Himself one of Rabbi Shapira's former students, Rabbi Weiss simply could not bring himself to issue anything other than a lukewarm statement of opposition to conscientious objection, which carried as little conviction as did his subsequent apologia (Meir and Rahav-Meir 2005: 39–60). During the disengagement operation itself, Rabbi Weiss and his staff kept a deliberately low profile – and well away from the main areas of military activity.[7]

More important than the causes of the military rabbinate's irrelevance are its consequences. With the senior IDF chaplain patently incapable of providing national–religious soldiers with coherent guidance, that task devolved on civilian religious authorities, whose institutional commitment to the IDF was less blatant. This situation further augmented the influence likely to be exerted on the behavior of the *kippot serugot* by the views expressed in the wider circle of the national–religious rabbinate.

The Intra-rabbinic Debate

Whereas the IDF (with the marginal exception of its rabbinate) thus presented an unambiguous position with respect to conscientious objection, attitudes within the national–religious community were far less monolithic. This was not unexpected. 'Religious Zionism', it bears repeating, is very much an umbrella term, which encompasses an assortment of lifestyles and forms of worship. Beneath the surface of shared values, there have long lurked deep divisions of attitudes and priorities amongst both the *kippot serugot* and their spiritual mentors – not just with respect to the importance of preserving the integrity of 'the Greater Land of Israel' (Don-Yehiya 1994) but also, and more fundamentally, regarding the continued contribution of the state of Israel, in its present form, to the fulfillment of Jewry's messianic vision (Inbari 2012: 108).

Given that background, there was nothing surprising in the fact that the intra-rabbinic debate on the conduct expected of national–religious troops assigned to disengagement duties was particularly intense. Within days of Rabbi Shapira's call to troops to disobey orders (above p. 111), 57 rabbis – including two principals of *hesder yeshivot* – signed a manifesto supporting his exhortation. But barely was the ink on that document dry before a further 80 rabbis – again, the roster included heads of (other) *hesder* academies and some *mekhinot* – published a counter-manifesto, adopting precisely the opposite position. There followed a round of intense exchanges between the two camps, which although invariably couched in the lingua franca of traditional intra-rabbinic disputation, occasionally violated the norms of scholastic cordiality (Bick 2007, Inbari 2012: 107–32).

---

7   Weiss, who was somewhat summarily retired from his post in 2006, subsequently published an autobiographical memoir of the dilemmas that he had confronted. Weiss 2010.

A tangled web of individual allegiances compounded the complexity of the situation thus created. The principals of some institutions owed ties of personal loyalty to Rabbi Shapira, with roots in a distant teacher–disciple relationship. Others were for similar reasons inclined to defer to the opinions of Rabbi Tzvi Tau, the charismatic head of the prestigious 'Har Ha-Mor' *yeshivah* in Jerusalem who for long declined to come out openly on conscientious objection one way or the other.[8] In yet a third category, the issue split single institutions right down the middle. Thus, in 'Birkat Mosheh', the large *hesder yeshivah* situated in the West Bank town of Ma'aleh Adumim, conscientious objection was advocated by the principal (Rabbi Nachum Rabinovitch), but vigorously opposed by one of the senior members of his faculty, Rabbi Chaim Sabato.

Much of the intra-rabbinic debate on the *tactics* to be adopted vis-à-vis disengagement was conducted behind closed doors.[9] Where the *principle* of conscientious objection was concerned, however, discussion was public and exerted an impact that extended beyond the confines of the academies. Indeed, echoes of the debate resounded in both the websites and newspapers that specifically cater to a national–religious audience, and especially in the popular pamphlets that various groups distribute in large numbers each Sabbath eve to synagogues up and down the country. Thus it was that 'The Expulsion' (*ha-gerush*) as disengagement was commonly termed by its opponents, became an even more divisive issue amongst this sector of the population than it was elsewhere in the country.

As both sides to the national–religious debate on disengagement appreciated, the arguments that they each adduced in the spring and summer of 2005 were not novel. In intellectual terms, the lines of battle had essentially been drawn as early as the dismantlement of Yamit in 1982, and had been reiterated with considerable passion in 1993, in the wake of the news that Israelis and Palestinian representatives had reached agreement at Oslo (Naor 2001). On both occasions, those who advocated refusal to obey orders based their arguments on the belief that the Jewish people possesses an exclusive, God-given and irrevocable right to possession of the entire Land of Israel, over which it is forbidden to relinquish sovereignty – no matter what the cost in blood and treasure. Those teachings were frequently buttressed, moreover, by the time-honored rabbinic contention that the relationship between human and Divine authorities is anyway akin to that of a slave to his master. Hence, when government orders conflict with God's commandments, only the latter are to be obeyed. Harnessed together, these two positions led to one conclusion. The IDF's true mission is to act as the instrument of God's will and to

---

8   Rabbi Tau's position was thought to be especially important, since he was a former teacher of rabbis Eli Sedan and Rafi Peretz, the principals of two of the largest of the *mekhinot*, at Eli and Atzmonah respectively. See also Inbari 2012: 67–70.

9   For a rare account of one such discussion (attended by all the *mekhinot* heads) see the recollections in an address delivered to his students by R. Eli Sedan, Sedan 2005. On day-to-day contacts between rabbis and the settlers prior to disengagement, during its course and in the immediate aftermath, see C. Ariel 2006.

facilitate the realization of His plan. Once its actions contradict that role, however, military orders necessarily become devoid of all authority. Indeed, they have to be disobeyed.

Ever since the mid-1980s, at the latest, opponents of conscientious objection had likewise appealed to the bar of hallowed texts and their traditional interpretations. The keystones of their theses, however, were entirely different. Even though many declared themselves personally opposed to Mr. Sharon's program (which, besides all else, several considered to be an act of political betrayal on his part), they regarded the theological rights and wrongs of disengagement per se to be a subsidiary issue. In advocating a review of the arguments advanced by proponents of national–religious conscientious objection, opponents of that course cited two alternative considerations, the importance of which they believed to surpass even the preservation of Jewish control over the Holy Land.

One is the altogether overriding value that rabbinic Jewish traditions have always placed on the preservation of human life (*pikuch nefesh*). The authors of the call to military disobedience adduced this principle as one reason for objecting to any territorial compromise, on the grounds that concessions on Israel's part would merely encourage her enemies to seek further gains, if necessary by force, and hence ultimately cause further bloodshed (Naor 1999). Opponents of that opinion, by contrast, argued that matters were far more complex – so much so that they doubted whether rabbis are empowered to make any unilateral judgment one way or the other. Rather, in this case they have to allow the country's political and military authorities to come to their own conclusions with respect to the relative costs and gains of a withdrawal from the territories. Indeed, rabbis must relate to politicians and generals in the same way that they have for centuries related to, for instance, medical authorities: as lay experts to whose professional advice rabbis conventionally defer when the observation of a specific commandment (such as abstinence from food on a mandatory fast day) raises issues of life and death. Since no one could guarantee that disengagement would not, as promised by its advocates, save some lives, no one possessed the *halakhic* right to prevent the implementation of that program.[10]

A second consideration adduced by rabbinic opponents of Rabbi Shapira's call to national–religious troops to refuse orders to participate in disengagement operations carried more community-centered overtones. Drawing on a distinguished tradition of teachings that preached the importance of preserving Jewish unity, opponents of conscientious objection invested the concept of mutual responsibility with a meta-eschatological meaning. From that perspective, they argued, adherence to Rabbi Shapira's pronouncement could only play havoc with the hallowed notion of national Jewish solidarity. Precisely because of the numerical prominence

---

10   Rabbi Ovadya Yosef, the *Sephardi* Chief Rabbi of Israel, had authoritatively presented this argument long before military disobedience became an issue; see above pp. 54–5. In 2005, too, Rabbi Aaron Lichtenstein, the highly respected principal of the Har Etzion *yeshivah*, dwelt at some length on this consideration, which he listed as the second of his main arguments in the densely argued plea that he published in the daily press. Lichtenstein 2005a.

of national–religious troops in the IDF, their conscientious objection would necessarily impair the cohesion of Israel's military and thus irrevocably damage this, the most obtrusive symbol of the miraculous renewal of renewed Jewish sovereignty. In the last analysis, therefore, what was most disturbing about Rabbi Shapira's pronouncement was the apparent irresponsibility with which it related to the possible consequences of its very implementation for the survival of the State of Israel. In the words of one rabbinic summary of this argument: 'Bad though disengagement is from a national–religious perspective, to refuse orders would be even worse' (Aviner 2004; see also Lichtenstein 2005b; Cherlow 2010: 108. Counter-arguments in Melamed 2004, Hankin 2005).[11]

The Contexts of the Debate

No single circumstance can adequately explain why, in the event, the overwhelming majority of *kippot serugot*, of all ranks, found the arguments in favor of participation in the disengagement operation to be more persuasive than Rabbi Shapira's warning that Heaven would never forgive them for doing so. In part, of course, that result may simply have reflected 'institutional conformity' – the inherent tendency of all soldiers in uniform to obey military commands, especially when the vast majority of the comrades-in-arms with whom they serve are prepared to do so. But in this case allowances must also be made for other possible causes. One might be sheer intellectual conviction; the troops may have found the theses adduced against conscientious objection to be, on their merits, more persuasive than those in its favor. Another could be the sociology of the debate. Although the two rival rabbinical camps were numerically almost equal, in terms of the personalities involved they were far less evenly matched. Certainly, Rabbi Shapira's name carried considerable authority in the national–religious community. So, too, did those of rabbis Elyakim Levanon, principal of the *yeshivat hesder* located in the settlement of Alon Moreh, and of Eliezer Melamed, principal of the *yeshivat hesder* located in the settlement of Bet-El, who were two of the most articulate and persistent advocates of conscientious objection. The vast majority of figures in this

---

11   Levy 2007b has argued that, 'the effective functioning of the Israel Defense Forces can be attributed to the degree to which it has become embedded primarily within the social networks of the national religious groups that serve within it. The army implemented the evacuation by leveraging the interest of those groups to reinforce the army's status as an apolitical and universal 'people's army' by which the groups could preserve their mobility within its ranks. Thus, what prevented the groups from initiating massive clashes with the evacuating troops was their assessment that a confrontation could have undermined the army's status and, by extension, that of the resisting groups – both within the IDF and in civilian society'. That seems to me to overestimate the Machiavellianism of the troops concerned and to underestimate the very real concern that their rabbis expressed, not for the status of their own group, but for the unity of the country as a whole. It also minimizes the role played by IDF officers in defusing potential tensions (on which see Minka-Brand 2005).

camp, however, tended to be somewhat obscure; they were known only to the small coterie of their immediate circles. Principally, this is because the *yeshivot* of which they were principals were invariably small – and in any case often not usually of the sort that encouraged their students to perform military service.

Many rabbinical opponents of conscientious objection were of an entirely different type. Several were principals of some of the largest *yeshivot hesder* and *mekhinot*, and hence enjoyed close relationships with substantial bodies of pupil–soldiers. Some had also established an independent following amongst even larger numbers of conscripts, of both sexes, by virtue of their extensive writings on issues of concern to national–religious youngsters. This was certainly so in the cases of rabbis Shlomo Aviner and Yuval Cherlow, respectively heads of *yeshivot hesder* in Jerusalem and Petach-Tikvah, who had been two of the most adamant opponents of conscientious objection from the very start. Both men had for long contributed regularly, and prolifically, to popular works of homiletics and *halakhic* literature (Aviner 1999a, 1999b, 2000; Cherlow 2002, 2003, 2005). Theirs were therefore virtually household names in the national–religious circles most likely to be interested in rabbinic opinion on whether or not to refuse military orders.

But to these considerations must be added, finally and, arguably, most decisively, the religious context of the debate. That context, I suggest, cannot be properly understood if, as is usually the case, analysis focuses exclusively on what was said and written by the spiritual and lay leaders of religious Zionism (a tendency that also characterizes the most recent, and fullest, account: Inbari 2012: 107–32). After all, from a practical point of view, all the rabbinic huffing and puffing mattered far less than did was what going through the minds of the rank and file of soldiers wearing *kippot serugot*. As the following paragraphs will show, once attention shifts to the internal discourse of those youngsters and their peers, the importance attached to disengagement assumes considerably less decisive importance. In fact, as a potential cause for disobedience to military orders it was, throughout the period preceding August 2005, overshadowed by other issues.

Herein, it is proposed, lays a supplementary, and far subtler, explanation for the operation's smooth implementation. National–religious soldiers did not obey orders solely because they had been conditioned to do so (by the IDF) and/or convinced to do so (by many of their own rabbis). Their behavior also owed much to the fact that, for the vast majority, disengagement touched only peripherally on the topics that they considered to be most salient as far as relations between themselves and the military were concerned.

Evidence for that contention initially surfaced in random interviews that I conducted with national–religious conscripts and junior officers in the months before and after the implementation of disengagement. The impressions thus formed, however, were substantiated by sources that provide additional authentic glimpses into the state of mind of young adults in the national–religious community. One body of evidence consists of the behavior of national–religious youngsters serving in the IDF. Throughout 2005, several critics of disengagement warned that its implementation would generate disillusionment with the Force, a sentiment that would be reflected in a drop in the willingness of religious Zionist youth to volunteer for combat duty and service as junior officers. In the event, nothing of the sort occurred. After disengagement, as before, the increase of *kippot serugot* continued to be a dominant fact of the IDF's sociology.[12] Moreover, subsequent to the disengagement, only a handful of national–religious troops voiced opposition to the prospect that they might be dispatched to carry out similar operations, most blatantly in December 2009 when a group of newly recruited soldiers publicly demonstrated against the dismantlement of the unauthorized West Bank outpost of Chomesh. The one rabbi who openly supported the soldiers (Rabbi Melamed of Beit El) was urged by other principals of *yeshivot hesder* to modify his stance. When he refused to compromise, his colleagues withdrew their opposition to the Minister of Defence's decision to remove his academy from the list of accredited *yeshivot hesder*, a move that deprived him of the right to receive Treasury funding. In response, Melamed announced that his academy would henceforth expect its pupils to apply for extended deferments of their military service (Inbari 128–30). But any hopes that he might have harboured of thereby renewing the debate with the national–religious community over the conduct expected of soldiers were disappointed. Rabbinical comment was minimal, and the reactions amongst prospective students subdued. Those who did wish to enlist in the IDF at an earlier age simply enrolled elsewhere.

Still more informative as indicators of sentiment amongst national–religious youth are the collections of epistolary exchanges that take place between rabbis and those individuals who turn to them for advice and/or instruction on a matter of relevance to their conduct as religiously observant Jews. Known in the traditional Jewish literature as *shutim* (an acronym for *she'elot u-teshuvot*, literally 'questions and answers', otherwise translated as 'responsa'), this form of communication draws on a tradition that stretches back for over a millennium and a half, and whose value as a source for an understanding of Jewish life has long been apparent to social historians (Katz 1998). The working hypothesis of the present chapter is that contemporary responsa serve a similar purpose with respect to orthodox youngsters serving in the IDF. Indeed, thanks to the adaptations of the genre to the circumstances relevant to that segment of the population, responsa provide an especially informative window into the thoughts and feelings of its members.

Two such adaptations are especially relevant in the present context. The first is the appearance of responsa specifically devoted to matters of relevance to military life. This is a sphere of human activity with which Jews had virtually no contact whatsoever throughout their Diaspora history, and which is consequently rarely even mentioned in the vast corpus of letters between rabbis and their correspondents that records every other conceivable topic of Jewish concern between medieval and modern times. Clearly, however, universal conscription, together with the prevalence of Israel's resort to military force as an instrument of policy, has wrought a change

---

12   An internal IDF audit published in 2010 showed that the proportion of graduates of national–religious high schools in combat infantry courses had risen since 2005, reaching a peak of 31.4 percent in 2007 ('B' 2010: 53).

of revolutionary proportions. Ever since 1948, responsa – indeed, entire volumes of responsa – specifically dedicated to military issues have become an increasingly prominent item on the orthodox Jewish bookshelf (see above pp. 89–97). Their authorship has added to their appeal. Most contemporary responsa on military matters are written by rabbis who have personally served in the IDF, often in field formations and sometimes at fairly senior ranks. Not incidentally, many also function as principals or senior faculty members in one or another of the *yeshivot hesder* and *mekhinot*, in which capacity they come into virtual daily contact with the successive cohorts of *kippot serugot* to whom they act as spiritual guides.

A second relevant feature of the contemporary responsa literature is its new format. Although (as noted above) many of today's exchanges between rabbis and their correspondents on military matters, as on others, are published in the traditional format of books, an increasing number are being posted on one of the several websites that specifically offer 'ask the rabbi' types of portals.[13] In addition, most of the *yeshivot hesder* publish (and sometimes post on the web too) weekly or bi-monthly newsletters, several of which also contain records of the issues with which student–soldiers on active service have recently corresponded with their teachers. The importance of these developments lies in their influence on the style and availability of the queries and responses. Electronic modes of communication lend themselves to a much more abbreviated and accessible style of writing than was considered de rigueur in the traditional responsa, which were customarily encrypted in highly technical and prolix rabbinic prose. In addition, e-mails allow for anonymity, speedy response, and almost instantaneous distribution to a virtually infinite audience.

Admittedly, the usefulness of this source as a research tool is restricted by several methodological difficulties. To what extent do the participants in the published epistolary exchanges constitute a representative sample of national–religious opinion? How can observers weigh the differences in editorial approach and style of the various available websites? Is it possible to ascertain the degree to which the website managers and/or the rabbis who are their respondents might have censored the questions posted, or otherwise influenced the timing and frequency of their appearance? But even when due note is taken of these question marks, the responsa literature – especially when collated with allied sources – does seem to place in proportion the types of issues that seem to be of most pressing concern to the contemporary generation of *kippot serugot*. In so doing, it also provides a means of gauging the extent of the inner turmoil generated amongst them by the disengagement program and its implementation in the summer of 2005.

The evidence demonstrates that Rabbi Shapira's call for orthodox troops to pronounce themselves conscientious objectors over disengagement clearly struck

---

13   The four main sites, all in Hebrew, are: <http://www.moreshet.co.il>; <http://www.kipa.co.il>; <http://www.moriya.org.il>; <http://www.yeshiva.org.il>. Each maintains a portal dedicated to responsa, which are catalogued by their subject matter. In addition to 'army and security', these categories include such topics as: ritual issues; blessings; Sabbath observance; personal matters; economics; medical ethics, etcetera.

several sensitive cords. This is apparent from the sharp rise in the number of appeals for rabbinic guidance with respect to conscientious objection that were thereafter posted on the internet, principally by young men and women who identified themselves as soldiers on active duty – and in one particularly interesting case from the wife of a battalion commander.[14] Nevertheless, even in this period disengagement was not the sole – and certainly not the principal – topic of concern to the *kippot serugot*. Most of their enquiries continued to focus on the conventional span of ritual and personal issues. More significantly still, even within the specific category of responsa dedicated to matters relating to the IDF, disengagement and its consequences did not constitute the most obtrusive topic of interest to the *kippot serugot*. Statistical analysis shows that they were far more troubled by a wide range of other issues: the relative merits of military service vis-à-vis torah study; Sabbath observance whilst on duty; interpersonal relations with secular troops; and gender relations in military units (S. Cohen 2008).

This list is instructive, principally because it reveals a basic continuity in the principal topics of concern to national–religious troops. Of all the items in the roster, only gender relations (to be discussed below) constitute a novel topic of *halakhic* enquiry. All the others have for several decades been staple items on the agenda of military-centered responsa. This finding dovetails with the conclusions of previous research, which had indicated that at the root of the dilemmas confronting national–religious troops in the IDF lies an existential tension between 'the scroll' (that is, religious obligations) and 'the sword' (military service), which runs far deeper than the surface friction generated by debates over the integrity of the greater Land of Israel. How to maintain Sabbath observance in a military environment, for instance, had been a primary bone of contention long before the issue of 'the territories' arose. Moreover, and as the voluminous literature devoted to adapting the do's and don'ts of the orthodox Sabbath code to service life amply demonstrates, the subject has remained at the very top of the national–religious serviceman's agenda ever since.[15]

Only marginally less persistent, likewise, are the dilemmas confronting national–religious youngsters (girls as well as boys) who, on the eve of their enlistment, have to chose between a full term of conscript service or registration

---

14	The enquiry also indicates that a high proportion of the husband's troops wore *kippot serugot*, and that the brigade was to be assigned to the disengagement operation. 'My husband is very much concerned, especially in view of the confusion on this that is so rife in the religious Zionist sector. What he finds most difficult is [the prospect of] confrontation with those of his troops who will refuse orders. How should he act? What about the rabbinic decisions in this matter? Is Rabbi Shapira's pronouncement definitive? Please help the confused' <http://www.moreshet.co.il/shut/shut2.asp?id=47658>; posted 26 October 2004, accessed 19 September 2012.

15	Sabbath observance, in its various forms, constitutes by far the largest single item covered in such comprehensive guides of religious law for the soldier as Kaufman 1994 and Binyamin and Cohen 2000. On the specific issue of the duty to disobey military orders involving a desecration of the sabbath, Schochetman 2004.

in one of the programs whose timetable combines military duty with torah study. And especially frustrating is the feeling that, even after decades of experiment, neither of these choices deserves to be judged entirely successful. The young religious recruit will still be bound to experience the shock generated by sudden close contact with conscripts from an entirely different – secular – background. The evidence provided by the responsa indicate that it is still true to say that:

> Quite apart from experiencing the alarm to which every conscript is submitted on entering the military framework, the religious soldier is estranged and struck dumb by the comportment of his secular comrades. Even their everyday speech contains phrases and terms which his own mouth, accustomed to prayer, is unable to utter and which his ears, attuned to words of wisdom, refuse to absorb (Levi and Furstein 1995).

By comparison, how to react to disengagement seems to constitute a relatively minor problem

That impression of priorities is confirmed when attention is turned to those responsa that concern gender relations in the military. This is a relatively new topic of enquiry, which shot to prominence in the late 1990s, when the IDF began integrating female soldiers into combat units. Because the new assignments place men and women in unavoidably close proximity (for instance within the confines of a single tank or APC) they necessarily offend the sensibilities of religious soldiers, who have been educated to observe traditional Judaism's stringent laws of 'modesty' (*tzeniyut*), which restrict gender relationships, especially prior to marriage. After some hard bargaining, the principals of the *hesder yeshivot* and *mekhinot* managed to come to an 'arrangement' with the IDF High Command, according to which troops in those frameworks were to have the option of serving in gender-segregated units (Sasson-Levi 2010: 180). As the responsa indicate, however, several areas of contention remained:

> I am currently in a military course for medics. The 'modesty' problems in this course are terrible – all the instructors are girls, as are many of the other participants .... The instructors demonstrate many of the exercises on themselves, and in the process uncover their bodies. When they ask the participants to do likewise, the result is an endless torrent of rude remarks .... In rest periods, too, it is hard to avoid licentiousness. The girls walk around immodestly everywhere, so that even the way to the synagogue is replete with forbidden sights. We are just a few religious troops here – and although we have tried to speak to everyone we can – instructors, officers etc. – nothing seems to help.[16]

---

16   <http://www.moreshet.co.il/shut/shut2.asp?id=49689>; posted 26.12.2004, accessed 19 September 2012.

No less significant than the frequency of such appeals for assistance and guidance is the tone and substance of the rabbinical responses that they generated. By any gauge these are distinctive. On other issues, including as we have seen on disengagement, the responses reveal various hues of opinion. With respect to gender issues, by contrast, they are uniformly emphatic. Jewish law (*halakhah*) can no more sanction concessions to the traditional regulations governing inter-gender modesty than it can tolerate unnecessary, and unauthorized, infringements of sabbath observance. As much is made plain in the published response evoked by the plea for assistance quoted above. The authority concerned (Rabbi Ratzon Arusi), although generally opposed to conscientious objection, not least with respect to disengagement, was in this case adamant that an exception had to be made:

> If matters are indeed as you describe, it is forbidden for you to be in that course … Should all the authorities refuse to deal with the matter then you will have to disobey orders, and go to prison.

The unambiguous and consistent nature of such statements seems to have sent the troops concerned a clear message, which served to delineate the borders of their right to refuse to obey military orders. From the *halakhic* point of view, only with respect to sabbath observance and gender issues was the legitimacy of conscientious objection absolutely firm. Where other issues of contention were concerned, all such claims rested on somewhat shakier ground.

Implications

At one level, the conclusions of this chapter seem self-evident. The absence of any large-scale incidence of conscientious objection on the part of national–religious troops during the summer of 2005 puts to rest many of the fears once generated by their prominence in IDF combat units. Ultimately, this segment of the force complement did not prioritize the preservation of 'the Greater Land of Israel'. The same is true of all but a minority of the persons whose advice the *kippot serugot* most often seek – the rabbis who teach in *yeshivot hesder* and *mekhinot*, and who (also) reply to questions posed on the internet. When pragmatic push came to doctrinal shove, they too largely decried conscientious objection.

Nevertheless, the evidence presented in this chapter also cautions against placing too sanguine an interpretation on what transpired in the summer of 2005. Closer scrutiny suggests that those who warned of the possibly fissiparous implications of the prominence of *kippot serugot* in IDF combat units were not altogether erroneous; their mistake was to look for the wrong symptoms. A less simplistic analysis of the available data indicates that a significant proportion of the national–religious complement does indeed consider its military service in the IDF to be contingent. But the roots of that attitude have far less to do with an ideological commitment to the settlement enterprise per se than is often supposed.

Far more substantive, rather, is their determination (a determination that is deliberately and unanimously fuelled by their rabbinic mentors) to preserve and enhance those elements of their lifestyles to which they attach intrinsic religious importance.

From that perspective, settlements possess essentially talismanic importance. They certainly signify a religious value, but by no means constitute the sum total of the *kippah serugah*'s interests. Like many of their rabbis, religiously observant soldiers, female as well as male, are by and large more troubled by other concerns: how can they best reconcile the need to perform military service with the religious duty to devote their time to the study the sacred texts? How can they avoid unnecessarily desecrating the sabbath? how can they harmonize military life with the observance of traditional laws of 'modesty'? And – perhaps most encompassing of all – how can they best preserve their distinctive identities in a military environment? These are issues on which no compromise is at all possible.

Of the several implications of these findings, two appear to be especially noteworthy. First, and at their most restricted level, they serve to underscore the strength of the impulse to segregation that characterizes the service patterns of many *kippot serugot*. Far from being universally committed to exerting an influence on the entire IDF, significant numbers are principally concerned to minimize as far as possible the impact of military norms on their own introspective world. That is why increasing numbers of the national–religious conscript segment now elect to perform their military service in the more sequestered structure of the *nachal haredi* (Drori 2005b); that is why they reacted so strongly in 2005–2006 to hints that the IDF might shut down segregated *hesder* companies; and that is why they may yet be receptive to post-2005 calls for them to 'disengage' from other keystones of secular society too (Aviner 2006).

The second set of implications of this chapter carries broader relevance, and casts light on relations between the IDF and its service complement as a whole. Recent research has altogether begun to question the validity of the conventional assumption that militaries justify their reputations as useful agents of social engineering. If anything, quite the opposite has often been the case (see below, pp. 127–142). Not least is this so with respect to the IDF. As numerous studies have pointed out, the multiple communities of which Israeli society is composed do not evince any single (let alone hegemonic) attitude towards military service. Different segments exhibit varying levels of propensity to enlistment in the IDF; they also harbor different expectations of the benefits and costs that, as citizen–soldiers they are likely to receive as a result of the military experience (Levy 2003, Kemp 2004). Edna Lomsky-Feder and Eyal Ben-Ari claim that the IDF has increasingly found it necessary to take account of that situation. Consequently, although still officially committed to the notion of a unified 'people's army', it has been compelled to 'manage' the diversity of its intake. It does so, they claim, by 'handling each group according to policies and on the basis of practices that are unique to it' (Lomsky-Feder and Ben-Ari 1999).

A study of the events of the summer of 2005, whilst ostensibly indicating the successes of that strategy, also points to its potential limitations. As we have seen, the IDF cannot claim exclusive credit for moderating inclinations amongst the *kippot serugot* to opt for conscientious objection where disengagement was concerned. Equally significant, if not more so, was the influence exerted by rabbinical opponents of military disobedience in this case. Hence, there exists no guarantee that the military formula adopted vis-à-vis this segment of its complement in 2005 will likewise work in the future. On the contrary, the evidence contained in the responsa, especially, indicates that the IDF, in its corporate capacity, has still to come to grips with the roots of the concerns that most of the *kippot serugot* find more troubling: their fears that the military environment impinges upon the values that give most salient expression to their group identity.

Should other segments of the population harbor anything like the same sentiments (Lomsky-Feder and Ben-Ari speak specifically of immigrants, women and non-Jewish minorities) the IDF will be compelled to reconsider some of the fundamental premises upon which its personnel policies have hitherto been built. Instead of functioning as a pro-active 'melting pot', it will be reduced to the far more passive status of an arena within which adherents to different Israeli identities seek to give expression to their individuality. Whether the IDF can fulfill that role without impairing its own corporate character as a unified fighting force deserves to be considered one of the most compelling of the issues on the agenda of societal–military relations in Israel in the years to come.

Chapter 8

Religion as a Nation-binder and Nation-divider: Interpersonal Relationships in the Israel Defense Forces[1]

Observers of Israel's politics and society have long commented on the comparatively high profile accorded to both religion and the military in the country's public and private life (Kimmerling 1991, Shafir and Peled 2002). Hitherto, however, they have adopted a segmented mode of analysis when examining the impact exerted by these two components of Israeli national identity. Religious attachment and military service are treated as distinct entities, each of which is assumed to move on an independent trajectory when influencing interpersonal relationships among citizens from different backgrounds. By contrast, this chapter proposes an integrative mode of analysis. Specifically, it examines the various ways in which religion and military service interact in Israel, especially when conscript soldiers who are committed to the maintenance of a traditionally Orthodox Jewish lifestyle serve alongside draftees who are not thus inclined. It asks whether that circumstance tends to ameliorate or to accentuate the differences between these two sectors. Although the answers to that question are necessarily *sui generis*, in the sense that they apply solely to the instance of Israel, this chapter maintains that their overall relevance might also be considerably broader and teach us much about the impact of an admixture of religion and military service in other societies too.

Ever since their establishment in 1948, the Israel Defense Forces (IDF) have conventionally been designated a 'people's army'. Of the several justifications for that depiction, undoubtedly the most obvious is the composition of the Forces. In Israel, salaried professional troops are vastly outnumbered by conscripts – men and women who are drafted for two to three years of service when aged 18 and are liable for mandatory terms of annual reserve duty for some 20 years thereafter. Manpower requirements undoubtedly provided the principal impetus behind Israel's original decision to institute conscription (Greenberg 2001). From the first, however, societal *desiderata* also loomed large – especially in the thinking of David Ben-Gurion, Israel's first prime minister and defense minister (he held both positions for much of the period between 1948 and 1963), the man who did more than any other to create the IDF and determine their structure. Indeed, as early as

---

1 The original version of this chapter appeared in: Jonathan Fox (ed.), *Religion, Politics, Society and the State* (Paradigm, Boulder, 2012), pp. 89–103. By permission of Oxford University Press, USA (www.oup.com).

1949 he determined that in the new state of Israel the military was to be given an overt role as a national melting pot (Ben-Gurion 1971: 81).

For many years, assessments of Ben-Gurion's efforts in that regard tended to be extremely favorable, particularly with respect to relationships between Israeli citizens with different degrees of commitment to the observance of traditional Judaism. In that area of social interaction, the IDF's achievement was thought to outstrip even its contribution to moderating differences rooted in class affiliation, ethnic origin, and gender. Writing in the late 1960s, one American observer went as far as to claim that, through the homogenizing mechanism of conscription, the IDF had over the previous two decades

> helped to break all barriers between men who lived their lives in vastly different cultural milieus. Boys from religious families could mix freely with antireligious boys from secularist left-wing kibbutzim, learning to give and take, to disagree while respecting the other's right to his own view, to refrain from excesses of behavior and find a deeper unity of purpose (Rolbant 1970, 154).

The purpose of this chapter is to examine whether that assessment remains valid. In part, the exercise is mandated by the appearance within the literature on military sociology of several new constructs to describe how recruitment policies impact, both positively and negatively, the overall fabric of society. But a fresh look at the subject is also mandated by the availability of new empirical data arising from developments in Israel in recent years, of specific relevance to the interface between military service and religious–secular relations. The structure of the chapter seeks to accommodate both considerations. It begins by identifying three alternative constructs of the societal consequences of conscription. Thereafter, it demonstrates how trends within Israeli society have generated shifts along the axes of those constructs over time.

Alternative Constructs

Ben-Gurion's vision of military service as a cauldron of new Israeli nationality was not, of course, original. As early as the mid-nineteenth century, the notion that conscription promotes national integration had become conventional in much of western and central Europe, whence it soon spread to polities as diverse as Meiji Japan, Czarist Russia, Brazil and – intermittently – the United States. Moreover, Israel's adoption of this credo paralleled the policies pursued in many of the post-colonial states established in Asia and Africa after World War II. There too, politicians, faced with the need to create cohesive national communities out of a jumble of loyalties and affiliations, turned almost instinctively to conscription. Like Ben-Gurion, they thus subscribed, albeit in broad terms and *avant la lettre*, to what the American psychologist Gordon Allport (1954) termed 'the contact hypothesis' (Allport 1954). Broadly speaking, they believed that conscription would not only foster 'acquaintance potential' among otherwise hostile groups, but that since military service typically requires men (and in Israel, women too) to perform common tasks in a highly structured environment that enforces their co-operation, while also sometimes placing them in situations of extreme vulnerability where their very survival depends on mutual trust, it would diminish inter-communal prejudice.

Although the view of armed forces as great 'nation-binders' retains much of its hold over both the official and popular imaginations, with time it has been subjected to various critiques (Krebs 2004). Broadly speaking, two alternative constructs of conscription's societal consequences have been formulated. One considers military service to do no more than mirror existing national divides. Evidence culled from several countries, it argues, shows that minorities – even when drafted – are never fully integrated into the military or given an equal opportunity to influence its culture. Rather, once enlisted they are expected to conform to norms that the majority has laid down as appropriate for the nation's soldiers. Because military values thus reflect those of the prevailing civilian hierarchy, enlistment in fact merely transfers divides and differentials from the civilian to the military setting, where they are replicated and reinforced.[2]

The second alternative construct is more radical, and goes as far as to depict military service as a 'nation-divider'. Most clearly associated with the work of Cynthia Enloe, this view argues that the experience of common service is more likely to exacerbate pre-existing societal discrepancies than (as the 'contact' enthusiasts maintain) to moderate them. Typically, it does so by restricting officer training, especially in prestigious combat units, to sectors of society (such as men) who in civilian life too are considered superior to others (Enloe 1980). In more extreme cases, this chapter shall argue, military service can even create societal schisms where none previously existed, most obviously by establishing different categories of citizenship based upon the performance/non-performance of military duty.

Application

An interesting facet of the relationships between religiously observant and non-observant troops in the IDF is the way in which, to varying degrees, they reflect all three of the constructs outlined in the preceding text.

Nation-binder

Undoubtedly the most compelling evidence in support of the contention that military service has indeed helped to moderate differences between religious and non-religious communities in Israel is provided by the recent growth in the number of troops from what is popularly known as a 'national–religious' Jewish

---

2   See, for example, Dietz et al. (1991), citing evidence from Ethiopia, Nigeria, China, Greece, Turkey and Israel.

background now drafted into IDF combat units. True, service in the Forces has always been fundamental to the ideology of this sector of Israeli society, which is currently estimated to constitute roughly 15 percent of the total Israeli Jewish population. Nevertheless, leaders of this community were from the first fearful that enlistment might dilute the religious attachment of new recruits, whom they therefore initially wished to have drafted in separate units of their own. When this suggestion was quashed on the grounds that it would prove a recipe for disunity ('the establishment of 'religious' units will merely lead to the establishment of 'antireligious' units'),[3] national–religious rabbinic mentors resorted to tactics that were less drastic, but more effective. Young religious males were discouraged from serving in combat units, where the risk of secular 'contamination' was deemed to be greatest, and steered in the direction of rear echelon support occupations, where they were more likely to remain under parental influence. Female graduates of the Orthodox Jewish school system were directed to apply for the exemptions from service that the Military Service Law permits to women who claim that the performance of military duty would conflict with their religious lifestyles.

Largely as a consequence of such directives, throughout the initial decades that followed the 1948 War of Independence, the profile of the IDF, certainly as far as the most prestigious combat formations were concerned, remained overwhelmingly secular. National–religious youths, although drafted in large numbers, made little impact on the overall character of the military organization. Hence, in his authoritative *Portrait of the Israeli Soldier*, published in 1986, Colonel (res.) Reuven Gal, a former chief IDF psychologist, did not think it necessary even to refer to them as a distinctive element in the Forces.

Today that approach would be impossible to sustain. As Chapter 1 pointed out (above pp. 11–12), the sight of a knitted skullcap (*kippah serugah*; the most obtrusive sign of male national–religious affiliation) in frontline combat formations, once comparatively rare, is now commonplace. If anything, ever since the late 1990s, graduates of the national–religious school system are thought to be over-represented – often by a ratio of three to one – in the ranks of infantry companies and their junior- and middle rank officers. In support units their profile is likewise high in several of the elite formations previously considered almost exclusively secular enclaves, such as the Computer Branch; the Intelligence Branch; and *Galei Tzahal*, the IDF radio station. Furthermore, where the men have led, women now follow. In the past, almost all female graduates of the national–religious school system elected to perform a year or two of civic service rather than of military duty. Of late, preferences have shifted. Whereas in 2010 barely one third of all graduates of national–religious high schools for girls had registered for the draft, the proportion was expected to rise to almost a half – equivalent to over 2,800 individuals – in 2013 (Agmon 2013).

---

3   Ben-Gurion's reply to a deputation of national–religious leaders, September 23, 1949, cited in Mo. Friedman 2005: 109–12.

No single cause can account for this development. Efforts to portray it as an indication of shifts in the societal prestige ('social convertibility' in the jargon of sociologists) attached to military service by different classes in Israel (for example, especially, Levy 2003, 2007) seem too sweeping to be viable. Probably more influential have been the steps taken within the more insular world of contemporary national–religious Jewry in order to overcome the fear that military service's secularizing influence might compromise the Orthodoxy of religiously observant troops.

The vital initial moves in that direction were initiated by Rabbi Shlomo Goren, the first IDF chief chaplain and, to date, the longest serving (he held the office from 1948 until his retirement from active duty over 20 years later). From the start determined to ensure that religiously observant troops could serve as equals in the IDF, Goren embarked on two pioneering initiatives. One was essentially intellectual: the formulation and promulgation of rabbinic solutions to the multitude of ritual problems that religiously observant soldiers confront on a regular basis during the course of their military service, especially with regards to Sabbath observance. The other was administrative: expanding the writ of the military rabbinate to include responsibility for ensuring that the IDF as a whole observed the basics of traditional religious custom (for example, with respect to dietary regulations) and that all units refrain from behavior likely to alienate religiously observant troops (Kampinsky 2008).

Goren's attainments were certainly impressive. Not only did he lay the groundwork for the formulation of an authoritative corpus of Jewish religious law (*halakhah*) with respect to military matters, an area hardly touched by traditional rabbinic enquiry for almost two millennia (Edrei 2007). With similar gusto he infused the military rabbinate with a sense of mission, gradually winning for it a mandate that far exceeded the largely decorative functions entrusted to chaplaincies in most modern armed forces. Goren's successors, especially of late, built on both foundations. As a result, graduates of national–religious high schools no longer have grounds to fear that enlistment might leave them exposed without answers to whatever threats military service might pose to their observant lifestyles. They now enjoy access to a massive corpus of rabbinic advice and instruction, much of which is available on the Internet, which specifically addresses the concerns and queries of male and female soldiers. Their ritual needs are also serviced by a large and vigorous military chaplaincy committed to equipping every IDF base with the facilities (synagogues, prayer books, etcetera and in some cases ritual baths, too) that observant Jews require on a regular basis.

Notwithstanding their significance, such measures have gone only halfway toward performing the nation-binding function that Ben-Gurion originally envisaged for military service where relations between observant and non-observant Jewish Israelis are concerned. Their net effect has been to enable religiously observant troops to become full members of the IDF – to be sure, a necessary first step toward establishing relationships with non-observant troops, but not one that of itself is sufficient to produce religious–secular amity. The 'contact hypothesis' requires a complementary framework, which might more directly foster and encourage mutual interaction and understanding between the two segments of the complement.

Goren's efforts in that regard were far more tentative and for the most part limited to the preparation of occasional introductory courses in Jewish customs and rituals, intended for troops from non-observant backgrounds. Aware of the limitations of so skeletal a program, more recent IDF chief chaplains, and especially General Rabbi Avichai Rontski (2007–2010) have sought to intensify the 'outreach' facets of the formation under their command. But in many respects their efforts have backfired, generating public criticism of the 'overenthusiasm' they are said to arouse. Thus, during the fighting in Gaza early in 2009, left-wing secular newspapers accused Rontski of displaying excessive 'missionary zeal' and of distributing materials that incited Israeli troops to unwarranted violence in the name of religious militancy.[4] More generally, he has also been charged with encroaching on turf that properly belongs to the IDF's Education Corps. Clearly unwilling to become embroiled in the ensuing outcry, Lieutenant General Gabi Ashkenazi, then the chief of staff, decided to defuse the situation. Besides laying down clear spheres of bureaucratic influence between the Education Corps and the rabbinate, he also attempted to divest the IDF of this hot potato, principally by intensifying earlier efforts to ensure that much of the religious instruction given to troops from a non-observant background was 'outsourced' to civilian educational institutions.[5] They, too, however, hardly provided a sustained bonding function. On the contrary, since the programs concerned are attended exclusively by conscripts from a secular background, they if anything send a signal to the participants that they and their religiously observant comrades-in-arms inhabit two very different cultural worlds.

Mirror

Whereas the 'nation-binder' construct is thus seriously flawed as an accurate depiction of conscription's impact on relationships between observant and non-observant Jewish troops, the 'mirror' model seems to enjoy relative validity. This also appears to be the case in other areas of Israeli national life. For instance, it has been found that conscription has done little to foster the integration into Israeli society of Druze troops. If anything, service in the IDF might even have intensified their sense of ethnic and societal marginality (Halabi 2006). Likewise,

---

4   BBC television programmed a summary of the charges under the title 'The Rise of Israel's Military Rabbis', which was shown early in September 2009. See <http://news.bbc.co.uk/2/hi/programmes/newsnight/8232340.stm> (accessed 19 September 2012).

5   See, especially, the program entitled 'Identity and Purpose', which has been conducted ever since 2002 by a private educational institution located in Jerusalem see <http://www.bmj.org.il/inner_en/30> (accessed 19 September 2012), and the 'Sabbath for Soldiers' programs initiated in 2011, which are likewise conducted in civilian locations see <http://www.idf.il/1086-11626-en/Dover.aspx> (accessed 25 February 2013). In general, Libel 2012.

the conscription of women has failed to improve gender equality in Israel at large. On the contrary, according to one school of thought, the way in which the IDF, perhaps unavoidably, maintains a gender hierarchy has itself become a justification for the preservation of chauvinistic stereotypes in civilian life too (Izraeli 1997, Sasson-Levy 2007). Finally, it has been noted that to a large degree soldiers from different class backgrounds, which themselves often parallel ethnic distinctions between Jews from western countries (*ashkenazim*) and of oriental origin (*mizrachiyim*), end up following different service patterns, often simply because the two groups possess different educational backgrounds and hence enter the IDF with different qualifications (Roumani 1991).

Conscription, it is here argued, has exerted a similarly limited integrative impact on relations between religiously observant and non-observant Jews in Israel. Indeed, whatever chances might once have existed that the draft would help to bridge the gulf between the two communities have receded over time, principally because that gulf has tended to become progressively wider. Over and above the demise in the general spirit of consociationalism that was once considered characteristic of intergroup relations in Israel (A. Cohen and Susser 2000), responsibility for that development lies principally with the schisms fostered by the existence of three distinct state Jewish school systems: one 'national' (that is, secular), a second 'national–religious', and the third 'independent' (that is, ultra-Orthodox or *haredi*). Inexorably, the differences between these frameworks have grown ever more pronounced – not just between the *haredi* and determinedly secular worlds, but between the generally less antagonistic non-Orthodox and national–religious communities too. Hence, although youngsters from the latter are encouraged to participate fully in every sphere of national life, including military service, they are taught to do so in educational frameworks that have become increasingly distinct from those attended by their non-observant counterparts. For instance, whereas in the non-religious community the mixed gender day school predominates, the national–religious world has witnessed the proliferation of single sex schools, many of the most prestigious of which (*yeshivot tichoniyot* and *ulpanot*) are also residential. After school hours, religious youngsters also attend youth movements of their own: *B'nei Akivah, Ezra,* or the Religious Scouts.

Field research, based on extended interviews and discussions with IDF troops and their junior officers, indicates that thanks to this multilayered background of organized segregation, by the time national–religious recruits are summoned to service in the IDF they constitute a group apart, products of an environment about which their non-religious counterparts know very little at all. Moreover, they have grown accustomed to patterns of behavior (gender relationships, language, dress, and entertainment) with which few non-observant draftees can empathize. True, a substantial minority of national–religious high school graduates looks forward to enlistment precisely because it promises to place them in an environment in which they might abandon an Orthodox lifestyle, and almost a third of each annual male national–religious cohort is estimated to do so (Laslo and Rich 2001). But most retain a high degree of attachment to traditional Jewish observances and seek, while on active duty, to avoid compromising the beliefs and norms that they have been educated to observe.

Of the several mechanisms that the national–religious community has developed to prepare its youth to meet that challenge, by far the most significant is the *mekhinah* (preparation) program, which enables prospective conscripts to delay their enlistment for a year during which they attend one of the *mekhinot kedam tzeva'iyot toraniyot* (pre-military Torah colleges) that has received approval from the IDF. This framework was initiated in 1988 when 20 young males enrolled in the first such institution, and has since grown by leaps and bounds.[6] (After considerable debate, *Tzahali*, a *mekhinah*-type institution for religious women who planned to enlist in the IDF, was established in 2006.) During their pre-enlistment year of grace, the students are put through an intensive regimen that includes both strenuous physical training, whose purpose is to ensure that they arc fit cnough to qualify for the most demanding of combat units, and intensive studies in traditional religious texts, designed to provide them with whatever 'spiritual fortification' they might require in order to retain their standards of religious observance while on service.

By all accounts, both aims are attained. Graduates of *mekhinot* constitute a vastly disproportionate number of combat personnel. Almost all continue to observe traditional Orthodox rituals while on service. Nevertheless, the record of the program hardly supports the 'contact' hypothesis. If anything, quite the contrary is the case. By definition, it caters exclusively to a constituency already committed to Orthodox Jewish observance. Non-Orthodox high school graduates who are interested in a similar program of pre-military fortification (intellectual and spiritual as well as physical) must therefore go elsewhere. That explains the foundation, over the past decade, of ten avowedly secular *mekhinot*, most of whose pupils are female, and another seven institutions of the same name that proclaim themselves to be mixed in terms of religious affiliation, but that in practice are overwhelmingly attended by non-Orthodox youngsters.

In other words, instead of providing an overarching framework that might institutionalize Orthodox–secular contact, the *mekhinot* in fact deepen existing differences. A review of the prospecti issued by the *mekhinot* confirms that finding. Whereas four of the mixed institutions and one of the secular institutions proclaim 'bridging the secular–religious divide' to be their principal educational aim, that goal is not mentioned at all in any of the mission statements published by the institutions that cater to observant pupils, which instead emphasize the need to 'fortify' the religious faith of their clientele prior to military recruitment.

The tendency toward segregation of observant and non-observant conscripts thus fostered by the pre-enlistment colleges is similarly apparent subsequent to enlistment, when it takes several additional forms.

---

6   As of 2012 there existed almost 30 similar colleges, whose combined annual enrolment of over 1,800 young men encompassed almost a third of the sum total of male graduates of the national–religious high school system. Knesset Center for Research 2012: 20.

Undoubtedly the most pronounced is the infantry formation that the IDF lists as Battalion 97 – *Netzach Yehudah* – and that is popularly known as the *Nachal Haredi*. An all-male unit originally established in 1999 with the purpose of encouraging young men from the ultra-Orthodox *haredi* community to perform military service, *Netzach Yehudah* from the start furnished its personnel with unique conditions: they were guaranteed that the kitchens on their base would conform to the most stringent standards of Orthodox dietary laws, they were to be granted unusually lengthy intermissions in training for daily prayers and study spells, and the soldiers (all male) were to be strictly quarantined from any contact with female staff. But the results produced by this arrangement largely belie the expectations of its architects (Drori 2005). Despite all the fuss, *Netzach Yehudah* makes very little impression on the *haredi* community, in which males of service age overwhelmingly take advantage of the legal loophole provided by the government's commitment to suspend the draft for any person whose full-time occupation is the study of the sacred texts known collectively as 'Torah' (for statistics see above pp. 5–6). By contrast, the segregated nature of the battalion's structure has proved increasingly attractive to male adolescents from the more conservative wing of national–religious Israeli society. By 2004 recruits from this segment already comprised over half of the unit's complement, and despite subsequent IDF efforts to place a cap on their proportions, continued thereafter to be principally responsible for the fact that the *nachal haredi*'s annual intake of new draftees more than tripled in the decade 1999–2008, from 31 to 115.

A more widespread articulation of the preference for segregated military service amongst national–religious high school graduates is provided by the network of 'arrangement academies of Jewish study' (*yeshivot hesder*). Personnel drafted within this framework, apart from being permitted an active conscript term that is considerably shorter than the norm (some 18 months instead of three full years), also serve in a social milieu that is often largely their own. True, *hesder* recruits are no longer deployed in homogenous companies. But many do undertake basic training (at least) in formations in which they constitute a sizable proportion. Moreover, because of the peculiarities of their service schedule, which ensures that bouts of military duty are interspersed with periods of study in the academies, the individual recruit is assured that – even when alone in a formation – his isolation from his fellow students is much shorter than it would have otherwise been. Such facets have undoubtedly augmented the system's popularity. A form of service that the Ministry of Defense in 1964 sanctioned as an experiment, to be carried out by just one academy that housed 30 students, now encompasses some 40 *yeshivot*, located across the length and breadth of the land, with an annual intake of some 850 students (about 12 percent of the total number of national–religious high school graduates). Over the past decade, a similar program has been instituted for women, who are now able to choose between three academies (*midrashot*) of their own (Rossman-Stollman 2005).

For all their growing popularity, the aforementioned frameworks still cater to less than a half of all national–religious conscripts. Most graduates of national–religious high schools, male as well as female, enlist in the IDF individually and are assigned to units on the basis of a formula that takes account of both their own preferences and their psychometric (standardized testing) scores. What is interesting, nevertheless, is that they too evince behavioral characteristics that are recognizably segregationist, often deliberately so. In many instances, the phenomenon finds expression in a tendency to gravitate toward specific units, such as the Education and Intelligence Corps in the case of women,[7] and elite combat companies (*sayarot*) in the case of men. This tendency is easily understood. After all, even youngsters educated toward full integration into the IDF (a message that, as noted, is most emphatically articulated by the pre-conscription colleges) find it easier to maintain their religious observances in the company of persons of their own kind.

But even when 'bunching' of that nature is not so pronounced, national–religious and secular troops will frequently find themselves proclaiming their differences. Thus, at their induction they will respond in different ways to the oath of allegiance to the IDF (whereas the standard response is 'I swear' ['*ani nishba'*], religious troops declaim 'I pledge' ['*ani matzhir'*]); they will find themselves attending different classes in the IDF's Sunday morning cultural programs; thanks to the introduction in 2007 of General Staff regulations that grant religiously observant troops the right to be provided with single sex training exercises (termed, not altogether euphemistically, *ha-shiluv ha-ra'ui* [appropriate integration]), they could find themselves undergoing courses of instruction that are parallel to – but separate from – those conducted in mixed gender settings (Sasson-Levi 2010); and even when that is not the case, they will almost certainly celebrate graduation from the program at different places of entertainment.[8]

Observation suggests that the schismatic impact thus generated is only marginally mitigated by the steps taken to ensure that, at other points on the military life cycle, even the most non-observant of the IDF's troops are exposed to Orthodox Jewish rituals and practices, such as attendance at a festive meal welcoming the advent of the Sabbath on Friday nights. Whatever feelings of affinity might thus be attained seem to be transitory and limited almost entirely to the time spent in uniform. Once religious and non-religious personnel leave the military framework, they revert to their separate lifestyles. Hence, very few of even the national–religious troops committed to the ethos of integration in uniform will, once off their base, maintain

---

7   In 2013, the IDF Manpower Directorate reported that over a quarter of all national–religious female recruits were posted to educational and manpower assignments; 13 percent served in intelligence; 16 percent in technical services and 6 percent in combat units. Agmon 2013.

8   Especially highlighted, in recent years, has been the increasing numbers of national–religious soldiers who have demonstrably excused themselves from attending official IDF events in which girl singers provide part of the musical repertoire. Although all such instances have been harshly criticized by the IDF Chief Rabbi (Peretz 2012), they have often been encouraged by some of his subordinates, thus generating unprecedented friction – not just between religious and secular troops – but within the religious community too.

much social contact with their non-religious buddies. As one such soldier remarked in conversation, 'The fact that I serve in a tank driven by a non-observant fellow soldier doesn't mean that I have to spend my leave with him, still less that I need invite him to my home so that he can meet my sister'.

Nation-divider?

Writing at the turn of the current millennium, the American political scientist Robert Putnam noted the difference between what he termed 'bridging' and 'bonding' types of social capital (Putnam 2000, 22–24). Bridging, he claimed, is created by networks that are outward looking and encompass people across diverse social cleavages. (His examples were the civil rights movement, youth service groups, and ecumenical religious organizations). Bonding social capital, by contrast, is the product of inward-looking frameworks that tend to reinforce exclusive identities and homogeneous groups (Putnam cited ethnic fraternal organizations, church-based women's reading groups, and fashionable country clubs). These distinctions are not necessarily comprehensive. After all, and as Putnam was himself quick to point out, many groups – indeed, perhaps most of those that aspire to be national in scope – can simultaneously bond along some social dimensions while bridging across others. The value of Putnam's taxonomy, therefore, lies not in its potential for 'either–or' classifications, but in its provision of a gauge by which we might audit organizations on a 'more or less' measure

Measured on that scale, the IDF must be judged far more of a bonding institution than a bridge. In practice, Israel's military-service patterns do not simply reflect existing differences between various segments of the country's population. In extreme cases, they can be said to exacerbate those divides, principally by making them even more prominent than they might otherwise have been. Hence, even when religiously observant and non-observant young people are drafted together, the contact established between the two groups hardly produces the bridging results envisaged by Ben-Gurion. Far from sensitizing them to those features of Israeli identity that they share, common military service can emphasize the extent to which they are different.

Two examples illustrate the extent of this process of exacerbation. The first concerns national–religious troops who come into daily contact with non-religious service personnel, sometimes in extremely cramped physical conditions; the second affects those members of the IDF who are recent arrivals from the Former Soviet Union (FSU).

Exacerbation Related to Close Contact between Observant and
Non-observant Troops

Even the most comprehensive of contemporary rabbinic compendia that discuss relations between observant and non-observant Jews in Israel make relatively few references to the ritual problems generated by the experience of common military service. By contrast, that subject figures prominently in the modern rabbinic literature devoted specifically to military life in Israel. Although I have been unable to find direct references to this topic in Rabbi Goren's writings, it recurs with noticeable regularity in other written sources that are now available in various printed and electronic formats. This growing corpus of evidence indicates that for many years now religiously observant soldiers have been asking whether Jewish law (*halakhah*) permits them to share food parcels with soldiers who they know will not recite a blessing on the products; can they can lend their transistor radios (whose use is forbidden on the Sabbath) to comrades who declare their intention of tuning in to the broadcast of a football match on that day? Can they partake of a Friday night festive meal prepared by troops who do not observe dietary laws? And – most frequently of all – may they include non-observant soldiers in a prayer quorum (*minyan*)?

It must be pointed out that, overwhelmingly, the answers given to such enquiries have deliberately leaned in a direction that, to a layman, appears remarkably tolerant.[9] Indeed, rabbinic responses are permeated with warnings against alienating non-observant brothers-in-arms, whose military service in itself warrants recognition as a religious duty of supreme importance and who their observant comrades are consequently duty-bound to do everything possible to befriend (for example, Rabinovitch 1994: 29–77). Nevertheless, the very fact that such questions crop up time and again testifies to the concern that they continue to cause. The implication is that common service – does not launder out the differences between observant and non-observant Jews, precisely because it brings them so closely together. As far as the religiously observant segment is concerned, quite the opposite may be the case. Juxtaposition with non-observant soldiers, especially those of the opposite sex, merely sensitizes the observant even more to the cultural gulfs that separate them from their comrades.

New Immigrants from the FSU

New immigrants from the Former Soviet Union (FSU), over 1,000,000 of whom have arrived in Israel since the early 1990s, now constitute almost a fifth of the country's entire population. Those of service age, whether as new recruits or as reservists, are enlisted as a matter of course. Their conscription, however, does not seem to have exerted the sort of integrative impact originally expected. Partly this is because recent arrivals from the FSU, unlike some earlier waves of immigration,

---

9   The basic text, referred to by virtually every subsequent rabbinic authority who writes on this subject, is a letter that Rabbi Yehudah Amital, the joint principal of one of the most prestigious of *hesder* academies ('Har Etzion'), addressed to his pupils on active service in 1971, and that was widely distributed in the academy's newsletter *Alon Shevut* (no. 10, 1971), pp. 15–18 (author's private collection). For a recent affirmation, which focuses on meals cooked by non-Jews, published in the IDF Rabbinate's journal, see Markovitch 2007.

tend to resist the 'melting pot' thesis and actively seek to preserve their cultural individuality – for instance, by sponsoring Russian language newspapers and theaters. But also noteworthy is the low level of enthusiasm that they evince for military service, which for many still carries Soviet connotations (Lomsky-Feder and Rapoport 2003).

For a substantial proportion of Israel's FSU population there exists yet another, and more salient, cause for the draft's failure to serve as an integrative agency. On their arrival, most FSU immigrants were granted Israeli citizenship on the basis of their fulfillment of the criteria of being Jews as defined in the country's Law of Return ('one who was born to a Jewish mother or converted, and does not subscribe to another religion'). But as many as a third gained entry by virtue of subsequent clauses in the Law that recognize the claims to Israeli citizenship of spouses of Jews, children of Jews and their spouses, and grandchildren of Jews and their spouses. As Professor Asher Cohen points out, the result has been to place some 300,000 new 'Jewish' immigrants in a strange, intermediary situation. On one hand they are full citizens; but on the other they are not designated Jews by either the rabbinate or the Ministry of the Interior (Ash. Cohen 2007). Thanks to conscription, IDF figures tell much the same tale. Ever since the late 1990s, FSU immigrants and their offspring have comprised at least 10 percent of every annual cohort of new recruits. However, because roughly one third of this number are invariably children of gentile mothers – a situation that bars them from receiving rabbinic recognition as Jews – the IDF now regularly enlists some 5–6,000 'non-Jewish' FSU immigrants each year.

Some of the soldiers in that category accept their classification with pride. Indeed, every year about 200 new inductees declare themselves to be adherents of the Russian Orthodox Church, and hence insist on swearing the Oath of Allegiance to the IDF on the New Testament (copies of which it is the duty of the Military Rabbinate to supply). A larger number seek to alter their status and take advantage of the special program for conversion to Judaism, named *Nativ*, which the IDF inaugurated in the year 2001 and which in many respects is specifically tailored to the cultural background of FSU immigrants. But the majority do not avail themselves of either option. Consequently, at the completion of their compulsory service the vast majority of non-Jewish FSU immigrant soldiers in the IDF find themselves in precisely the same anomalous situation they were in when they first donned uniform two to three years earlier. By virtue of their performance of military duty, they can claim to have undertaken what they and many members of the general Israeli public regard to be the most significant rite of passage to identification with the Jewish state and all it represents in terms of Jewish identity and survival. Yet according to traditional Jewish law they are still non-Jewish and hence not considered by Orthodox Jews to be fully integrated members of the majoritarian Jewish–Israeli collectivity.

The abrasive results to which that situation can lead have on various occasions intruded on the Israeli public discourse with stark brutality. One early instance occurred in January 1970, when Chanan Frank, a new immigrant who had been

persecuted by the Soviet authorities for demanding the right to emigrate from
Russia to Israel, felt compelled to write an open letter to the then–prime minister
of Israel, Golda Meir. Frank, whose father was Jewish but whose mother was not,
protested that a proposed change in the Law of Return would disqualify him from
being registered as Jewish on his Israeli ID. Hadn't he struggled against the Soviet
authorities as a Jew, Frank asked? More pertinent still, hadn't it been as a Jew that
he had enlisted in the IDF and been severely injured in action against the Egyptian
foe? Frank wrote:

> Did I lose both my legs for the homeland or am I mistaken and this is not
> my homeland at all? Because I thought of myself as a Jew, I made 'aliya'
> [immigration] to Israel and was drafted into the army but it seems that all this is
> not sufficient. What must I do to be a Jew? (For reactions, Hadari 2002: 170–2).

Since the 1990s, the enlistment in the IDF of far larger numbers of people
whose status in Orthodox Jewish law is similar to that of Frank has transformed
what was once a rare curiosity into a widespread phenomenon. It has also resulted
in the appearance of cases that are, if anything, even more tangled and tragic. One
that occasioned particular debate concerned Lev Paschov, an immigrant from the
FSU born to a Jewish father and killed while on active duty in southern Lebanon
in August 1993. Since Paschov was the son of a non-Jewish mother who had never
converted, and hence did not fit the Orthodox Jewish criteria for definition as a Jew,
the military rabbinate originally buried him in a section of the military cemetery
designated for gentiles. This action was in accordance with the letter of the law,
which mandates that all burials in Israel, civil as well as military, must conform
to religious norms and that corpses of Jews hence be segregated from non-Jewish
corpses. Only subsequent to a public hue and cry were Paschov's remains later
reinterred in ground originally consecrated for exclusive Jewish use. Even so, the
entire incident left a bad taste (not least with some rabbis in the national–religious
community; see Shaviv 1994a). It demonstrated that far from diluting differences
in Israel between observant Jews and other citizens (in this case an immigrant
soldier), even death on the battlefield in a common could show how wide apart
the various groups in fact are.

Conclusions

The evidence presented in this chapter confirms suggestions put forward by
other scholars who have cast considerable doubt on the ability of conscription
to eradicate deep-rooted divisions within national societies. An examination of
relations between Jewish troops in the IDF who do observe the customs and rituals
mandated by traditional Orthodox Judaism and those who do not indicates that
even when wearing the same uniform those two segments of the Forces continue to
follow different lifestyles. Not even extended and intimate contact during service

is guaranteed to bridge the gulfs that in civilian society divide the religiously observant from the non-observant. On the contrary, in extreme cases the military might even provide an arena in which their differences can find new expression.

If such is indeed the case, it might also be possible to draw another conclusion, the relevance of which could likewise extend beyond the confines of the Israeli instance. Religious preferences, which in the case of Judaism are amenable to rough measurement along a scale of attachment to traditional dos and don'ts, can be remarkably resilient. This is especially the case when they are inculcated through the agency of a multilayered system of educational frameworks, both formal and informal, and thereafter buttressed by supplementary support institutions. Under those circumstances, religion proves itself capable not just of surviving even the most persistent of secularizing pressures (such as are presented by the experience of military service) but even of emerging from those experiences with renewed strength. The implications of that finding, if confirmed by other studies, cannot be exaggerated. Ever since the dawn of organized warfare, commanders have appreciated the value of religion as a source of combat motivation and willingness to self-sacrifice (Van Creveld 2008, 98–100). Perhaps the time has come to recognize that military activity and military organizations might likewise function as sources for the strengthening of religious identification rather than (or perhaps in addition to) national affiliation.

Chapter 9
Warfare in Contemporary Jewish Law: Varieties of Analytical Frameworks

Warfare was noticeably marginalized in the vast library of pre-modern legal codes and philosophical tracts that transmitted normative Judaism. During the high middle ages, especially, rabbinic authors overwhelmingly restricted their comments on military conduct to sporadic snatches of scriptural exegesis. With the titanic – but singular – exception of Maimonides (Moses ben Maimon; Egypt, 1135–1204), none of the authoritative medieval codifiers of traditional Jewish law even summarized the random regulations respecting the application of armed force scattered in biblical and talmudic sources. In this respect, the Jewish legal canon (known by the generic term *halakhah* [lit: 'way']) differed markedly from its parallels in other religious cultures, and especially in western Christendom, where protracted concern with 'just war' issues fuelled a majestic progression of learned enquiries into the precise components of both the *ius ad bellum* and the *ius in bello*.

The discrepancy between Jewish and gentile interest in matters military is easily explained. Although warfare had undoubtedly played a crucial role in the formation of Israel's national identity during both the biblical and post-biblical eras, its status as a topic of practical interest was abruptly terminated by Rome's destruction of the second Jewish commonwealth in 70ce, and her savage suppression of the 'Bar-Kochba' rebellion in Judea some 65 years later. Thereafter, all but the most innocuous traces of Jewry's martial heritage were expunged from the national consciousness. Instead, with exile and subjugation becoming increasingly dominant motifs of their experience, Jews the world over deliberately adopted the stance of a non-bellicose people. Hence, rabbinic enquiries into the religious implications of a resort to arms were exceptional. Generation after generation of spiritual guides to the children of Jacob depicted war as the trade of Esau. 'For the Jews, it belonged either to their mythical past or to their messianic future, but not to their present' (Luz 1987: 53).

As was pointed out in Chapter 2 (above pp. 27–8), that attitude first began to change in any significant measure in the wake of Emancipation, when increasing numbers of Jews chose to enlist for military service, initially in western and central Europe and the United States, thereafter in the Austro-Hungarian Empire, and ultimately in South Africa and Australia too. Conscription, introduced in western Europe during the nineteenth century and adopted by all the belligerents of the two world wars, further increased the number of Jewish men and (in World War II) of women in military uniform. Rabbinic authorities could no longer ignore the *halakhic* issues generated by such phenomena, undoubtedly the most politically sensitive of which was the fact that Jews were often being sent into battle against fellow Jews (Penslar 2008).[1]

Nevertheless, old attitudes died hard. Bereft of clear *halakhic* precedents for dealing with the numerous ritual and ethical challenges confronted by religious soldiers, even Jewish military chaplains tended to tip-toe around such issues. Of all the great rabbinic authorities of the 19th and early 20th centuries, only R. Yisrael Meir Ha-Kohen ([Kagan], 1838–1933, the '*Hafetz Hayim*') published what purported to be a comprehensive guide to ritual observance whilst on service that he entitled *Sefer Mahaneh Yisrael* ('The Book of the Camp of Israel') 1881. But that pioneering effort, originally addressed to Jews conscripted into the armies of the Austro-Hungarian Empire, was of little practical value. Its author could not give his readers the benefit of any personal experience of military life; neither did his slim volume reveal any awareness of the technological revolutions (such as electricity) that were revolutionizing the soldier's trade (Achituv 2002). Most important of all, the *Hafetz Hayim*'s initiative was never followed up. Even at the close of World War II, war-related *halakhah* continued to constitute one of the great lacunae of all Jewish libraries.

Such is no longer the case. In recent decades, warfare – broadly defined – has become a subject of intense rabbinic interest, especially in Israel where the ubiquity of armed conflict has been particularly marked. As a result, questions that for centuries received no attention whatsoever in Jewish sources, now constitute areas of avid religious inquiry. What, if anything, do the canonical sources have to say about the justice of warfare in general and about the ethics of specific modes of warfare in particular? Can the sacred texts accommodate a perspective that regards national security (as opposed to personal safety) as a categorical imperative? And on a more prosaic level, how might the dictates of traditional orthodox practices, with regards for instance to sabbath observance and dietary regulations, be reconciled to the practicalities of military life? It is no exaggeration to say that the quest for responses to these and similar enquiries has revolutionized the traditional Jewish legal corpus. Military-related matters, an area of human endeavor that was for two millennia almost totally devoid of rabbinic instruction, has ever since the 1950s become a thriving field of *halakhic* inquiry. *Dinei tzavah u-milkhamah* ('[religious] laws relating to the military and war'), transmitted by means of a swelling tide of detailed pronouncements and rulings, many of which are publicized in electronic formats, now constitute an integral part of the curriculum in all modern academies of rabbinic learning.

Previous scholarship has already supplied both general appraisals of this new corpus, as well as detailed reviews of some of the discreet themes that it analyzes. (J.D. Bleich 1983; Inbar 1987; Ravitzky 1996; Blidstein 2002; Luz 2003; Broyde 2007; Rozenak 2007; Eisen 2011). In a more synoptic sense, much of the

---

1   For specific illustrations of sensitivity to this issue during World War I, see Saperstein 2008: 303–8. The other great military-related issue of rabbinic concern (especially in Tsarist Russia) was the fulfillment of conscription quotas. See Zalkin 2006, Judith Bleich, 2007.

literature has been subjected to overall mapping, and has been surveyed in terms of its authorship, content and format (Lubitch 2009 and Chapter 6 above pp. 85–106). Still lacking, nevertheless, is a comprehensive examination of the interpretational strategies that contemporary rabbis employ when approaching topics about which there exist no immediately obvious prior rulings to which they might refer.

The present chapter aims to repair that deficiency. Its point of departure is the observation that, where military-related issues are concerned, contemporary Jewish rulings frequently exhibit an even greater degree of divergence than is usually the case in other fields. Consequently, religiously observant soldiers in the Israel Defense Force (IDF) commonly discover that rules of conduct prescribed by one rabbi can be proscribed by another. Only in part can such variations in opinion be attributed to political–ideological causes, of which undoubtedly the most salient are the right–left divides on national security issues that plague Israeli society overall. Where matters of religious doctrine and practice are concerned, the differences of opinion between *halakhic* authorities express a more profound clash, which focuses on the identity of the legal perspectives that have to be brought to bear when analyzing war-related issues. In their starkest terms, the issues at stake can easily be summarized: are the traditional categories of *halakhic* analysis, the overwhelming majority of which were painstakingly refined over centuries of microscopic forensic activity in exclusively non-martial contexts, sufficiently flexible to be applied to situations of modern armed conflict too? If not, which alternative investigative frameworks does traditional Jewish jurisprudence make available for possible adoption?

Although usually presented in essentially theoretical terms and often couched in the archaic mixture of Hebrew and Aramaic that has always been the *lingua franca* of rabbinic discourse, such questions are by no means devoid of contemporary practical importance. On the contrary, as far as many men and women in Israeli military service are concerned they touch upon issues of crucial and immediate concern. One reason is the IDF's increasing involvement in non-conventional and 'low intensity conflict', forms of military activity that necessarily exacerbate friction between combatants and non-combatants and thereby vastly expand the span of moral dilemmas concerning which troops in the field seek guidance (Ford and Am. Cohen 2012). But more specifically responsible for the relevance of the rabbinic discourse has been the sharp rise that has recently taken place in the number of religiously observant troops serving in IDF combat units. Official military sources are reluctant to publicize the precise sociological components of Israel's force structure, which incorporates a delicate admixture of troops from a variety of Jewish and non-Jewish backgrounds. Independent studies, however, indicate that graduates of orthodox Jewish high schools now constitute over a third of the rank and file in the IDF's four infantry brigades (almost three times their proportion in the overall population), where they also make up over 40 percent of the junior officer corps. Moreover, prior to their enlistment, at least half of all-male religious draftees participate in one of the several paramilitary programs of advanced Jewish studies that have been multiplied fourfold during the past decade, establishments in which they forge especially close bonds of association with their rabbinic mentors (for statistics see above pp. 11–12).

The influence that those formative experiences exercise on the conduct of national–religious soldiers is evident throughout their military careers. Indeed, in many cases it is fortified during the course of service, principally thanks to the efforts that the rabbis invest in maintaining contact with their alumni, who they regularly visit on base and to whom they send periodic electronic newsletters. In so doing, they establish a communications network that serves two allied purposes. For one thing, it sensitizes the rabbis to what are, by the standards of traditional *halakhah*, the entirely novel range of religious and ethical challenges confronted by the troops in the field. At the same time, the communications network enables rabbis to explain to a comparatively wide audience the criteria and frameworks of analysis that they have adopted when advising troops how to respond to the challenges that individual soldiers now confront on an almost daily basis.

A review of that literature in its various formats – the data base stretches from individual articles and occasional analyses of discreet topics published during the 1950s, to the flood of encyclopedic summaries of *dinei tzavah u-milkhamah* and compendia of rabbinic responses to individual enquiries on that field that began to characterize the rabbinic discourse during the 1990s – suggests that four principal modes of analysis can be identified.

- One coopts into the military setting jurisprudential mechanisms and principles that traditional *halakhah* has conventionally applied in non-military contexts. To put matters another way, in this scheme of things *dinei tzavah u-milkhamah* are 'regularized', and thereby incorporated into a *halakhic* framework that is essentially concerned with civilian norms and standards.

- A second mode of analysis espouses an entirely contrary approach. Warfare, it recognizes, constitutes an altogether exceptional activity – most obviously because it legitimizes the shedding of another person's blood, a deed otherwise strictly forbidden. *Dinei tzavah u-milkhamah* cannot therefore be approached simply as branch of 'normal' *halakhah*. Rather, they have to be granted an autonomous juridical status and hence regulated on their own terms.

- A third approach adopts what will here be termed a 'meta-*halakhic*' perspective. Its point of departure is that military-related activities often give rise to consequences that transcend the immediate effect that they produce. From a religious perspective, the specific rights and wrongs of an individual deed cannot therefore be adjudicated solely by the strict application of accepted *halakhah*. Even *dinei tzavah u-milkhamah* that recognize warfare's exceptionalism have sometimes to be modified in order to accommodate the general benefit of the community.

- The fourth and final school of thought is in many respects the most radical. Acknowledging the paucity of traditional *halakhah*'s experience with war-related matters, and indeed the universal dearth of military-related expertise at the disposal of Jewry's traditional legal authorities, this approach advocates a posture of rabbinic abstinence where warfare is concerned. Thus seen, *dinei tzavah u-milkhamah* cannot grow out of the *halakhah*; they can only be grafted on to it. Their source will be 'extra-*halakhic*', in the sense that they will be determined by the opinions and customs of professional military experts, including – where appropriate – non-Jews.

Table 9.1   Taxonomy of contemporary *halakhic* strategies respecting war

Framework	Regularization	Autonomy	Meta-*halakhic*	Extra-*halakhic*
	Halakhic principles developed in civilian contexts are co-opted into the military setting.	Military-related commandments are granted status as an autonomous *halakhic* corpus.	General considerations are applied to halakhah in the military sphere.	Reference to military-related criteria that originate outside recognized halakhah.
Example	• Pursuer (*rodef*) • Saving of life (*pikuah nefesh*).	• Self-endangerment • Fighting on sabbath (*ad ridtah*).	• *Hillul/Kiddush ha-shem* • Morale.	• International norms • Opinion of military experts.
Requirement	*Transfer* of existing halakhah to new setting.	*(Re)discovery* of relevant halakhot specific to warfare.	*Accommodation* of halakhah to general principles.	*Deference* of halakhah to non-*halakhic* authority.
Focus of analysis	Individual/ community.	Community/polity.	Polity/Jewish collectivity.	Jewish collectivity/ International society.

The pages that follow will illustrate each of these divergent perspectives and address their separate methodological strategies and heuristic implications. Before embarking on that exercise, however, it is important to offset any impression that the taxonomy outlined here might reflect a chronological progression. At no stage in the argument will it be suggested that contemporary rabbinic thought on warfare has marched at a uniform pace and in successive stages from the first framework of analysis ('regularization') to the fourth ('extra-*halakhic*'), passing through phases of 'regulation' and a 'meta-*halakhic*' analysis en route. Matters have been far more complicated, with the result that the overall picture is somewhat chaotic. Where *dinei tzavah u-milkhamah* are concerned, rabbinic opinion, quite apart from being fragmented, also moves simultaneously along several different time scales. Hence, it is not uncommon to find that methodological approaches which in the 1980s had begun to appear outdated were by the first decade of the twenty-first century enjoying a revival. Whilst many of these shifts can be attributed to changes in the IDF's military operational environment, others ought more properly be traced to ideological process at work within the more insular world of Jewish orthodox academe. Where appropriate, the following discussion will seek to address the influence exerted by both considerations.

Regularization

'Regularization', defined as the application to one area of activity judicial standards and rules developed in entirely different settings, deserves to be considered one of the most embedded methods of *halakhic* investigation and adjudication. As the talmudic sources attest, it was frequently resorted to in the embryonic stage of rabbinic discourse. Indeed, numerous passages record the efforts that the talmudic sages invested in identifying parallelisms between different situations and categories and, where these observations were upheld, to transferring judgments reached in one context to the other. Subsequent rabbinic authorities very much enhanced that tradition (Katz 1998). Especially was that so once the advent of modernity and technological innovation made it necessary to find a way of retaining traditional *halakhic* standards (for instance with regard to sabbath observance) without requiring orthodox practicing Jews to have no contact whatsoever with the changes (such as, in the above example, electricity) that were revolutionizing every walk of life. Deploying a heady combination of stunning erudition and mental gymnastics, *halakhic* decisors (*posekim*) found it possible to circumvent the need to construct an entirely new legal code to incorporate such changes. Pouring new wine into old bottles, they subsumed even the most modern of devices into the categories developed by generations of earlier authorities.

Two examples illustrate the adoption of similar techniques where war-related matters are concerned. The first is the application to military affairs of the principle that 'regard for human life' (*pikuah nefesh*) supersedes even the rules of behavior governing sabbath observance. The context in which this principle is analyzed in the Talmud (tractate *Yoma*, folio 85a) leaves no doubt that it was originally formulated with the physical health of individuals in mind. *Pikuah nefesh* sanctioned the cooking of warm food for a sick person on the sabbath or extinguishing a light so that s/he might sleep. In conformity with that background, the principle was in subsequent generations expanded. It was applied to such matters as personal hygiene (a topic codified on the basis of the *pikuah nefesh* principle in the massive seventeenth-century corpus known as the *Shulhan Arukh* [section *Yoreh De'ah*, Chapter 116]) and to the categories of persons enjoined to eat on the Day of Atonement (Ibid., section *Orah Hayyim* 618).

Not until the nineteenth century, however, did any rabbinic authority suggest that the same principle – which by association could incorporate actions taken to ward off any danger to life – might justify the act of taking up arms on the sabbath in self-defense.[2] And not until after the establishment of the IDF in 1948 was the supremacy of *pikuah nefesh* over conventional sabbath prohibitions extended to cover future military eventualities as well as current operational circumstances. In this new interpretation, troops did not have to wait until they were actually

---

2 See Kagan 1881, Chapter 28 and the note added to the contents page (referring to text page 114 line 4): 'And of course … if the matter touches on *pikuah nefesh* it is a commandment to violate the sabbath'.

assaulted before using their weapons on the sabbath. The need to maintain Israel's army in a constant state of readiness – and thereby deter the enemy from attacking in the first place – could likewise be defined as *pikuah nefesh*. As such, it supplied a *halakhic* justification for taking on the sabbath all steps deemed consonant with that aim, even during times of relative military quiet (Soloveitchik 1982).

A second example illustrative of the application of interpretative strategy 'regularization' to military affairs is provided by the similarly expansive reading applied since 1948 to the traditional *halakhic* rulings respecting the *rodef* (lit. 'pursuer'; see above p. 162). Here, too, the setting for this legal category is entirely civilian in origin. Talmudic sources (for example, tractate *Sanhedrin* folio 72a) entitle an individual whose life is patently being threatened by another person (even when no intent to murder can be ascertained) to attack the 'pursuer' who, if no other option is available, can be killed. In other words, situations of 'pursuit', a category also extend to thieves disturbed by a householder in the dead of night during the course of a break-in (see Exodus 22:1), obviate the conventional need for due legal process of investigation, warning and punishment by judicial authority. In this case, the rule of thumb is to follow the formula enunciated in the fifth-century collection of exegetical teachings known as the *Tanhuma* (see Chapter 3): 'If someone comes to kill you; strike him to death first'.

Since the source of that saying is found in a commentary on the biblical commandment to go to war against the Midianites, who were accused of threatening to corrupt the Children of Israel's morals in the wilderness (Numbers 25:17–18), its application to contemporary military situations is not altogether surprising. It has indeed been employed to provide *halakhic* legitimacy for pre-emptive IDF strikes against enemy forces massed on the border with clear intention of attack – as were, for instance, the Egyptians on the eve of the Six Days War in 1967 (for example, Ha-Levi 1980: 343). Far more inventive is the manner in which regulations regarding the *rodef* have likewise been 'regularized' in order to justify what might otherwise be considered military operations undertaken with the purpose of inflicting collective punishment on non-combatants.

The *locus classicus* for this application is a pioneering essay written in 1954 by R. Shaul Yisraeli (1909–1995), who at the time was widely regarded as one of the most authoritative rabbinic figures in Israeli orthodoxy. The immediate occasion of Yisraeli's text was the operation carried out against the Arab village of Kibye by Israeli troops on the night of 14th–15th October 1953 in response to an act of terror perpetrated by Palestinian raiders against Jewish Israeli civilians two nights earlier. One of a series of 'reprisal raids', the distinction of the Kibye operation lay in the high number (over 60) of deaths that the IDF troops inflicted on the civilian population. As the analyses by Roness (2010) and Eisen (2012) demonstrate, Yisraeli's text is open to various interpretations. Nevertheless, its general thrust is unmistakable. Contrary to Professor Yeshayahu Leibowitz (1903–1994), an orthodox Jewish philosopher who immediately condemned the IDF action as an act of brutality that contradicted traditional Jewish moral standards (Leibowitz 1992), Yisraeli found the raid to be consonant with *halakhah*, especially since he was under the mistaken impression that it had been carried out by private Jewish vigilantes, not IDF troops. After all, he argued, there was no reason why the category of *rodef* should not be expanded so that the license it allowed for extra-judicial action could be applied as much to an entire enemy community as to an individual foe. The logic then became fairly straightforward:

> Since according to available estimates the [civilian Arab] population [of the villages in the area of Kibye] encourages the actions taken by the terrorists in several ways, behavior that undoubtedly helps to increase their motivation to expand their activities in the future, it can be said that the entire population is in this case in the category of a *rodef* who it is permitted to kill in order to save [our] lives (Yisraeli 1954: 112).

Autonomy

Undoubtedly the most serious defect in the interpretive strategy here defined as 'regularization' is that it deprives warfare of its moral and legal distinctiveness. It assumes that the battlefield is an arena of activity to which the norms of behavior that are considered right and proper in everyday civilian life can be applied. Self-evidently, that is not the case. As jurists and philosophers have long recognized, and as Michael Walzer (2011) has recently reiterated, 'the practice of war … . has its own law and its own morality. By definition, it doesn't take place in civil society. It is a longstanding human practice (however uncomfortable we are with it), which represents a radical break with ordinary social life'.

One obvious reflection of war's uniqueness is provided by the radical transformation that it mandates in the application of the sixth of the Ten Commandments. In civilian situations, bloodshed is categorically outlawed and defined as murder; it can be tolerated only in the most extreme of circumstances – and even then solely a last resort. By contrast, in situations of 'war', provided hostilities have been declared and initiated by legally empowered authority, killing – even on a large-scale and in an organized and purposeful manner – becomes a norm of behavior. Soldiers are expected to shed the blood of their enemies during the course of battle, just as they are also required to place their own lives at risk by performing actions that in other contexts would be considered suicidal.

Occasional indications that orthodox Judaism has always recognized the legal singularity of warfare can be identified in several of the ancient and medieval codes and commentaries. Some of these texts merely affirm the deviations from conventional rules of behavior that the Biblical sources permitted to the children of Israel during wartime; the spectrum ranges from theft, now categorized as the lawful taking of booty (Deuteronomy 20:14) to sexual intercourse with gentiles [the '(captive) woman of beautiful countenance'(Deuteronomy 21:10–15)]. But others add a number of ritual concessions (for example, the 'four prohibitions that the rabbis abrogated in a military encampment' [Mishnah *Eruvin* 1:10]). Texts such as these, however, are few and far between. Hence, even as late as the early nineteenth century it was still possible for one codifier to admit to being unable to find a *halakhic* discussion of the way in which a soldier's duty to place himself in situations of danger could possibly be reconciled with the overall commandment transmitted in Leviticus 18:5 to take care of one's life ('And you shall live by them').[3]

The person who first sliced that particular Gordian knot was Rabbi Abraham Isaac Kook (1865–1935), the Lithuanian-trained scholar who founded an entire school of 'national–religious' thought and also had the distinction of serving as the first (Ashkenazi) Chief Rabbi of mandatory Palestine. Deeply affected by the moods of nationalism and militarism that engulfed Europe during the first World War, Kook (who for the first three years of the conflict resided in Switzerland), undertook what was, for an orthodox rabbi, an entirely revolutionary investigation into the religious implications of the bloodletting that he witnessed all around him. His conclusions were equally radical. 'War', he wrote, 'constitutes a *halakhic* category entirely distinct from any other'. He surmised that such must always have been the case. However, since the body of texts that during the bygone days of Jewish independence had transmitted *dinei milkhamah* has long been lost, the relevant corpus must now be reconstructed. That task could never be accomplished simply by seeking to apply civil law to military situations. Instead, rules of behavior relevant to this area of Jewish legal activity have to be considered autonomously.[4]

In the years since the establishment of the IDF as the military arm of an independent Jewish state, Kook's approach has won considerable (albeit by no means universal) acceptance, especially amongst right-of-center national–religious Israeli Jews. Consequently, it has become increasingly common for the rabbinic authorities who counsel that sector to apply to concrete military situations Kook's thesis that, precisely because the battlefield environment is so different from any other known to *halakhah*, it has to be judged in accordance with rules and standards that are similarly *sui generis*. With that axiom in place, it obviously stands to reason, for instance, that a combat medical orderly on service in the IDF must risk his life by entering a minefield in order to save the life of a wounded comrade. In warfare, the prohibitions derived from 'And you shall live by them' have to be entirely discounted. Instead, other norms take precedence. In the phrase used by one of modern Israel's earliest and most respected *halakhic* authorities (Waldenberg 1972: 205): 'Just as it is impossible to make inferences from what is permitted in war to other circumstances, so too is it impossible to transfer the prohibitions of other circumstances to war'.

---

3   R. Joseph ben Moses Babad (Poland, 1800–1874), *Minhat Hinukh* [a commentary on an earlier exposition of the Pentateuch's 613 'written' commandments], no. 425. His rather lame conclusion was 'this matter requires further investigation'.

4   Rabbi Kook projected this thesis in the course of four letters (dated 1916–17) to Rabbi S.Z. Pines of Zurich, printed in Kook's collection of responsa: *Mishpat Kohen*, nos. 142, 143, 144 and 148. For a thorough analysis: Rakover, 2000.

Once thus set in motion, what is here termed the 'autonomous' *halakhic* approach to war-related issues gathered a momentum of its own. So much is this so that in recent years it has begun to generate the development of a school of thought that expands the unique status of *dinei milkhamah* to topics that seem to be once removed from the life and death arena of actual armed conflict. Sabbath observance presents an especially obtrusive example, and one that was developed with particular energy by Major General Rabbi Shlomo Goren (1917–94), the IDF's first and most influential chief chaplain (he held office from 1948 to 1971). Applying the 'war as a special category' argument, Goren posited that there was no need to resort to the plea that the need to preserve life (*pikuah nefesh*) permitted soldiers to violate the sabbath whilst on active duty. On the contrary, the commandment to pursue a just war (that is, one of self-defense) to a victorious conclusion made it imperative for soldiers to violate the sabbath – not just when battle was under way, but also during intervals of apparent calm, in order to maintain the military's state of readiness (Goren 1983: 88–109).

Later authorities, some of them who served under Goren's command in the IDF rabbinate, have extended that argument yet further. No action undertaken by a Jewish soldier in a military setting can be analyzed in accordance with rules that, although certainly hallowed by tradition, were self-evidently formulated and developed for an entirely non-military environment. All realms of battlefield behavior, including battlefield ethics must – rather – reflect the influence of divinely inspired teachings composed with the uniqueness of the military backcloth specifically in mind. Hence (Rozen 2002: 135): 'Although we are all in favor of ideals and of educating [young soldiers] to correct behavior, it is obvious that all such considerations give way, not just to the 'command of life' [that is, self-survival] … but also to the commandment to carry out war 'until [the enemy] is subdued' [*ad ridetah*; Deuteronomy 20:20]'.

From an analytical perspective, just as significant as the conclusions thus posited by exponents of the 'autonomous' approach are the methods whereby those conclusions are reached. 'Regularization', it will be recalled, relied on the time-honored talmudic procedure of transfer: conclusions reached in a civilian setting were applied to a military context. That methodology cannot be employed, however, once warfare is recognized to constitute a unique category of *halakhic* analysis. Instead, scholars have resorted to the alternative of searching the traditional corpus for whatever traces they could identify of texts with a possible bearing on war-related activities that, in the older atmosphere of deliberate disinterestedness in such matters, had previously been overlooked.

Here, too, Rabbi Goren took the lead, in particular when calling attention to one scrap of ancient exegesis on Deuteronomy 20:20 ('until [the enemy] is subdued'), which intimates that need for victory in war provides its own validity for sabbath violations (Goren 1983: 88–109). More recent rabbinic research has gone much further, progressing along two parallel paths:

- One has been charted by those scholars who have deliberately widened the scope of Goren's somewhat complicated reading of the commentary on

Deuteronomy 20:20, the application of which he restricted entirely to the confines of sabbath observance. In the new reading, however, *ad ridetah* (now taken to mean '[the pursuit of war aims] until the absolute defeat of the enemy') has become a prooftext for an approach that stresses warfare's *sui generis halakhic* status in numerous additional areas, extending from interpersonal relations between religious and secular soldiers within a military unit to troop conduct towards Palestinian civilians (Shenwald 2002). In other words, it adumbrates a thesis that shifts the emphasis of rabbinic enquiry from the need to reconcile military activity with other commandments to a perspective that stresses the need to prioritize the successful pursuit of the war over almost all other *halakhic* considerations.

- A second methodological extension of Goren's approach has displayed an alternative form of resourcefulness. Acutely aware of the paucity of war-related texts in the traditional Jewish *halakhic* corpus, several young rabbis have invested their considerable intellectual energies and talents in a quasi-archeological search for such teachings in other classes of texts, prominent amongst which are medieval and early modern rabbinic commentaries on the books of the Bible, many of which had been hidden from view by centuries of scholarly neglect. One prime example is the commentary composed in the sixteenth century by Rabbi Judah Loew (1525–1609, better known as the 'Maharal of Prague') on Genesis Chapter 34, which relates how two of the 12 sons of Jacob indiscriminately put to the sword an entire Canaanite township in response to the rape of their sister Dinah by Hamor the son of Shechem. Loew justified that action by describing it as an international conflict (which has its own rules and in which even the 'collateral' killing of innocent bystanders is an accepted norm) rather than as a feud between one family and another (a situation that prohibits any harm to non-involved persons). As Blidstein (1996: 36) has shown, this reading attained enormous popularity during the first *intifadah*, when the status of Palestinian non-combatants became a highly emotive topic of debate in national–religious circles, and when Goren's earlier and more conservative analysis seemed to be overtaken by events (Edrei 1996). In the atmosphere of tension now existing, even R. Yisraeli's attempt to tar Palestinians with the collective brush of the category of 'the pursuer' (above pp. 149–50) seemed inadequate. 'It is inconceivable that the rules of warfare are no more than extensions of those of *rodef*. Rather, there exists a term "war" that possesses independent [*halakhic*] status' (Amital 1994).

The Meta-*halakhic* Perspective

Typically, *halakhah* has always adhered to a culture of biblical exegesis and judicial decision-making that places a premium on a word by word interpretation of the Scriptures and on strict attention to the details of observance and worship that they proscribe. Even when the sublimity of certain general rules of behavior is recognized, they are never left at the level of abstractions. In the hands of rabbinic masters, accordingly, 'Love thy neighbor as thyself' (Leviticus 19:18) became a springboard for the elucidation of (amongst other things) the ways in which Jews should show respect for the dead. Likewise, in Maimonides' great code ('Laws of Mourning' 14:2 and 'Laws of Neighbors' 14:5), 'And thou shalt do what is good and right in the eyes of your Lord' (Deuteronomy 12:28) is particularized as an indication of the value of compromise in civil disputes.

At the same time, however, there also exists within *halakhah* a readiness to consider the wider implications and consequences of individual actions and, when necessary, to subordinate the specific dictates of prior individual rulings to the mandate of more general values that take into account the wider impact of a discreet action. Thus, *tikkun olam* (generally translated as 'social responsibility') was at a very early stage of the rabbinic enterprise endowed with a *halakhic* status that allowed the sages of the Mishnah to suggest ways of circumventing the biblical prohibitions on financial transactions involving payment of interest. Likewise, *kevod ha-beriyot* ('respect for human dignity') has long constituted a guideline in *halakhic* decision-making in the area of medical ethics (respectively, Mor 2011; Rakover 1998). Increasingly, considerations of a similarly general nature have intruded upon the contemporary rabbinic discourse concerning *dinei tzavah u-milkhamah*.

By far the most prominent demonstration of that process has been the realignment of the ancient principle of *hillul ha-shem* (literally: 'desecration of the Divine name'). For centuries, this concept (together with its antithesis *kiddush ha-shem* ['sanctification of the Divine name']) was employed as a standard of personal ethical behavior; right action glorifies the Almighty, whilst unethical behavior brings His name into disrepute. Medieval European communities added another layer of meaning. Apostasy constituted an ultimate desecration of the Divine name; by the same token, the martyrdom of Jews qua Jews earned the accolade of *kiddush ha-shem*.

As Lubitch (2010) shows, in modern Israeli national–religious' rabbinic literature the terms have undergone a process of further reinterpretation. I suggest that this change has incorporated the elevation of *kiddush ha-shem* and *hillul ha-shem* to the status of yardsticks for the measurement of the *halakhic* legitimacy of conduct in a military setting too. In this reading, what determines the permissibility or impermissibility of specific battlefield actions is not the extent to which they might be licensed (or outlawed) by the letter of rabbinic law – or even by the Bible itself. Rather, standards are much more flexible, and to a large extent determined by inherently subjective assessments of the impact that an individual military actions is considered likely to exert on the Jewish image in the world at large. Thus:

> On the one hand, it is clear that any action taken by a gentile that injures or shames a Jew – because he is a Jew – constitutes a *hillul ha-shem* and hence has to be stopped at all costs. On the other hand, we can also cause a *hillul ha-shem* by undertaking actions that are 'exceptional and cruel' when attempting to stop the gentile. This is because a *hillul ha-shem* is not defined by what pure

halakhah permits or forbids but by whether or not our action does or does not accord with what the gentiles expect of us in terms of their standards of 'moral' conduct (Sharir 2005: 437).

More specifically, rabbinic advice to soldiers on active service was:

Even though the Bible explicitly sanctions the taking of booty [Deuteronomy 20:14), today it would not be permitted to follow the letter of that law. One reason is that today all spoils belong to the IDF, and not to the individual soldier. Another is that we are duty-bound to take heed of international attitudes. Press pictures of IDF soldiers looting would cause a massive *hillul ha-shem* (Aviner 1995; see also Rimon 2002, Rozenfeld 2003).

Much is added to the force of that argument by *halakhic* traditions indicating that the application of *hillul ha-shem* as a guide to specifically military ethics boasts an extremely long pedigree (Charlap 2005). Folio 46a in the Talmudic tractate *Gitin* (redacted in the sixth century) records that a desire to avoid *hillul ha-shem* likewise explains why, according to the Biblical account (Joshua 9:18ff), Joshua had spared the Gibeonites from the destruction initially commanded by God. Joshua had given the Gibeonites his word that he would spare them; no gentile would have accepted a subsequent plea that the oath had been extracted under false pretenses (the Gibeonites had originally claimed to be members of a more distant people than was in fact the case). Any breach of that promise – even though justified by the strict letter of *halakhah* – was rendered impossible by the consideration that it would have been bound to sully the reputation of God's chosen people, and thereby bring about a *hillul ha-shem*. In weighing the rights and wrongs of their own military conduct, is the implication, Israeli troops must take into account precisely the same considerations.

Their everyday behavior at the IDF checkpoints dotted throughout Judea and Samaria provides a case in point. By the beginning of the twenty-first century, several rabbis were appealing to the Joshua precedent in order to argue that the legitimacy of the harassment of Palestinian civilians could not be assessed solely by reference to the Biblical lists of do's and don'ts vis-à-vis hostile civilians – which, according to some interpretations, in these matters tend to be very permissive indeed (Broyde 2007). On the contrary, troop actions at checkpoints had to place far greater weight than the Bible generally allows on the impression that the behavior of soldiers was likely to create amongst the international community.[5]

A second meta-*halakhic* consideration that has similarly begun to affect the substance of *dinei tzavah ve-milkhamah* is troop morale. Growing sensitivity to the impact exerted on the soldier's battlefield performance by his state of mind has

---

5   The most explicit enunciation of this case that I have found is located in an essay written in the spring of 2004 by R. Avraham Avidan, principal of the Sha'alvim *yeshivat hesder*, and included in the monthly newsletter sent to all his students (on file with the author).

encouraged numerous contemporary rabbinic authorities to introduce into *dinei tzavah u-milkhamah* a degree of flexibility that in most other contexts would have been considered far too radical to be acceptable (Gutel 2006). The extent to which that is so became starkly apparent whenever the Israeli government agreed to exchange a large number of terrorists in return for a handful (sometimes a single) IDF soldier held captive. One such trade was completed in 1985 ('the Jebril deal') and another in 2011, when Israel released over 1,000 Palestinian prisoners, who were collectively responsible for 569 Israeli deaths, in return for Sergeant Gilad Shalit, the young Israeli soldier who had been abducted by a Hamas unit over five years earlier and since then held in isolation.

On both occasions, some rabbinic authorities certainly considered the price far too high, and decried such deals on the grounds that they directly contradicted the traditional *halakhic* prohibition against paying exorbitant ransoms (a prohibition born out of fear that kidnappers would only thus be encouraged to undertake similar actions in the future; Mishnah, *Gittin* 4:6). Others, however, called attention to the meta-*halakhic* aspects of the case. IDF captives, they argued, were not private individuals but soldiers. Were the government to abandon them, the effect on the fighting spirit of other soldiers (who would fear the same fate) would be disastrous. In this case, therefore, the traditional prohibition against paying captors an exorbitant price simply did not apply (Shaviv 1990). As one contemporary rabbinic analysis of the Shalit case pointed out, the relevant criteria had been established by R. Yisraeli some five decades earlier:

> Since our soldiers went out to war for the State and in its name to protect the people living in Zion … an unwritten but self-understood obligation exists that the state must use all its options, without jeopardizing its overall security, for their release in the case of their fall. And just as the obligation stands in the case of their injury, heaven forbid, in war, so too the demand to act in every possible way for their release from captivity is of no less importance (Gisser 2012: 132).[6]

Even more obtrusive, because far more common, is the extent to which morale has intruded into the rabbinic discourse with respect to sabbath observance, an area that altogether warrants consideration as a litmus test of rabbinic flexibility (and inflexibility). For some years now it has been common to adduce troop morale as a *halakhic* justification for the IDF practice of giving precedence, even on the sabbath, to the transport of fallen soldiers away from the battlefield. Simply put, survivors would be disheartened – perhaps decisively so – were they to think that their dead comrades were not receiving the respect they deserve (Gutel 2004; cf. Wong 2005). More recently, in January 2009, the same framework of argument was advanced in order to grant, *post facto, halakhic* sanction to military chaplains

---

6   The reference is to Yisraeli 1975: 75.

who had travelled on the sabbath to be with the IDF ground forces about to enter the Gaza Strip during 'Operation Cast Lead'.

> Since the preservation of fighting spirit is so important for the fulfillment of the commandment of war, it seems that we must approach every subject associated with the soldiers' state of mind .... as though it were a case of true *pikuah nefesh* (Roness 2009).

Perhaps most remarkable of all, however, is the way in which contemporary halakhah has widened the circle of persons whose morale has to be considered. During the course of a groundbreaking ruling, R. Sh. Z. Auerbach (1910–1995), one of the most authoritative of contemporary *halakhic* decisors in Israel, included within that category not just the soldiers themselves, but immediate members of their family too. Hence, he ruled, in order not to cause parents undue anguish, soldiers could go home on leave prior to the sabbath – even though there was a strong likelihood of their being summoned back to base within a matter of hours, an order that would require them to travel and thereby desecrate the Holy Day (cited Kaufman 1994: 255).

Extra-*halakhic* Influences

Rabbinic authorities have never claimed a monopoly of the knowledge required to come to decisions concerning each and every one of the areas of life, private as well as public, governed by *halakhah*. Although insistent on maintaining the all-embracing status of the traditional Jewish codes of law, they have always acknowledged the limitations of that principle. One obvious consequence has been *halakhah*'s recognition of the validity of non-*halakhic* expertise in some areas of crucial concern, such as medical science. Thus, doctors have traditionally received what amounts to a rabbinic commission to assess whether or not a sick person may eat or drink on the annual Day of Atonement, which under any other circumstances is a mortal sin. In this case, *halakhic* procedure is clear: rabbis sanction whatever conduct medical expertise prescribes.

Equally noteworthy is the position traditionally accorded in *halakhah* to non-Jewish inputs. True, matters in this area are much less straightforward. Whilst some concessions to non-Jewish practice were mandated by obligations that gentile suzerains periodically imposed on Jewish behavior, others reflected a recognition that, in specific areas of life, pragmatic self-interest warranted the adoption of non-Jewish law (Hanshke 2009). And above all there was the influence exerted by the ebb and flow of a particular Jewish community's interaction with its host society. But even when most quarantined from such stimuli, *halakhah* accepted that in some areas of behavior Jewish practice could be (often had to be) governed by non-Jewish norms and rules. So much was this so that the phrase *dina de-malkhuta dina* ('the law of the land is law') became accepted as a norm of Jewish public life.

Precisely because the canonical texts of traditional *halakhah* provide so few precedents for decisions on war-related topics, *dinei tzavah u-milkhamah* might have been thought especially susceptible to the two types of extra-*halakhic* inputs noted above. A review of the current literature, however, reveals that resistance to that possibility has in fact been just as pronounced. Within 'national–religious' Israeli Jewry, especially, two major camps have consequently emerged: one far more inclined to include within *dinei tzavah u-milkhamah* extra-*halakhic* opinions than the other.

Deference to Non-rabbinic Expertise

Whether or not *halakhah* should on issues of 'grand strategy' take account of the judgments of persons who are not rabbis but whose biographies justify their claims to political and military expertise (and who also carry the burden of ultimate responsibility for whatever decisions are reached) has come to constitute a major point of contention. True, no rabbinical authority has questioned the decision-making autonomy of the statesmen – and stateswomen – and generals who have periodically sent IDF soldiers into battle, or demanded that they include in their considerations whatever *halakhah* might have to say about the initiation of hostilities. That has not been the case, however, where peacemaking is concerned. Since almost all of Israel's efforts to reach agreements with her neighbors have involved the withdrawal of IDF forces from areas under Jewish military control (and in some cases the dismantlement of Jewish settlements established in regions considered integral to the Jewish people's God-given homeland), they have injected into scholarly debates on this subject a spiraling tone of invective.

Opponents of those initiatives have argued that, where so cardinal an issue is concerned, the only opinion worthy of attention is that of the *halakhah*. Soon after the announcement of the 1993 Oslo, R. Shlomo Goren emerged from his retirement to thunder:

> It is clear that according to the *halakhah* a soldier who receives an order which contradicts the laws of the *Torah* must obey the *halakhah* and not a secular instruction … . *A fortiori* is it forbidden to obey a military order that contradicts the commandment of settling the Land of Israel, which is equivalent to all the [other] commandments of the Torah (Goren 1993).

As far as other authorities were concerned, however, matters were not so clear-cut. As early as 1975, when the prospect of territorial compromise was still very much a theoretical issue, Rabbi Yosef Dov Soloveitchik (1903–1993; who although not resident in Israel possessed enormous prestige amongst many rabbis in the national–religious Israeli community) had publicly reminded readers of a popular Tel-Aviv daily:

When one is required to feed an ill person on Yom Kippur it is done on the advice of experts: i.e. the doctors. In the area of territory, policy and *pikuah nefesh* – the experts are the chief of staff and the leadership of the IDF, and the government of Israel. If they will conclude that it is possible to compromise over territory without threatening the life of the *yishuv* [Jewish community in Israel] and the existence of the state, we should rely on them' (cited Helfgot 2005: 236).

This became a recurrent refrain. Precisely the same medical example was cited in 1990 by the Sephardi Chief Rabbi of Israel (*Rishon le-Tziyon*), R. Ovadya Yosef, who concluded: 'If the commanders of the army, together with the political experts, determine that retaining the territories entails *pikuah nefesh*, we rely on their judgment and permit the cessation of territory' (Yosef 1990). Rabbi Soloveitchik's reasoning was likewise cited in the summer of 2005 by his son-in-law, R. Aaron Lichtenstein, the principal of one of the most prestigious of Israel's *hesder* academies, in an open letter which queried the *halakhic* basis of a right-wing rabbinic manifesto calling upon IDF soldiers to disobey orders to implement the disengagement from the Gaza Strip:

> What advice would His Honor [R. Avram Shapira, the principal of the *Merkaz Harav* academy, who was behind the manifesto, see above pp. 111–12] give to a disciple of my revered teacher, Rabbi Yosef Dov Soloveitchik, of blessed memory, who resolutely asserted that there is no prohibition to hand over portions of the Land of Israel to the nations of the world when there are considerations of saving lives, and even said that when we come to define these considerations, we must take into account the views of military and political leaders? (Lichtenstein 2005b).

An even more extreme version of that line of reasoning was voiced in 2010, when debate over the *halakhic* legitimacy of what was then still a putative swop of numerous terrorists for sergeant Gilad Shalit had yet to reach full crescendo. As one rabbi wrote: 'On this question, in my opinion the *halakhah* is neutral, and leaves the tactical consideration to the [judgment] of the governing state leadership' (Rozen 2010).[7]

Adoption of Non-Jewish Norms as Halakhic Guidelines

Equally intense has been the debate over the extent to which *dinei tzavah u-milkhamah* might, or indeed should, take cognizance of norms of behavior that originate in non-Jewish sources. In this case, attention has focused on topics that the western tradition classifies as *ius in bello* concerns, and specifically on the search for appropriate standards of IDF conduct vis-à-vis the Palestinians.

---

7 Similar sentiments in Yisraeli 1975: 76. 'In sum, the matter [whether a prisoner exchange would endanger state security] is a matter for consideration and decision by the defence authorities'.

At an abstract and very general level, the notion that the quest for such guidelines need not be limited to specifically *halakhic* sources has a somewhat distinguished rabbinic pedigree. By the nineteenth century, at the latest, it was being taken for granted that since 'it is the way of the world that both sides suffer casualties in war', once hostilities commence Jews too need not be too squeamish when considering the rights and wrongs of causing injury during the course of hostilities. Hence, it was asserted, whilst it is true that: 'The Holy One Blessed be He specified that a person is punished [for murder] at a time when it is proper that he should act in a fraternal manner', different rules apply during periods of war, 'which are times of hatred and killing'. Consequently, once battle commences 'no punishment at all is meted out'.[8] In his essay on the Qibya operation (above p. 149–50), R. Shaul Yisraeli pursued the same line of thought. Presenting international norms as a form of *dina de-malkhuta dina*, he surmised that:

> in this case [Kibye] too, we must examine whether a military response of this kind is generally accepted practice amongst the nations of the world. Because if that is the case, then all the parties to hostilities must be considered to have agreed [to this form of action] which therefore should not be considered illegal bloodshed (Yisraeli 1954: 202).[9]

Since the outbreak of the first *intifada* in 1987, and the increasing involvement of IDF troops in violent conflicts with Palestinian irregulars and non-combatants, the parameters of debate have shifted considerably. One obvious reason is the heightened exposure of the Israeli population at large, and of the settler communities in Judea, Samaria and (until 2005) the Gaza strip especially, to murderous acts of terror. But another development has been the attention paid during the same period to the do's and don'ts of military counterterrorism by the western legal community. Over the past 30 years, especially, international humanitarian law (IHL) has moved from the margins to the very center of the international legal arena, leading to the establishment of several international tribunals specifically mandated to adjudicate situations of military occupation and to provide institutional interpretations of the international laws of armed conflict. Thus, as from the mid-1990s war crimes' tribunals were created by the United Nations Security Council and by special agreements with states. In 2003 a permanent International Criminal Court with wide jurisdiction began to operate. On another level, several states began to apply, sometimes vigorously, the doctrine of universal jurisdiction, which allows national courts to adjudicate international crimes.

Several studies audit the ways in which these developments have intruded upon Israel's secular legal conduct and, more specifically, on the IDF's culture and structure. For instance, decisions handed down by Israel's Supreme Court in cases

---

8   Babad, *Minhat Chinukh* no. 425 and Rabbi Naftali Tzevi Judah Berlin (1816–1893), *Ha-Amek Davar*, commentary to Genesis 9:2.

9   For a detailed analysis of Yisraeli's attitude to international law, which also refers to more recent developments in international humanitarian law, see Roness 2007.

affecting military behaviour in the Territories have shown an increasing sensitivity to IHL (Am. Cohen and S. Cohen 2011: 143–71). For its part, the IDF has also sought to adapt to the new environment. One major step in that direction was taken in 1995, when Ehud Barak (then Chief of the IDF General Staff) formally adopted a 'code of ethics', entitled *Ruah Tzahal* ('The Spirit of the IDF'), the content of which was clearly affected by IHL – although the term itself was carefully kept out of the text. Furthermore, in the year 2000 an entire military unit (the International Law Department; *Dabla*) was established under the Judge Advocate General's command with the purpose of providing instruction and advice to Israeli combat officers on IHL and the laws of armed conflict. In some views, *halakhah* cannot remain indifferent to this environment. On the contrary, rabbis have to face up to the fact that, given the paucity of traditions in this area, they must consider giving due weight to what one particularly sensitive and prolific principal of an academy (R. Yuval Cherlow) preferred to term 'natural ethics' when formulating *halakhic* responses to the moral dilemmas posed by modern warfare (Cherlow 2002).

Perhaps not unexpectedly, most rabbinic responses to that argument have not been enthusiastic. Altogether, indeed, of all the four interpretative strategies outlined in this chapter, the 'extra-*halakhic*' approach (characterized by an appeal to the bar of non-Jewish norms) is that which has been most criticized in recent literature. One immediate reaction to R. Cherlow's suggestion rejected 'with both hands the rush of the contemporary house of study to appease the media stricken public by projecting the basics of *Torah* in a humanistic light' (Rozen 2002). Less emotionally, other commentators cite common sense. International law, they point out, is after all basically a figment of the legal imagination. Since even the most liberal of western nations only abide by its principles when it suits their interests to do so it cannot possess any inherent compelling power over the IDF (Sharir 2005). But notwithstanding the emphatic manner in which such positions are expressed, there lingers a suspicion that their authors are not entirely convinced that combat ethics is not an area in which *halakhah* might indeed need to look to external sources for guidance (Gutel 2006). Perhaps that is why the current rabbinic discourse on this subject still rehearses themes (such as the *halakhic* status of the IDF's traditional adherence to 'purity of arms') that in both secular and religious quarters were voiced several decades ago (Chazan 2009; Don-Yehiya 1993).

Implications: A Matter of Perspective?

Are the four interpretative strategies outlined in this chapter little more than mental constructs – intellectual paradigms that in effect speak only to the cognoscenti who have a personal or scholarly interest in *dinei tzavah u-milkhamah*? Or do they perhaps reflect political orientations that carry wider relevance?

My own tentative conclusion is that the latter is the case. This is not because these four strategies can be aligned with positions favored by persons who stand on the right or the left of the Israeli political spectrum – either with respect to the 'peace process' and what it might entail or with reference to the long list of other issues that concern religion and the Jewish state. Rather, each of the four strategies seems to me to be the outgrowth of even more fundamental distinctions of perspective with respect to the dimensions of the subjects that *dinei tzavah u-milkhamah* ought to address.

Regularization (the transfer to a military setting of *halakhot* originally developed in non-military settings) reflects an individualistic perspective. In this view, the dangers confronted today by Jews living in the Land of Israel, civilians as well as soldiers, are essentially personal. Their lives are threatened by their non-Jewish neighbors, and hence *halakhah* requires them to do their utmost to defend themselves. Given that mindset, there exists no need whatsoever to reinterpret existing *halakhah*, still less to reinvent a corpus relating to warfare that might be presumed to have been lost. The rules of battlefield combat, for instance, are perfectly clear, and adequately set down in the existing codes. For centuries, those sources have taught that no individual is entitled to assume that the blood running through the veins of any other person is redder than his own (Babylonian Talmud, tractate *Sanhedrin* folio 74a) – least of all when the other person is a gentile.

In some versions, that ruling certainly applies to an Israeli soldier held captive, whose release in return for hundreds of murderous terrorists would necessarily endanger the lives of other Jews. It also provides a rule of thumb for deciding whether *halakhah* permits IDF soldiers to carry out orders to cause the death of one of their comrades who they observe being led into captivity (Goldstein 2001). In the most warped and grotesque of recent renditions (*Sefer Torat Ha-Melekh*, published in 2010 under the auspices of an especially fundamentalist and right-wing academy located in Samaria), the 'individualistic' perspective has also been understood to require the strict application to all gentiles – qua gentiles – of the unabashedly aggressive conduct that, in this much maligned reading, *halakhah* justifies against gentiles on the grounds that whatever inclination there may be to exercise moderation in warfare is negated by the teaching: 'If someone comes to kill you; strike him to death first' (A. Shapira and Elitzur 2010).

An *autonomous* approach to war-related issues, by contrast, grows out of a state-centered focus. Those who adopt this interpretative strategy adopt, therefore, what in other contexts would be considered a quintessentially Clausewitzian view of the political consequences that wars must entail. In the words of one recent rabbinic formulation (which bear all the marks of a direct polemic against *Torat Ha-Melekh*):

> War is not measured on a *personal* gauge, but on a *communal* gauge. [The fact
> that] an individual Jew happens to come into conflict with a gentile does not turn
> a personal confrontation into a general war. Only when one *community* fights
> against another can the confrontation be considered warfare (Ariel 2010: 375;
> emphasis in original).

At its most sophisticated, this perspective has given rise to a classification of military situations that clearly differentiates between separate categories of international hostilities. Only in their least structured form (indiscriminate 'disturbances'), can these be said to permit individuals to respond on their own initiative, and thereby carry out what could be termed 'the duty to fight' (*mitzvat lehimah*). True 'warfare', however, is distinguished by the fact that it constitutes a Divinely ordained commandment (*mitzvat milkhamah*) which has necessarily to take into account the general welfare of the polity as a whole (Gutel 1994; Lau 2003). Translated into the almost metaphysical terms favored by one school of Rabbi Kook's disciples, true warfare thus attains powers of metamorphosis that are depicted in terms which would not appear out of place in one of Hegel's essays:

> When a community fights no account is taken of an individual as an individual. This is a different level of reality. When the people of Israel confronts the reality of war – suddenly the calculation changes, suddenly each individual is only one limb in the body of the community … This is a level of spiritual revelation that … inspires the will to self-sacrifice, increases the love of the Almighty and the desire for *kiddush ha-shem* … In war we cease to be individuals. We become a collective (Tau 1983: 20–1).

There is more to this outlook than wishful thinking. A state-centered perspective, however phrased, also has severely practical *halakhic* consequences. Necessarily, it affects decisions for war and peace, and hence was mobilized in opposition to exhortations that religious soldiers disobey orders during the 2005 disengagement:

> It is inconceivable that every soldier or officer in uniform, together with his rabbi … might assume the function of the Chief of Staff, Foreign Minister, Minister of Defense and Prime Minister. The issue is not one of individual conscience … but the renewal of the awareness of legitimate authority and the promotion of sensitivity to collective responsibility (Lichtenstein 2005a).

More recently, the same state-centered perspective has likewise been used to influence the rationale affecting *halakhic* opinions on the justification of accepting the exorbitant terms demanded by Sergeant Shalit's captives for his release. In this reading, the threat posed to the personal safety of individual Israelis by the danger that hundreds of terrorists will be set free pales in importance when compared to the damage that would be caused to the notion of the State and all it stands for were an IDF soldier to be left in hostile hands. Hence, the mishnaic prohibition against the payment of an exorbitant price is irrelevant.

> [It] made no reference to a person taken captive during the course of a general war, and certainly not to a soldier who was sent into battle as a conscript to fight on behalf of the state … the subject of Shalit [is not a personal issue] but has to be considered part of a special *halakhic* framework appertaining to war, the state and the army (Gisser 2011).

Meta-halakhic interpretative strategies relative to *dinei tzavah u-milkhamah* adopt a perspective that is even wider in terms of its scope. Although certainly cognizant of warfare's character as a political action likely to most immediately affect the fortunes of the Jewish state, its focus is broadened to incorporate the impact that war-related activities undertaken by Jews might also in the long-term exert on the welfare of Jewish communities worldwide.

In some respects, this perspective is deeply embedded in traditional rabbinic thinking. For instance, concern for the welfare of Jewry at large has long been adduced as an excuse for the otherwise unjustifiable manner in which the biblical figure of Mordechai is reported to have encouraged Esther to offer her body to King Ahasuerus, and thereby contravene explicit religious guidelines respecting sexual mores. Bluntly put, there was no other way of saving Jewry from annihilation (Passamaneck 2003: 133–54). In the modern age, similar rationales were adduced by diaspora rabbinic authorities when ruling that Jews not attempt to avoid the draft, despite the near certainty that army service would require them to violate the sabbath and other ritual commandments.[10]

Since the IDF's adoption of conscription in 1948, the welfare of Jewry at large has also figured as a consideration in at least two other military-related contexts, both of more specific concern to Israel. The first, and certainly the most important in terms of its numerical impact, centers on the ultra-Orthodox (*haredi*) contention that the survival of the Jewish people is altogether independent of military activity and depends entirely on the study of the *Torah*, a duty so sublime that it outweighs all other religious obligations put together. Distilled from centuries of reverence for scholasticism, that teaching was repeated even at the height of the Holocaust by influential *haredi* rabbis in Europe. It is also consistently advanced by their successors, in both the Diaspora and the State of Israel. Notwithstanding the differences in context, the message remains the same. Scholarship, far from being just an intellectual exercise, is essentially a sacrament: the prime means whereby

----

10   See, for instance, the warnings about the dire consequences that could flow from any suspicion that Jews were draft dodging voiced by Rabbi David Tzvi Hoffman (1843–1921), the undisputed spiritual leader of neo-orthodoxy in late nineteenth-century Germany. Even the dangers of sabbath violations had to give way to the near certainty that draft dodging danger that 'is bound to bring about a *hillul ha-shem* because Jew haters will say that altogether Jews do not obey the country's laws'. Hoffman 1926). Almost precisely the same line of reasoning was adopted by Rabbi Soloveitchik in the 1950s, when ruling that rabbinical students at Yeshiva University be encouraged to enlist rather than take advantage of their exemption from the draft. One reason was that, absent sufficient Orthodox candidates, 'reform and semi-reform rabbis would fill all the vacancies [for military chaplains] and thus be afforded the opportunity to spread their influence among thousands of young men – the soldiers of today and the leaders of tomorrow'. But in addition: 'such a state of affairs would not remain an internal issue within the confines of the Jewish community, but would necessarily also affect our relationship with the non-Jewish community. … it might affect the political status of the Jew in this country and prove disastrous. This alone is a legitimate reason for subsuming the coercive situation under the class of pikuah nefesh' (Helfgot 2005: 55–6).

Jews achieve communion with God and re-enact the theophany at Mount Sinai. Hence, Torah study guarantees Divine protection. Absent that gift, this-worldly military agencies are powerless. Critics of the deferments (in effect exemptions) that by 2020 are expected to be granted to one in every four Jewish Israeli males of draft age warn of the catastrophic implications for Israel's societal cohesion; but *haredi* spokesmen remain insistent that their contribution to the defense of Jewry justifies whatever price has to be paid. As Rabbi Eliezer Menachem Shach (1898–2001) one of the most authoritative of all leaders of *haredi* Jewry once famously declared: 'Other than the *Torah* we have no security; neither soldiers nor the IDF will help us' (cited Doron 2008: 504).

An altogether different (and somewhat surprising) version of the Jewry-wide perspective that flows from the meta-*halakhic* strategy is to be found in justification that Rabbi Soloveitchik is reported to have provided for the fact that Israeli soldiers, by endangering themselves whilst on military service, are violating the commandment 'And you shall live by them'. His initial arguments follow time-honored rabbinic conventions and are not especially remarkable. Drawing on earlier rabbinic discussions as to whether a person is permitted to interrupt the flight of an arrow that threatens to strike at several other individuals, they lead to a straightforward conclusion: 'We can say that a danger to the community makes permissible a danger to the individual … it is by placing himself in serious danger that the individual lessens the danger to the community of which he is a part. Hence, his action is not considered to endanger himself but to save himself (and others)'. The next part of the analysis is somewhat trickier. Surveying the dangers threatening Jewish survival in his age, R. Soloveitchik concludes that the greatest is posed by assimilation in the Diaspora. Hence, anything that delays that process is praiseworthy, whereas anything that threatens to accelerate it is to be decried. This leads, finally, to what by any criterion other than a meta-*halakhic* perspective deserves to be considered a leap in the dark:

> And it appears that would the Jewish state in the Land of Israel to disappear, assimilation in America and Europe would be very much greater … . Hence, we can say that the self-sacrifice of individuals who are killed in the Land of Israel comes under the category of individuals who place their lives in possible danger in order to save many others from certain danger (cited in Schechter 1994: 98).

Finally, note must be taken of the perspective that underlies the fourth type of interpretative strategy identified in this chapter: the *extra-halakhic framework*. In this case, the focus of attention seems to go beyond the confines of the Jewish people altogether, and to encompass humanity at large. Hence, the wars currently being waged against the State of Israel are not fought by the enemy in order to attain material assets, such as territory or access to resources. Rather, they are essentially 'expressive', in that their purpose is to eradicate what the Jewish people stands for in the world and to impose an entirely different way of life and set of values. Thus seen, Jewish soldiers in the IDF do not fight solely on behalf of the interests of the state that they have sworn to defend. They are in the vanguard of a struggle between forces of good and forces of evil, the dimensions of which are truly cosmic in their compass. As a recently retired chief rabbi of the IDF put it: 'When the IDF goes to war, its purpose is not to kill in order to destroy the world. The entire function of the war should be to eradicate the evil and corruption that exist in the world' (Rontski 2006: 227).

In some quarters, this interpretation of Israel's geo-strategic situation has spawned a viewpoint that empowers rabbis as strategic as well as spiritual authorities. As such, they are entitled to a voice in both the definition of war aims and the determination of the methods by which it is to be waged (Seeman 2005). Alternative conclusions, however, have also been drawn:

- For one thing, and as has already been seen, sensitivity to the enormity of the consequences of military action has sometimes resulted in the pronouncement of what amount to self-denying rabbinic ordnances. These relinquish all but the faintest claims to rabbinic input in many classes of military affairs and instead place the onus of responsibility for strategic decision-making entirely on senior generals and politicians.

- More interestingly, awareness of the cosmic dimensions of Israel's wars has also prompted an interest – albeit still hesitant – in what the IDF's potential allies in the fight against evil, all of whom are heirs to a vastly richer tradition of combat morality, might have to say about battlefield ethics. For example, much though Rabbi Cherlow might deny the charge that he had issued a call 'to be cognizant of the winds of humanism blowing in the world', in point of fact that is precisely what he does do (Cherlow 2003). As he admits: where military matters are concerned, the modern rabbis' task is 'to confront the Jewish – torah inspired – and Divine concept of morality with the western – Christian – secular concept of morality'. Cherlow has no doubt that, on examination, the former will be found superior. Nevertheless, it suffers from so many lacunae that the former too will often have to be followed. Implicit in this position (although certainly not directly articulated) was the suggestion that – given the patent inadequacy of traditional *halakhic* sources in the area of combat morality – *dinei tzavah u-milkhamah* might have to adopt international norms not just as a general 'standard' of conduct but, in addition, as a specific set of 'rules' to which Jewish soldiers are as committed to adhere as any other.[11]

It is far too early to attempt to predict which (if any) of the four interpretational strategies outlined in this chapter might eventually be accepted as preferable to others. As has repeatedly been stressed, by the standards of a tradition that

---

11   On the difference between a general rule (such as the duty to drive safely), which qualifies as a 'standard' and a specific rule (for example, a reduced speed limit in an urban area), see Sullivan 1992.

is used to measuring the time devoted to analysis of any subject in terms of centuries, the current discourse on war-related issues must be considered still in its infancy. Moreover, that discourse is constantly being modified and refined as a result of the persistent pressure exerted on its content by the multiplicity of novel military situations in which Israeli troops find themselves involved. Precisely for those reasons, however, it deserves to be considered one of the most fascinating developments in contemporary Jewish political life. How *dinei tzavah u-milkhamah* are addressed and analyzed – and, consequently, how practicing Jewish men and women in Israeli military service are advised to behave by their spiritual guides – provides an insight into the ways in which this segment of Jewry is responding to the moral challenges posed by the need to exercise armed force. The variety of interpretational strategies that have been developed in an effort to frame that response bears testimony to the enormity of the intellectual efforts being invested in the task.

Chapter 10
Epilogue:
From *Haredi* Non-enlistment to
an All-volunteer IDF?

This book has focused on the revolutions occurring in public perceptions of the role played by Judaism in the Israeli military and, more generally, on the changing role of Jewish religious issues in the wider framework of relationships between the IDF and Israeli society. Briefly summarized, the transformations have involved shifts of tone as well as substance. During the decades that immediately followed the declaration of Israel's independence in 1948, the overall tenor of discourse on the nexus between religion and military service, within military and civilian circles alike, was emphatically affirmative. Notwithstanding occasional evidence of friction between observant and non-observant troops, religion was, overall, thought to be a source of unit cohesion. For one thing, the practice of traditional Jewish rites and practices was said to help bind the vast majority of military personnel to the common legacy of cultural associations and collective myths that lie at the root of Israel's Jewish identity. Additionally, common service on the part of men and women educated in separate 'religious' and 'secular' environments seemed to create an atmosphere of harmony that effectively quarantined the IDF from the intra-Jewish dissensions that otherwise permeate Israeli society and politics. Since the early 1990s, however, that image has become increasingly difficult to sustain. Religion, far from exerting a homogenizing influence on the IDF, is now more often regarded as a source of tension.

As previous chapters have shown, a variety of circumstances have contributed to this transmutation. Some are political, such as the injection of religious *motifs* into the acrimonious debates that frequently erupt over the future disposition of the Territories conquered by the IDF in 1967, and the fate of the Jewish settlements subsequently established in those areas. Other causes for the change in mood deserve to be considered more deeply cultural, especially when related to the possible impact of the increasing prominence of 'national–religious' soldiers on the cohesion of the Force. Since the advent of the new millennium, however, the concerns raised by both of those developments have been overshadowed by yet a third: the exponential growth in the numbers of ultra-orthodox (*haredi*) citizens who claim – and are granted – indefinite draft deferments on the grounds that 'the study of the *torah* is their profession'. The current prominence of *haredi* non-service in Israeli public discourse places an entirely new complexion on the wider subject of the intersection between Judaism and the IDF. Therein lays the justification for placing discussion of the issue in the concluding chapter of the present book. Hitherto, it has proved possible – even if increasingly difficult – to meet the challenge of religiously-based friction in the IDF by adopting a series of accommodations. Each adjustment has, of course, necessitated a degree of change to one part or another of the framework within which tensions between religion and military service have been played out. Overall, nevertheless, the superstructure holding 'religious' and 'secular' components of the Force together has proved remarkably resilient, with the result that several of the institutions and practices established as long ago as 1948 still play a vital role in ensuring that religiously-based frictions are contained within manageable bounds. The distinction of *haredi* non-service lies in that it threatens to upset that delicate balance. This time, it appears, no amount of tinkering with the system will suffice. Instead, a major overhaul of the overarching framework seems to be required.

This chapter seeks to explain why that is so. It begins by tracing the stages by which the issue of *haredi* non-service has moved from the periphery to the center of Israeli public debate over the links between religion and military service, and identifies the actors chiefly responsible for that realignment. Thereafter, attention shifts to the underlying inferences and implications of *haredi* non-enlistment. At this level, the principal argument is that the significance of the phenomenon lies in the ways in which it straddles two of the most crucial current debates in Israeli public life: the proportionate degrees of Israel's commitment to being democratic as well as Jewish; and the extent of the justification for the IDF's continued characterization as a 'people's army'. That intersection of issues, it will be argued, explains why the consequences of whatever resolution is found for the problems posed by *haredi* non-enlistment are unlikely to be restricted solely to the realm of relations between the 'religious' and 'secular' wings of Israeli society. Because the phenomenon impinges so blatantly on the demographic complexion of Israel's armed forces, its effects will necessarily also extend to the far wider realm of military–organizational reform.

The Significance of *Haredi* Non-enlistment

At the level of ideology, which perforce carries considerable weight in a state that owes its establishment to the fusion of several variants of the Zionist idea (Shimoni, 1995), *haredi* draft deferments generate friction because of what they represent. They signify nothing less than the irreconcilability of the ultra-orthodox and Zionist conceptions of security. Non-*haredim*, even when religiously observant, overwhelmingly posit the dependence of Israel's security on material assets. The lesson most derive from the Holocaust, especially, is that the survival of an independent Jewish polity in the land of Israel must in the last analysis depend on the state's acquisition and utilization of all available weapons of war, including nuclear bombs. For *haredim*, however, 'security' constitutes far more than a physical condition. At its most sublime, it is a state of salvation, brought about by the metaphysical reconciliation of Jews to their Maker. Material assets are irrelevant to the attainment of that goal. It can only be reached by devotion, prayer and – above all – by incessant study of the sacred texts generically designated *torah*, a duty so sublime that it outweighs all other religious obligations put together. Distilled from centuries of reverence for scholasticism, the mantra that *torah* saves, physically as well as spiritually, was repeated even at the height of the Holocaust by several of the most influential *haredi* rabbis in Europe. (Schweid 1994) It is likewise advanced by their successors in the State of Israel. Notwithstanding the differences in context, the message remains the same. Scholarship, far from being just an intellectual exercise, is a sacrament: it constitutes the prime means whereby Jews achieve communion with God and hence attain Divine protection. Absent that gift, this-worldly military agencies are powerless.

As long as the *haredi* community amounted to little more than a small sect, essentially consisting of a remnant of a way of life that had been savaged by the Holocaust, such notions could be regarded with a mixture of tolerance and disdain. That was certainly Ben-Gurion's opinion. His original promise, made as early as 1947, that in the future state of Israel a few hundred *haredi* students would receive draft deferments, was predicated on the prediction that the entire arrangement would rapidly become obsolete. After all, ultra-Orthodoxy would soon succumb to the forces of progress, as represented by Zionism and modernity, and thus inexorably wither away.

As matters turned out, however, nothing of the sort occurred. On the contrary, the *haredi* world is now experiencing a renaissance of unprecedented scope and, from a *haredi* point of view, near-miraculous proportions (Rose 2006, 2008). Thanks in part to one of the highest birth rates in the western world, *haredi* communities have expanded and branched out, establishing vibrant and near-autonomous enclaves in various Israeli towns and cities, as well as in specific areas of the United States, Canada, the United Kingdom, France, south America, Australia and Belgium too. More to the point, in Israel, especially, *haredim* have come closer than ever before to realizing their ideal and establishing 'a society of learners', one in which a life devoted to scholarship is not reserved solely for the gifted few but is made available to virtually all (provided that they are of the correct sex). *Haredi* conventions assume, as a matter of course, that the males of the community will be enrolled in a *yeshivah* virtually at birth, and remain full-time students for much of the remainder of their lives. The family's financial needs are met by the incomes attained by the student's spouse, by donations received from wealthy members of the community at home and abroad, by social security child support payments and, most significantly, from government stipends to *yeshivah* students, payment of which *haredi* political parties have for the past three decades managed to ensure will be guaranteed in every Israeli national budget.

Haredim consider the resultant situation to have come as close as is imaginable to the construction of heaven on earth. To non-*haredim*, however, it appears to be a grotesque and costly anomaly (Berman 1999). Not only are *haredi* males, as a group and without reference to their individual cerebral talents and state of health, granted official leave to avoid the physical risks that citizens who are drafted into military service face as a matter of course. Worse still, in return for an assertion that they are devoting themselves to full-time *torah* studies, an assertion that no government agency ever seeks to verify, *haredim* also receive from the State a student stipend that, in effect, ensures their dependence on the political leadership that has lobbied for its payment.

Public pressure to put a stop to that feedback loop of incentives to *haredi* non-service (and, in economic terms, non-productivity) was surprisingly slow to gather momentum. In other areas of public interest, military as well as social, Israelis were by the 1980s evincing an increasing readiness to take to the streets – so much so that mass demonstrations had by then already become a feature of the country's political life (Lehman-Wilzig 1992). But for as long as the preferential treatment granted to *haredim* appeared to be a fairly limited phenomenon, unfair but not intolerable, that particular issue seemed immune to the trend. Besides, the delicacy of the balance between the major political blocs in the *Knesset*, which frequently gave *haredi* parties a decisive voice in determining the composition of the ruling coalition, also inhibited incitement to protest. After all, which politician would dare run the risk of antagonizing the *haredim* and thereby reducing his or her chances of attaining, or retaining, high office?

Ultimately, the initiative for change came from Israel's Supreme Court (ISC). This was not an entirely unexpected development. Contrary to the stand-off and non-interventionist posture that it had studiously cultivated during the first decades of Israel's statehood, the Supreme Court had ever since the late 1970s begun to play an increasingly active role in domestic public life. As a result, and following precedents already set in such other western democracies as France, Germany, Italy and especially the United States, Israel thereafter began to experience a growing degree of judicial involvement in value based political affairs (Segev 2008). This development found particular expression in the changes that took place in the ways in which the Supreme Court acted in its capacity as the country's High Court of Justice. It dismantled many of the institutional and legal barriers that had thereto impeded direct petitions, in the process becoming the most accessible of all supreme courts in the western world. Any person, organization or legal entity that considered itself to have been wronged by any action taken by the government or any part of the executive could petition the ISC (whereas only 381 appeals had been lodged in 1970, the numbers grew to 802 in 1980, to 1,308 in 1990, and to 2,209 in 1994; Barzilai 1999: 19). Still more significantly, the Court matched its readiness to entertain claims against governmental agencies with a willingness to intervene in matters thereto considered political and hence outside the judiciary's jurisdiction. Especially was that so once Justice Aharon Barak, who was appointed to the bench of the Court in 1978 and became its President in 1998, embarked on a policy of 'judicial activism', which propelled the Supreme Court to the very forefront of public policymaking.

Barak's initiatives affected several areas of Israeli national security concern (Am. Cohen and S. Cohen 2011). Their effect on the issue of *haredi* non-service was, however, especially pronounced. Prior to the late 1980s, the Supreme Court – even though overwhelmingly composed of persons whose outlooks and lifestyles differed very markedly from those of *haredim* – had persistently refused to even consider the petitions on this issue that had been tabled with persistent regularity by Mr. Yehudah Ressler, a Tel-Aviv lawyer. Ressler, the judges repeatedly ruled, possessed no 'standing' in the case since he could not prove that he had suffered personal damage as a result of the government's grant of *haredi* exemptions. In what way, then, could he expect to receive recompense from the Court? But in 1988, Justice Barak, who presided over a discussion of yet another Ressler petition, began to take a significantly different tack. The prime criterion that the Court had to consider, he now argued, was not that of 'standing' but the 'reasonableness' of the government's conduct. At this particular juncture, he ruled, *haredi* draft deferments could still be said to meet that test – just. However, he warned that the time was fast approaching when such might no longer be the case (High Court Judgment [HCJ] 910/86, Ressler Vs Minister of Defense, 1988).

Exactly a decade later, in 1998, Barak ruled in response to another petition (presented on that occasion by a professor of law) that the quantity of *haredi* deferments had indeed begun to exceed the bounds of 'reasonableness'. True, he was still reluctant to proclaim the entire arrangement to be unconstitutional. But he did rule that he would be forced to do so unless the *Knesset* introduced legislation regulating the issue (HCJ 3267/97, Rubinstein Vs Minister of Defense, 1998). The Government (led, rather confusingly, by Ehud Barak – no relation to Aharon Barak) attempted to deflect that ultimatum. First, it established a commission of enquiry, chaired by former Supreme Court Justice Zvi Tal, with a mandate to formulate a new system that would somehow square the circle, by satisfying both *haredi* demands that draft deferments remain in place and the Court's insistence that they be kept to a 'reasonable' level. After two years of near-herculean labor, the commissioners claimed to have accomplished the impossible. *Haredim*, they proposed, should be given several choices: they could enlist for shortened terms, opt to substitute civic service for military duty (both abbreviated) and – in both cases – defer any decision on the matter for a year or two beyond the mandatory draft age of 18.[1] Seizing on this complicated panacea, the Government eventually incorporated the main body of Tal's suggestions into a Service Deferral Law which, after a testy debate, Israel's parliament passed into law in July 2002. The vote clearly reflected the unhappy mood of the *Knesset*. Fifty one members voted in favor, 41 opposed, five abstained and 22 demonstratively absented themselves from the chamber.

Even before the new law come into force, it was clear that it could not be considered the last word on the issue of *haredi* draft deferments. Indeed, incorporated into the legislation was a clause specifying that this was to be regarded as a temporary arrangement, which would have to be reviewed every five years. Sensing a change in atmosphere, opponents of draft deferments decided not to wait that long. As early as July 2005, one group petitioned the Supreme

---

1   The various options are described in some detail in Bick 2010.

Court on the grounds that, notwithstanding the passage of the new law, nothing had been done to put it into effect. Specifically, the Government had failed to establish any of the administrative machinery required in order to draft *haredim* and ensure their service in either the military or civilian posts. As a result, the number of *haredi* enlistments had in fact declined. Although the justices shared the petitioners' disappointment with the situation, the truth of which was also admitted by defense counsel for the Government, by a vote of seven to two they nevertheless decided to grant the Government further time in order to rectify it. (Justice Aharon Barak, nearing the end of his presidency of the Court, sided with the majority; HCJ 6427/02, Movement for Quality of Government in Israel Vs The Knesset, 2005). With audible relief, members of the *Knesset* seconded that exercise in wishful thinking. Hence, in 2007 by a vote of 56 to nine, and without much argument at all, the Service Deferral Law was extended for a further five years.

The indefatigable Mr. Ressler was not so easily fooled. With good reason, he suspected that coalition considerations would prevent any Government from attempting to coerce *haredim* to enlist in large numbers. (The general election held in 2009 provided further confirmation. Mr. Netanyahu's Likud party, which eventually put together a government, had won less mandates than its prime rival, Kadimah [26 Vs 27]). Hence, he once again petitioned the Supreme Court, arguing that the injustice inherent in massive *haredi* exemptions from military service had clearly become intolerable. Citing data provided by both the State Comptroller and the IDF, he showed that the hopes invested in the Service Deferral Law had been utterly misplaced. Instead of exercising the options for various forms of service contained in the law, the vast majority of *haredim* were simply ignoring its provisions. Common sense demanded that the entire arrangement therefore be declared unconstitutional.

This time, the Court – by a majority of nine to three – agreed. Justice Dorit Benisch, who had succeeded Barak as President of the ISC in 2006 and wrote the principal opinion, in the late spring of 2012 declared herself convinced that, given the facts on the ground, the law originally passed in 2002 clearly suffered from faults that were not simply administrative, and hence susceptible to eventual repair, but inherent ('genetic'). Instead of promoting equality of burden sharing, a basic characteristic of any democracy, it in fact exacerbated differentials between *haredi* and non-*haredi* segments of society, which had now become entirely disproportionate. Under no circumstances, therefore, could the existing Law be renewed. Instead, it must be left to die a natural death when its term expired on August 1st 2012 and replaced by alternative legislation (HCJ 6298/07, Ressler Vs the *Knesset*, 2012).

Benisch's ruling created havoc. Initially, Prime Minister Netanyahu attempted to resort to the time-honored stalling device of appointing yet another commission of enquiry, with a mandate to come up with a solution to the problem. However, he disbanded this body as soon as it became evident that the commissioners, who were chaired by *Knesset* member Yochanan Plessner, were formulating a scheme that, because it would involve enlisting large numbers of *haredim*, would prove politically unacceptable. One result was that the Kadimah party, which had agreed to enter Mr.

Netanyahu's coalition only a month previously, in July 2012 attacked him for giving in to *haredi* blackmail and stormed out of the Government, leaving the Prime Minister with a reduced majority. Secondly, and yet more pertinently, the disbandment of the Plessner Commission left the entire issue of *haredi* service up in the air. Consequently, the August 2012 deadline for the expiry of the 2002 Law came and went without any replacement in sight. Besides, since the *Knesset* was in summer recess, no alternative could in any case be tabled. To all intents and purposes, therefore, anarchy prevailed. Formally, all-male *haredim* were now liable for the draft. But no effective machinery was in place in order to bring them to induction centers.

Matters were even further complicated by the results of the general elections to the *Knesset*, held on 22 January 2013, nine months earlier than the date mandated by law. Mr. Netanyahu had calculated that by bringing forward election day he could benefit from the upswing in his personal popularity ratings induced by his effective appearance at the United Nations General Assembly in New York the previous September and what was perceived to be his adept handling of the military confrontation with the *Hamas* organization in Gaza (Operation 'Pillar of Cloud', mid-November 2012). Those hopes proved ephemeral. Although the right-wing alliance led by Netanyahu (*Likud-Beitenu*) emerged as the largest party in the *Knesset*, with 31 seats (out of 120), that number was 11 less than the figure he had previously commanded. The real electoral laurels went elsewhere: first to *Yesh Atid* ('There is a Future', an entirely new party founded just a year previously by a well-known journalist and TV personality, Mr. Yair Lapid), which gained 19 seats and thus became the second largest party in the *Knesset*; and then to *Ha-Bayit Ha-Yehudi* ('The Jewish House', a remodeled version of the old National-Religious Party, led by a successful businessman and another political novice, Mr. Naftali Benet), with 12. Combined, then, these two leaders controlled as many parliamentary seats as did Netanyau.

Notwithstanding their differences on many foreign policy and security issues – Lapid broadly campaigned on a centrist platform whilst Benet leaned far more obviously to the national–religious right – the two men had much in common. Both were representative of Israel's urban upper-middle classes; both held out visions of social change and 'new politics'; and most importantly both insisted that Israel's *haredi* community had for far too long shirked its civic duty to carry a fair share of the country's economic and security burdens. Building on that basis of broad agreement, they quickly formed an 'alliance', pledging that neither would enter into a coalition agreement with Netanyahu until they had jointly received assurances that the new government would take the necessary steps to ensure what they termed 'burden sharing' – broadly recognized to be a euphemism for sizable *haredi* enlistment and a concurrent reduction in stipends received by *haredim* who were not part of the labor market.

For once, *haredi* parties were powerless to negotiate away those threats by the sort of wheeling-dealing that had in the past characterized the process of coalition formation. Even though they too had increased their share of the vote in 2013, together gaining 18 seats (three more than in the previous parliament), this was insufficient a number to enable Netanyahu to form a majority coalition (requiring 61 seats) in which they would participate and either Lapid or Benet would not. The result was deadlock. Lapid and Benet made it plain that they regarded the enlistment/non-enlistment of *haredim* as a litmus test for their right to be considered equal citizens of the polity in which they live. But *haredi* leaders were equally adamant that they could not possibly cooperate with any government that was prepared to divert significant numbers of *haredi* males, especially those in their late teens and early twenties, from the full-time study of the *Torah*. As one rabbinic authority wrote in an open letter published in the *haredi* press:

> For this is the essence of our existence and our task in life. And if they [the Israeli authorities] take this away from us, it will be the most enormous catastrophe to befall us because we will not be able to fulfill the Almighty's wish. It is a matter of life and death (Steinmann, 2013).

Other spokesmen were even more uncompromisingly adverserial, warning that *haredim* would 'in their thousands and tens of thousands' go to prison rather than enlist. 'The study of the Torah is non-negotiable' (R. Iskar Dov Rokach ['the Rabbi of Belz'], cited in Ben-David 2013).

Future Scenarios

Discussions about how to unfreeze that stalemate are no longer restricted to members of the judicial elite, who dominated the Tal Commission in the year 2000. Each of the non-*haredi* Jewish political parties that participated in the 2013 elections put forward some form of solution to the problem of 'burden sharing'. Both before and after the elections, so too did researchers at the think tanks that seek to shape public opinion (Elran and Ben-Meir 2012, Ben-Basat et. al.2013) and several columnists in the national press, from both extremes of the political spectrum (for example, Ben 2012, Avneri 2013, Pollak 2013, Weinberg 2013).

Almost without exception the proposals thus tabled rest on two propositions, both of which had also been premised in the Tal Report. The first is the need for gradualism. Hence, even those who advocate the drafting all *haredi* 18 year-olds males (and it is noteworthy that most proponents of *haredi* enlistment are prepared to grant exemptions to limited percentages of especially gifted *torah* students) preach the virtues of an incremental approach. The numbers of *haredim* enlisted, they promise, will be ratcheted up in annual installments stretched over a protracted period. The second proposition is that whatever specific scheme is adopted will have to be consonant with the notion that national service – and specifically national service in the armed forces – would remain both a military necessity and a societal norm.

Self-evident though the latter proposition is often made to seem, its validity is in fact sometimes called into question. Significantly, this is not because of differences of opinion with respect to the equity of *haredi* exclusion from a system of universal conscription but because of reservations as to the necessity of that system's continuation. From this perspective, complicated computations involving the proportion of *haredim* to be drafted each year really place the cart before the horse. A prior question is whether their service is required at all.

Of late that has become an increasingly pertinent enquiry. After all, ever since the 1990s doubts have in any case been cast on the validity of the IDF's claim to constitute an all-inclusive 'people's army'. One flaw in that depiction, as left-wing domestic critics of Israel's military never tire of pointing out, is exposed by the consistency with which all Israeli governments have deliberately acquiesced in the non-enlistment of the vast majority of Israel's Arab citizens – a policy that reinforces their marginal societal status (Kimmerling 2001, Kemp 2004). Other observers with less blatantly ideological axes to grind, adopt a milder tone, but nevertheless highlight with equal force additional deviations from the ideal of universal service. Under Treasury pressure to rationalize its work force, they point out, the IDF has since the 1980s evinced a growing willingness to adopt what amount to differential draft policies – granting early discharges from duty to conscripts who it judges to be superfluous whilst offering salaries to those whom it would like to see 'sign on' for a year or two of professional service. Pouncing upon such indications, individual academics, journalists and a motley assortment of internet bloggers have sporadically suggested that it is high time to reform the IDF, most drastically by altogether abandoning conscription and bringing Israel's military into line with those of other western democracies by transforming it into a professional and all-volunteer force (S. Cohen 1995, Shelach 2003; Yehezkeli 2009).

Admittedly, no person in senior military or political office has ever seconded so drastic an idea. But a growing number have conceded that operational and financial considerations certainly warrant the construction of a 'smaller and smarter' IDF, a project that would necessarily require the reduction of IDF manpower and a greater reliance on labor-saving military technology. In 2009, the then Chief of the General Staff (Lt.-General Gabi Ashkenazy) went one step further and suggested that Israel retain only the façade of universal conscription, principally by instituting a program of compulsory civic service, which would be staffed by persons for whom the IDF had no use. As pundits pointed out, without acknowledging the fact, the Chief of Staff was barely a whisker away from suggesting that the IDF be turned into an all-volunteer force (Pfeffer 2009, accessed 19 September 2012).

Precisely because it seems so intractable, the phenomenon of *haredi* non-service could, in the long-term, supply the final push required to shift public and official opinion in that direction. *Haredim*, after all, are no more likely to agree to perform civic than military duties (logically, since the former constitutes as much a digression from *Torah* study as does the latter). And even were a new government coalition prepared to coerce them to enlist *en masse* in the IDF, whatever benefits might accrue to the military from their service is likely to be far outweighed by the costs. At the very least, all *haredim* would demand the right to be granted conditions of duty equivalent to those presently enjoyed by servicemen in the *Netzach Yehudah* and *Shachar* programs (above pp. 5–7): kitchens that conform to the strictest standards of Jewish dietary laws; extra leisure time for prayer and study; and – above all – service in an environment that observes strict gender segregation. In their evidence to the Plessner commission in 2012, IDF representatives claimed that, if push came to shove, they were prepared to meet all such requirements.[2] But they also left the commissioners in no doubt that the costs involved would be considerable, not just in financial and administrative terms but also, and especially, because of the negative impact that an influx of *haredim* would exert on current IDF programs directed at gender integration in all units.

Given that audit of swings and roundabouts, it is not far-fetched to surmise that military planners as well as politicians might well consider that they stand to lose more from *haredi* conscription than to gain, and that they (and the country as a whole) would benefit by unconditionally excusing all *haredim* from the draft. One former CO of the IDF Manpower Branch has indeed publicly advocated such a scheme (Stern 2009: 281–8). It is inconceivable, however, that the Supreme Court, in its present mood, would ever sanction a policy that provided blanket service exemptions to just one specified group in Israeli Jewish society. Equity would require an all-or-nothing arrangement: either every citizen is subject to conscription, or all are excused and the IDF hence transformed into an organization in which service is entirely voluntary. Given so stark a choice, the pressures for institutional military renovation unleashed by the religiously-motivated phenomenon of *haredi* non-service might indeed dovetail with those independently being generated by the operational, technological and financial arguments in favor of the establishment of an all-volunteer IDF. Combined, they might even create a mood capable of investing that outcome with an aura of inevitability.

Only with the assistance of a supreme leap of faith, spiced with a heavy dose of naïveté, is it plausible to imagine that the transformation of the IDF into an all-volunteer force would remove religious frictions from the list of issues threatening to undermine military cohesion in Israel. On the contrary, one of the massive ironies of the present situation is that the abandonment of conscription, even if it does remove the stigma presently attached *haredi* non-enlistment, could well exacerbate other divisions that have their roots in religious commitments. That prediction would seem to carry particular weight once consideration turns to the effect of a transition to an all-volunteer force on the IDF's composition. Even under present conditions (see above p. 11) troops who have graduated from national–religious educational institutions comprise a disproportionate segment of IDF combat troops. They are still more conspicuous in the complement of junior and middle rank officers. It is generally agreed that the abandonment of conscription will accentuate those trends.

---

2   Plessner, 2012, 65–7, accessed 19 September 2012.

True, many secular troops will still be attracted to service: some because they seek a challenge; others because they hope to receive professional qualifications; and in yet a third category because they wish to make service in one of the armed forces their career. Even so, they are likely to be increasingly outnumbered by troops from a national–religious background, who also bring to service a sense of religious mission.

Under those circumstances, the challenges presented by the intersection between religion and military service will continue to be a source of debate and analysis. As such, albeit in a new guise, the need to formulate appropriate responses will remain high on the agenda of public concern.

References

Achituv, Y. 2002. From the Scroll to the Sword (Hebrew), in M. Bar-On, ed., *Shenei Evrei ha-Gesher*. Jerusalem: Yad Ben-Zvi, 414–434.

Agmon, G. 2013. News conference, Brig-Gen. Gadi Agmon, IDF Manpower Directorate, 24 February. <http://www.idf.il/1133-18361-HE/Dover.aspx> (accessed 25 February 2013).

Alkobi, G. 2003. *Tzava Ha-Shem*. Kochav Ya'akov, privately printed.

Allport, G.W. 1954. *The Nature of Prejudice*. Menlo Park, CA: Addison-Wesley.

Almog, O. 2000. *The Sabra: The Creation of the New Jew*. Berkeley: University of California Press.

Alon, Y. 1960. *Masach Shel Chol*. Tel-Aviv: Ha-Kibbutz Ha-Meuchad.

Amitai, Y. and Minka-Brand, H. 2010. Now and in Other Days: Motivating Troops to Carry Out Operations about Which there is Public Controversy, *Ma'archot*, 429: 12–21.

Amital, Y. 1987. The Wars of Israel According to Maimonides (Hebrew), *Techumin*, 8: 454–483.

Amital, Y. 1994. IDF Rules of Engagement in the Light of *halachah* (Hebrew), *Oz*, 1: 184–92.

Aran, G. 1986. From Religious Zionism to Zionist Religion: The Roots of Gush Emunim. *Studies in Contemporary Jewry*, 2: 116–43.

———. 1997. The Father, the Son and the Holy Land, in R. Scott Appleby, ed., *Spokesmen for the Despised: Fundamentalist Leaders in the Middle East*. Chicago: University of Chicago Press, 294–327.

———. 2013. *Kukizm. Shorshei Gush Emunim*. Jerusalem. Carmel.

Ariel, C. 2006. I Will be With Him in Trouble [Psalms 91:15]: (On the activities of the 'rabbinic staff' in the Katif bloc (Hebrew)), *Tzohar*, 26: 81–102.

Ariel, I. 2003. A Reserve Soldier to Whose Unit a Female Soldier was Attached (Hebrew), *Tzohar*, 17: 37–46.

Ariel, Y. 1998. *Shut Be-Ohalah shel Torah*. Kefar Darom: Machon ha-Torah.

———. 2003. Theft from a Gentile during War (Hebrew), *Techumin*, 23: 11–17.

———. 2010. *Halakhah Beyameinu*. Kfar Darom: Machon Hatorah.

Aryeh, N. 2002. Concerning the Initiation of Optional and Mandatory Wars (Hebrew), in E. Shenwald, ed., *Sefer Harel*. Chispin: The Golan Hesder Yeshivat, 88–10.

Artson, B. 1988. *Love Peace and Pursue Peace: A Jewish Response to War and Nuclear Annihilation*. New York: United Synagogue of America.

Avidan, M. 2006. *Masa Bahar*. Sha'alvim: Sha'alvim Hesder Yeshivah.

Aviner, S. 1995. Spoils of War (Hebrew), *Ateret*, 4: 1–2.

——. 1999a. *She'elot u-teshuvot be-inyan tzniyut ba-tzavah*. Jerusalem: Machon Ma'archot Yisrael.

——. 1999b. *Me- Hayyil le- Hayyil*. Jerusalem: Sifriyat Chava.

——. 2000. *Al Diglo*. Jerusalem: Sifriyat Chava.

——. 2004. With Love and Faith (Hebrew). *Be-ahavah u-ve-emunah*, 429: 12.

——. 2006. I Secede, (Hebrew), *Ma'ayanei Ha-Yeshuah*, 234: 1.

Avneri, U. (2013). Equality of Burden-sharing. A Disaster for the IDF (Hebrew), *Haaretz*, 14 February. <http://www/haartez/co/il/misc/2.444/1/1929690> (accessed 17 Feb. 2013).

Azarya, V. 1983. The Israeli Armed Forces, in M. Janowitz and S.D. Wesbrook, eds, *The Political Education of Soldiers*. Beverly Hills: Sage, 118–20.

Azaryahu, M. 1999. The Independence Day Military Parade: A Political History of a Patriotic Ritual, in E. Lomsky-Feder and E. Ben-Ari, eds, *The Military and Militarism in Israeli Society*. Albany: SUNY Press, 89–116.

'B' 2010. The Proportion of Skullcap Wearers in the IDF Tactical Command (Hebrew), *Ma'archot*, 432: 50–57.

Barkai, H. 2004. The Real Costs of the War of Independence (Hebrew), in A. Kadish, ed., *Milkhemet ha-Atzma'ut Tashach-Tashat*. Ramat-Efal: Ministry of Defense, 2: 759–91.

Bar-On, M. 2006. Rear Personnel, Front Personnel: Images of the Rear amongst the Combatants of 1948 (Hebrew), in M. Bar-On and M. Chazan, eds, *Am Be-Milkhamah*. Jerusalem: Yad Ben-Zvi, 467–92.

Baron, S.W. 1977. Review of History, in S. Baron and S. Wise, eds, *Violence and Defense in the Jewish Experience*. Philadelphia: Jewish Publication Society, 3–14.

Bar-Lev, M. 1988. The '*Hesder Yeshivah*' as an Agent of Social Change in Israel, *British Journal of Religious Education*, 11: 38–46.

——.1989. *Bimshoh ha-Yovel*. Tel-Aviv: Midreshet Noam.

Bartal, Y. 1997. Heroes or Cowards? Jews in Polish Armies (1794–1863), in Y. Bartal and Y. Guttman, eds, *Kiyum ve-Shever*, vol. 1. Jerusalem: Shazar Center, 353–67.

Barzilai, G. 1999. Courts as Hegemonic Institutions: The Israeli Supreme Court in a Comparative Perspective, *Israel Affairs*, 5: 15–33.

——. and Inbar, E. 1996. The Use of Force: Israeli Public Opinion on Military Options, *Armed Forces & Society*, 23: 49–80.

Ben, A. 2013. The Solution for Burden Sharing is Simple: A Professional Army (Hebrew). *Haaretz* 3 July. <http://www.haaretz.co.il/news/politi/1.1746739> (accessed 7 March 2013).

Ben-Basat, A. Dehan, M. and Kremnitzer, M. 2013. *Haredim Le-Tzahal*. Jerusalem: Israel Democracy Institute.

Ben-David, D. (ed.) 2010. *Doch Ha-Umah 2009*. Jerusalem: Taub Center for the Study of Social Policy in Israel.

Ben-David, E. 2013. 'We Will All Go to Prison, Not to the Army!' (Hebrew). *Jewish Daily News* 7 February. <http://www.jdn.co.il/news/185164> (accessed 11 February 2013).

Ben-Dor, G. 1973. The Military and the Politics of Integration and Innovation: The Case of the Druze Minority in Israel, *Asian and African Studies*, 9: 339–70.

Ben-Eliezer, U. 1984. The Palmach as a Mirror of its Generation (Hebrew), *Medinah, Mimshal ve-Yachbal*, 23: 29–48.

———. 1998. *The Making of Israeli Militarism*. Albany: SUNY Press.

———. 1998b. Is a Military Coup Possible in Israel? Israel and French-Algeria in Comparative Historical–Sociological Perspective, *Theory and Society*, 27: 311–349.

———. 2000. Do Generals Rule Israel? (Hebrew), in H. Herzog, ed., *Chevrah ba-Marah*. Tel-Aviv: Ramot, 235–269.

Ben-Gurion, D. 1955. *Tzavah u-Bitachon*. Tel-Aviv: Ma'arachot.

———. 1971. *Yihud ve-Yi'ud*. Tel-Aviv: Am Oved.

Ben-Hamu, S. 1982. Concerning the Law of Military Spoils in War – in Israel's Wars (Hebrew), *Noam*, 24: 143–156.

Ben-Meir, Y. 2005. The Disengagement: An Ideological Crisis, *Strategic Assessment* 7, available at: <http://www.inss.org.il/publications.php?cat=25andincat=andread=72> (accessed 19 September 2012).

Ben-Yehuda, N. 1995. *The Masada Myth: Collective Memory and Mythmaking in Israel*. Madison: University of Wisconsin Press.

Berman, E. 1999. Subsidized Sacrifice: State Support of Religion in Israel, *Contemporary Jewry*, 20: 167–200.

Bick, E. 2007. Rabbis and Rulings: Insubordination in the Military and Israeli Democracy, *Journal of Church and State*, 49: 305–327.

———. 2010. The Tal Law: A Missed Opportunity for 'Bridging Social Capital' in Israel, *Journal of Church and State*, 52: 298–322.

Binyamin, M. and Cohen, Y. 2000. *Index Le-hilkhot Tzavah*. Atzmonah: Otzem Academy.

Blau, Y. 2000. Ploughshares into Swords: Contemporary Religious Zionists and Moral Constraints, *Tradition*, 34: 39–60.

Bleich, J.D. 1983. Pre-emptive War in Jewish Law, *Tradition*, 21: 1–39.

———. Survey of Recent *Halakhic* Periodical Literature: Nuclear Warfare, *Tradition*, 22: 84–88.

Bleich, J. 2007. Military Service: Ambivalence and Contradiction, in L. Schiffman and J. Wolowelsky, eds, *War and Peace in the Jewish Tradition*. New York: Yeshiva UP, 415–76.

Blidstein, G. 1983. *Ekronot Medini'im be-Mishnat ha-Rambam*. Ramat Gan: Bar-Ilan UP.

———. 1996. The Treatment of Hostile Civilian Populations: The Contemporary *Halakhic* Discourse in Israel, *Israel Studies*, 1: 27–45.

———. 2002. The State and the Legitimate Use of Force and Coercion in Modern *Halakhic* Thought, *Studies in Contemporary Jewry*, 18: 3–22.

Brenner, U. 1979. In and Out of Uniform (Hebrew), *Kathedra*, 13: 169–75.

Broyde, M.J. 1996. Fighting the War and the Peace: Battlefield Ethics, Peace Talks and Pacifism in the Jewish Tradition, in J. Patout Burns, ed., *War and Its Discontents*. Washington, DC.: Georgetown University Press.

———. 2007. Just Wars, Just Battles and Just Conduct in Jewish Law: Jewish Law is Not a Suicide Pact! in L. Schiffman and J. Wolowelsky, eds, *War and Peace in the Jewish Tradition*. New York: Yeshiva University Press, 1–44.

Bruner, B. 2002. The Oath of Allegiance to the IDF (Hebrew), *Tzohar*, 11: 17–24.

Chamitovsky, Y. 2007. 'War of the *Torah*': Image and Reality in the Mishnaic and Talmudic Academies (Hebrew), *Moed*, 17: 41–66.

Budai-Heiman, R. 2012, The Female Religious Choice of the IDF (Hebrew), in: R. Gal & T. Libel,(eds)., *Bein Ha-Kipah la-Kumtah*, Modan: Ben Shemen, 549–576.

Carmy, S. 2007. The Origin of Nations and the Shadow of Violence: Theological Perspectives on Canaan and Amalek, in L. Schiffman and J. Wolowelsky, eds, *War and Peace in the Jewish Tradition*. New York: Yeshiva University Press, 163–99.

Charlap, Y. 2005. *Hillul Ha-shem* as a Factor in *Halakhic* Decision-making (Hebrew), *Techumin*, 25: 392–400.

Chazan, M. 2009. The Dispute in Mapai over 'Self-restraint' and 'Purity of Arms' during the Arab Revolt, *Jewish Social Studies*, 15: 89–113.

Cherlow, Y. 2002. *Reshut Ha-Rabim*. Petach-Tikva, Petach-Tikvah Hesder Academy.

———. 2002. Questions Respecting Military Ethics (Hebrew), *Tzohar*, 11: 97–104.

———. 2003. Response to R. Rozen (Hebrew), *Tzohar*, 12: 138–9.

———. 2003. *Reshut Ha-Yachid*. Petach Tikva, Petach-Tikvah Hesder Academy.

———. 2005. *Reshut Ha-Tzibbur*. Petach Tikva, Petach-Tikvah Hesder Academy.

———. 2010. *Shut Hitnatkut*. Tel-Aviv: Miskal.

Cohen, A. and Cohen, S. 2011. *Israel's National Security Law: Political dynamics and historical development*. London: Routledge.

Cohen, A. 2007. Non-Jewish Jews: Non-*Halakhic* Approaches to the Question of Joining the Jewish Collective, in S. Cohen and B. Susser, eds, *Ambivalent Jew: Charles Liebman in Memoriam*. New York: JTS Press, 157–172.

———. 2009. The *Kipa* and the Helmet – Image and Reality in the Public Discourse on Religious Zionism and Military Service (Hebrew), *Amadot*, 1: 95–114.

———. and Susser, B. 2000. *Israel and the Politics of Jewish Identity: The Secular-Religious Impasse*. Baltimore: Johns Hopkins University Press.

Cohen, S. 1995. Israel's Defense Force: From a 'People's Army' to a 'Professional Force', *Armed Forces & Society*, 21: 237–254.

———. 1997. *The Scroll or the Sword? Dilemmas of Religion and Military Service in Israel*. London: Harwood.

———. 2005. 'Unlicensed' war in Jewish Tradition: Sources, Consequences and Implications, *Journal of Military Ethics*, 4: 198–213.

——. 2007a. The Re-discovery of Orthodox Jewish Laws Relating to the Military and War in Contemporary Israel, *Israel Studies*, 12: 1–28.

——. 2007b. The Quest for a Corpus of Jewish Military Ethics in Modern Israel, *Journal of Israeli History*, 26: 35–66.

——. 2008. The Inner World of the Religious Soldier (Hebrew), *Psychologia Tzeva'it*, 3: 15–32.

——. 2009. *Israel and its Army: From Cohesion to Confusion*. London: Routledge.

——. 2012. The intrusion of the military into the world of religious Zionist *Torah* Scholarship (Hebrew), in: R. Gal & T. Libel (eds)., *Bein Ha-Kipah la-Kumtah*, Modan: Ben Shemen, 359–400.

Cohen, T. 2004. 'And all the Women Followed Her'. On Women's Religious Leadership in Modern Orthodoxy, in J. Wertheimer, ed., *Jewish Religious Leadership: Image and Reality*, vol. 2. New York: Jewish Theological Seminary, 715–56.

Coser, L. 1974. *Greedy Institutions: Patterns of Undivided Attention*. New York: Free Press.

Deichovsky, S. 2003. Preferences in the Saving of Lives in the Community (Hebrew), in A. Sabag, ed., *Kelavie Shachen*. Merkaz Shapira: Ha-machon ha-Torani.

De Vaux, R. 1961. *Ancient Israel: Its Life and Institutions*. New York: McGraw-Hill.

Dewar, M. 1985. *The British Army in Northern Ireland*. London, Arms and Armor Press.

Dietz, H., Jerrold E. and Roumani, M. 1991. *Ethnicity, Integration and the Military*. Boulder, CO: Westview Press.

Don-Yehiya, E. 1993. Religion and Political Terror: Religious Jewry and Retaliation during the 1936–1939 'Arab Revolt' (Hebrew), *Ha-Tziyonut*, 17: 155–190.

——. 1994. The Book and the Sword: The Nationalist Yeshivot and Political Radicalism in Israel, in M. Marty and R. Scott Appleby, eds, *Accounting for Fundamentalisms*. Chicago: University of Chicago Press, 264–301.

Dorff, E. 1991. Bishops, Rabbis, and the Bomb, in D. Landes, ed., *Confronting Omnicide: Jewish Reflections on Weapons of Mass Destruction*. Northvale, NJ: Aaronson, 164–195.

——. 2002. *To Do the Right and the Good: A Jewish Approach to Modern Social Ethics*. Philadelphia: Jewish Publication Society.

Doron, A. 1988. *Medinat Yisrael ve-eretz Yisrael*. Tel-Aviv: Ha-kibbutz ha-Meuchad.

Drori, Z. 2005. *The Israel Defence Force and the Foundation of Israel: Utopia in Uniform*. London: RoutledgeCurzon.

——. 2005b. *Between Faith and Military Service: The Nahal Haredi Battalion*. Jerusalem: Floersheimer Institute for Policy Studies.

——. 2006. Society Strength as a Basis for Military Power: The State of Israel in the Early 1950s, *Israel Affairs*, 12: 412–29.

Edrei, A. 2005. Divine Spirit and Physical Power: Rabbi Shlomo Goren and the Military Ethic of the Israel Defense Forces, *Theoretical Inquiries in Law*, 7: 255–297.

——. 2006. Law, Interpretation and Ideology: The Renewal of the Jewish Laws of War in the State of Israel, *Cordozo Law Review*, 28: 187–227.

Ehrenberg, Y.M. 1998. *Devar Yehoshua*. B'nei Berak: privately printed.

Eilam, Y, 1979. *Ha-Haganah*. Tel-Aviv: Zmora, Bitan, Modan.

Eisen, R. 2011. *The Peace and Violence of Judaism*. New York: Oxford University Press.

——. 2012. War, Revenge and Jewish Ethics. Rabbi Shaul Yisraeli's Essay on Kibiyeh Revisited, *AJSReview*, 36: 141–63.

Eiskovits, R. 2006. Intercultural Learning among Russian Immigrant Recruits in the Israeli Army, *Armed Forces & Society*, 32: 292–306.

Eizental, A. 2002. Deterrence – a Torah Perspective (Hebrew), in E. Shenwald, ed., *Sefer Harel: tzevaiyut yisra'elit be-aspeklariyah* toranit. Chispin: The Golan Hesder Yeshivah, 247–268.

Elran M. and Ben-Meir Y. (eds). 2012. *Giyus Haredim Le-Tzahal*. Tel-Aviv: National Institute for Strategic Studies.

Engelhard, Y. 1993.The Halakhic Problem of Ceding Territories of the Land of Israel: Law and Ideology (Hebrew), *Ha-Praklit*, 13: 13–34.

Enloe, C. 1980. *Ethnic Soldiers: State Security in Divided Societies*. Athens: University of Georgia Press.

Ezrachi, Y. and R. Gal, eds, 1995. World Views and Attitudes of High School Students with Respect to Subjects Concerned with Society, Security and Peace (Hebrew; draft report). Zichron Ya'akov: The Carmel Institute for Social Studies.

Feierberg, H. 2004. An Excellent Generation (Hebrew), *Eit-Mol*, 177: 12–14.

Feinstein, M. 1966. *Igrot Mosheh*, part 8: *Yoreh Deah*. New York: Metivta.

Ford, C. and Cohen, Am. (eds.) 2012. *Rethinking the Law of Armed Conflict in an Age of Terrorism*. Washington, DC.: Lexington Books.

Fox, J. and Sandler, S. 2004. *Bringing Religion into International Relations*. New York: Palgrave Macmillan.

Frank, Z.P. 1976. *Har Tzevi*. Jerusalem: Machon Frank.

Friedman, M. 1986. Life tradition and book tradition in the development of ultra-orthodox Judaism, in H. Goldberg, ed., *Judaism Viewed from Within and from Without*. Albany: SUNY Press, 235–256.

——. 1990. This is the Chronology of the 'Status Quo': Religion and State in Israel, in V. Pilovsky, ed., *Ha-Ma'avar me-Yishuv la-Medinah*. Haifa: Haifa University Press, 47–80.

——. 1991. *Ha-Hevrah ha-Haredit*. Jerusalem: The Israel Center for Israel Studies.

Friedman, M. 2005. *Ha-Yechidot ha-Datiyot Ba-Haganah u-va-Palmach*. Ramat Gan: Bar-Ilan University Pres.

Frisch, H. 1993. The Druze Minority in the Israeli Military, *Armed Forces & Society*, 20: 51–67.

Gabriel, R. 1984. *Operation Peace for the Galilee*. New York: Hall and Wang.

Gal, R. 1986. *A Portrait of the Israeli Soldier*. New York: Greenwood.

——. 2012. The IDF in [the Process of] Theocratization- So What? (Hebrew), in: R. Gal & T. Libel (eds). *Bein Ha-Kipah la-Kumtah*, Modan: Ben Shemen, 587–613.

Gelber, Y. 1984. *Bein Britim, Aravim ve-Germanim*. Jerusalem: Yad Yitzchak Ben-Zvi.

German, G. 2003. *Melekh Yisrael*. Bnei Brak: Moreshet.

Gisser, A. 2011. We Do Pay an Exorbitant Price for Soldiers (Hebrew), *Mekor Rishon*, 21.10.2011, p. 12.

——. 2012. The Shalit case: Responsibilities of the Jewish State, *Conversations* (The Journal of the Institute for Jewish Ideas and Ideals) 14: 126–132.

Gogol, D. 1919. Stepsons (Hebrew), *Kuntres*, 2: 35–7.

Goldstein, E. 2001. The 'Hannibal Procedure' in Halakhah (Hebrew), *Techumin*, 31: 157–165

Goren, R. 1989. Advancement of the Weak versus the Promotion of Excellence in the IDF, *Sekirah Hodshit*, 37: 3–6.

Goren, S. 1983–1992. *Meishiv Milkhamah*. 4 vols. Jerusalem: Idra Rabah.

——. 1992. The *Halakhic* Status of Judea, Samaria and the Gaza Strip (Hebrew), *Ha-Tzofeh*, November 20, 1992.

——. 1993. Disobedience to an Order (Hebrew), *Biton Moetzet Rabbanei Yesha*, 14 Dec. 1993, p. 1.

——. 1996. The Siege of Beirut in the Light of the Halakhah (Hebrew), *Sefer Torat Ha-Medinah*. Jerusalem: Idra Rabah, 402–23.

Gorenberg, G. 2006. *The Accidental Empire. Israel and the Birth of the Settlements, 1967–1977*. New York: Holt.

Granit-Hakohen, A. 2011. *Ishah Ivriyah el ha-Degel*. Jerusalem: Yad Ben-Zvi.

Greenberg, Y. 2001. *Am Lochem*. Sdeh Boker: The Ben-Gurion Research Center.

——. 2006. Military Recruitment of Manpower for Vital Services and Economic Enterprises (Hebrew), in M. Bar-On and M. Chazan, eds, *Am Lochem*. Jerusalem: Yad Ben-Zvi, 133–54.

Gutel, N. 1992. The Loud Silence of the IDF Rabbinate (Hebrew). *Meimad* 8–10.

——. 1994. The *Halakhic* Bounds of the Hasmoneans' Wars (Hebrew), *Shanah be-Shanah*, 229–49.

——. 2004. Considerations of Precedence in the Identification and Removal of IDF Fallen on the Sabbath (Hebrew), *Techumin*, 24: 383–394.

——. 2006. The *Halakhic* Weight of Morale in War (Hebrew), *Sinai*, 138: 98–110.

——. 2006b. Warfare in an Area Full of Civilians (Hebrew), in Y. Ha-Levi, ed., *Ha-Milkhamah ba-Terror*. Kiryat Araba: Makhon Le-Rabaney Yishuvim.

Guvrin, P. 1976. *Tzav Keriyah Tashach*. Tel-Aviv: Ma'arachot.

Hadari, Y. 2002. *Mashiach Rackuv al Tank*. Tel-Aviv: Ha-Kibbutz ha-Meuchad.

Hadari-Ramage, Y. 1995. War and Religiosity: The Sinai Campaign in Public Thought, in S. Troen and N. Lucas, eds, *Israel: The First Decade of Independence*. Albany: SUNY Press, 355–74.

Halabi, R. 2006. *Ezrachim Shevei Chovot*. Tel-Aviv: Ha-Kibbutz ha-Meuchad.

Halberstadt, Y.Y. 1996. *Divrei Yetziv*. Netanya: Tzantz.

Ha-Levi, H.D. 1980. The Law of 'Someone who Comes to Kill You' in Our Public Life (Hebrew). *Techumin*, 1: 343–56.

Hankin, Y. 1994. Killing a Captive Terrorist (Hebrew), *Keshot*, 2: 3–5.

——. 2005. Obedience to a [Military] Order that Contravenes the *Torah* (Hebrew). *Ha-Tzofeh*, 5 August 2005, B3.

Hanshke, Y. 2009. The Ways of the Gentiles as a *Halakhic* Consideration (Hebrew), *Tzohar*, 34: 39–54.

Harrison, M. (ed.) 2000. *The Economics of World War II: Six Great Powers in International Comparison*. Cambridge: Cambridge University Press.

Helfgot, N. (ed.) 2005. *Community, Covenant and Commitment: Selected Letters and Communications of Rabbi Joseph B. Soloveitchik*. Jersey City: Katav.

Hendel, Y. 1950. *Anashim Acheirim Heim*. Merchavia: Ha-Kibbutz Ha-Artzi.

Henderson, W. 1985. *Cohesion: The Human Element in Combat*. Washington, D.C.: National Defense University Press.

Hertz, J. 1941. *A Book of Jewish Thoughts*. London: Eyre and Spottiswoode.

Herzl, T. 1895 (new edn. 1946). *The Jewish State*. New York: Zionist Press.

Herzog, I. 1972. *Heichal Yitzchak*. Jerusalem: Herzog Fund.

High Court Judgments

Movement for Quality of Government in Israel Vs The Knesset. 2005; HCJ 6427/02.

Ressler Vs Minister of Defense. 1988; HCJ 910/86.

Ressler Vs the Knesset. 2012; HCJ 6298/07.

Rubinstein Vs Minister of Defense. 1998; HCJ 3267/97.

Hoffman, D. 1926. *Melamed le-Hoil*. Frankfurt: Charmon.

Holzer, E. 2002. The Use of Military Force in the Religious Zionist Ideology of Rabbi Yitzchak Ya'akov Reines and his Successors, *Studies in Contemporary Jewry*, 18: 74–94.

Horowitz, A. 1972. Booty Consisting of Forbidden Foods taken by the IDF in our Times (Hebrew), *Noam*, 15: 212–238.

Horowitz, D. and Lissak, M. 1989. *Trouble in Utopia: The Overburdened Polity of Israel*, Albany: SUNY Press.

Inbar, E. 1987. War in Jewish Tradition *Jerusalem Journal of International Relations*, 9: 83–9.

Inbari, M. 2012. *Messianic Religious Zionism Confronts Israeli Territorial Compromises*. Cambridge: Cambridge University Press.

Izraeli, D. 1997. Gendering Military Service in the Israel Defense Forces, *Israel Social Science Research*, 12: 129–166.

Johnston, A. 1995. Thinking about Strategic Culture, *International Security*, 19: 32–64.

Kadish, A. 1996. A Professional or Popular Army? The IDF at the End of the War of Independence (Hebrew), *Ma'archot*, 349: 52–4.

——. (ed.) 2004. *Milkhemet ha'Atzma'ut: Diyyun Mechudash*. Tel-Aviv: Ministry of Defense.

Kagan, Y. 1881. *Sefer Machaneh Yisrael*. Mishkaltz: privately printed.

Kahana, Y. 1948. Military Service in the Responsa Literature (Hebrew), *Sinai*, 23: 129–161.

Kampinsky, A. 2008. Religion, Army and Society in Israel: Changes in the Military Rabbinate, 1948–2006 (Hebrew), unpub. Ph.D. thesis, Bar-Ilan University.

______. 2012. The Military Rabbinate and its Influence on the 'Theocratization' Process in the IDF – Image and Reality (Hebrew), in R. Gal and T. Libel (eds). *Bein Ha-Kipah la-Kumtah*, Modan: Ben Shemen, 309–336.

Karpi, D. (ed.) 1997. *Igrot Ze'ev Jabotinsky*, vol. 3. Jerusalem: Jabotinsky Institute.

Kasher, A. 1996. *Etika Tzeva'it*. Tel-Aviv: Ministry of Defense.

——. 1997. Interview in *Haaretz* (Hebrew) weekend supplement, January 23, 1997, p. 16.

Katz, J. 1998. *Divine Law in Human Hands: Case Studies in Halakhic Flexibility*. Jerusalem: Magnes.

Katzenstein, P. (ed.) 1996. *The Culture of National Security: Norms and Identity in World Politics*. New York: Columbia University Press.

Kaufman, Y. 1994. *Ha-Tzavah ke-Halakhah*. Jerusalem: Kol Mevaser.

Kedar, N. 2002. Ben-Gurion's 'Mamlachtiyut': Etymological and Theoretic Roots, *Israel Studies*, 7: 117–33.

Kelsay, J. 2003. Al-Shaybani and the Islamic Law of War, *Journal of Military Ethics*, 2: 63–75.

Kemp, A. (ed). 2004. *Israelis in Conflict: Hegemonies, Identities and Challenges*. Brighton: Sussex University Press.

Khaled, Abou El Fadl. 1999. The Rules of Killing at War: An Inquiry in Classical Sources, *The Muslim World*, 89: 144–57.

Kimelman, R. 1968. Non-violence in the Talmud, *Judaism*, 17: 316–334.

——. 1970. The Rabbinic Ethic of Protest, *Judaism*, 19: 38–58.

——. 1991. The Ethics of National Power: Government and War from the Sources of Judaism, in D.J. Elazar, ed., *Authority, Power and Leadership in the Jewish Polity: Cases and Issues*. Lanham: University Press of America, 247–94.

Kimmerling, B. 1985. *The Interrupted System: Israeli Citizens in War and Routine Times*. New Brunswick: Transaction.

——. 1985b. Between the Primordial and the Civil Definitions of the Collective Identity, in E. Cohen, M. Lissak and U. Almagor, eds, *Comparative Social Dynamics*. Boulder: Westview, 268–82.

——. 2001. *The Invention and Decline of Israeliness: State, Society and the Military*. Berkeley: University of California Press.

Kliot, N. 2005. *Decision-making on Settlement Evacuation in Israel, Compensation and Resettlement: Sinai 1982 Vs Gaza Region and North Samaria 2005*. Jerusalem: Floersheimer Institute for Policy Studies.

Knapp, M. 2003. The Concept and Practice of Jihad in Islam, *Parameters*, 33: 82–94.

Knesset. Center for Research and Information, 2012. *Report on the Application of the Service Deferral Law* (Hebrew). <https://www.knesset.gov.il/mmm/data/pdf/m03076.pdf> (accessed 19 September 2012).

Kook, A.I. 1993. (3rd edtn.) *Orot ha-Techiyah*. Jerusalem: Mosad Harav Kook.

Kook, Z.Y. 1969. *Lintivot Yisrael*. Jerusalem: Mosad Harav Kook.

Krebs, R. 2004. School for the Nation? How Military Service Does Not Build Nations and How It Might, *International Security*, 28: 85–124.

Krim, E.M. 2001. *Kishrei Milkhamah*. Jerusalem: Machon Maarachot.

Lamm, M. 1978. After the War – Another Look at Pacifism and Selective Conscientious Objection (SCO), reprinted in M. Kellner, ed., *Contemporary Jewish Ethics*. New York: Sanhedrin, 221–38.

Laslo, A. and Rich,Y. 2001. *Survey of 12th Grade Students in National-Religious High Schools–5759: Research Report*. Ramat Gan. Bar-Ilan University.

Lau, B. 2005. *Mi-Maran Ad Maran*. Tel-Aviv: Yediot.

Lau, Y.M. 2003. *Yachel Yisrael*, vol. 3. Jerusalem: privately printed.

Lavie, Y. 2007. *Halakhic* Definitions of a Civilian War in the Rear, *Machaneichah*, 2: 269–86.

Lehman-Wilzig, S. 1992. *Wildfire: Grassroots Revolts in Israel in the Post-socialist Era*. New York. SUNY Press.

Leibowitz, Y. 1992. After Kibyeh in: Leibowitz, *Judaism, Human Values, and the Jewish State*. Cambridge: Harvard University Press, 185–90.

Levi, Y. and Furstein, A. 1995. It's not easy to be a Religious Soldier (Hebrew), *Zera'im*, 8: 8–9.

Levy, Y. 2003. *Tzavah Acher le-Yisrael*. Tel-Aviv: Yediot.

——. 2006. The War of the Peripheries: A Social Mapping of IDF Fatalities in the Al-Aqsah intifada, *Social Identities*, 12: 309–324.

——. 2007a. *Israel's Materialist Militarism*. Lanham: Lexington.

——. 2007b. The Embedded Military: Why did the IDF Perform Effectively in Executing the Disengagement Plan? *Security Studies*, 16: 382–408.

——. 2008. The Linkage between Israel's Military Policies and the Military's Social Composition: The Case of the Al Aqsa Intifada, *American Behavioral Scientist*, 51: 1575–89.

——. 2009. An Unbearable Price: War Casualties and Warring Democracies, *International Journal of Political and Cultural Sociology*, 22: 69–82.

——. 2012. Israel's Death Hierarchy. Casualty Aversion in a Militarized Society. New York: New York University Press.

Libel, T. 2012. From a 'People's Army' to a 'Jewish People's Army' (Hebrew), in: R. Gal & T. Libel (eds). *Bein Ha-Kipah la-Kumtah*, Modan: Ben Shemen, 205–242.

Lichtenstein, A. 1981. The Ideology of *Hesder*, *Tradition*, 19: 199–217.

——. 2005a. Do Not Disobey Orders! (Hebrew), *Ha'aretz*, 19.7.2005.

——. 2005b. Open letters to R. Avraham Shapira and R. Avraham Sylvetsky, August–September 2005. Both available at: <http://www.etzion.org.il/hitnatkut/hitnatkut.htm> (accessed September 19, 2012).

Lieberman, I. 2004. Religious Zionism: Towards Segregationalism (Hebrew). Unpublished Ph.D. thesis, Bar-Ilan University.

Liebman, C. 1968. The Orthodox Rabbi and Vietnam, *Tradition*, 9: 28–32.

———. and Don-Yehiya, E. 1983. *Civil Religion in Israel: Traditional Religion and Political Culture in the Jewish State*. Berkeley: University of California Press.

———. 1984. *Religion and Politics in Israel*. Bloomington, Ind.: Indiana University Press.

———. and Katz, E. (eds) 1997. *The Jewishness of Israelis*. Albany: SUNY Press.

Lomsky-Feder, E. and Ben-Ari, E. 1999. From 'The People in Uniform' to 'Different Uniforms for the People': Professionalism, Diversity and the Israel Defense Forces, in J. Soeters and J. van der Muelen, eds, *Managing Diversity in the Armed Forces: Experiences From Nine Countries*. Tilburg: Tilburg University Press, 157–86.

———. (eds) 1999. *The Military and Militarism in Israeli Society*. Albany: SUNY Press.

———. and Rapoport, T. 2003. Juggling Models of Masculinity: Russian-Jewish Immigrants in the Israeli Army, *Sociological Inquiry*, 73: 114–137.

Lubitch, R. 2009. Army and War in Religious Zionist Thought, (Hebrew), *Amadot*, 1: 115–38.

———. 2010. The Terms '*Kiddush Ha-shem*' and '*Hillul Ha-shem*' in Religious Zionist Thought (Hebrew), *Shaanan*, 16: 113–46.

Lustick, I.S. 1988. *For the Land and the Lord*. New York: Council on Foreign Relations.

Lutwak, E. and Horowitz, D. 1975. *The Israeli Army*. New York: Harper and Row.

Luz, E. 1987. The Moral Price of Sovereignty: The Dispute about the use of Military Power within Zionism, *Modern Judaism*, 7: 51–98.

——— 2003. *Wrestling with an Angel: Power Morality and Jewish Identity*. New Haven: Yale University Press.

MacCoun, R.J. 1993. What is Known about Unit Cohesion and Military Performance, in: *Sexual Orientation and U.S. Military Personnel Policy: Options and Assessment*. Santa Monica: Rand, 283–331.

Malkhin, A. 2007. *Ha-Aktivist*. Tel-Aviv: Am Oved.

Mandelkron, A. 1994.The Command to Make Peace Offers in War (Hebrew), *Oz*, 163–183.

Maoz, Z. 2006. *Defending the Holy Land: A Critical Analysis of Israel's Security and Foreign Policy*. Ann Arbor, MI: University of Michigan Press.

Markovitch, H. 2007. Cooking by Gentiles in the Army (Hebrew), *Machaneichah*, 1: 145–54.

Marks, R. 1994. *The Image of Bar Kokhba in Traditional Jewish Literature: False Messiah and National Hero*. Pennsylvania: Pennsylvania State University Press.

Markovizky, J. 1995. *Gachelet Lochemet*. Tel-Aviv: Ministry of Defense.

Meir, Y. and Rahav-Meir, S. 2006. *Yamim Ketumim*. Tel-Aviv: Yediot.

Melamed, Z. 2004. Opposition to the Evacuation of Settlements (Hebrew), *Ba-Yom Ha-Shevi'i*, 26 October 2004, A3.

Michaelson, M. 1982, The Military Rabbinate (Hebrew), in I. Kfir and Y. Erez, eds, *Tzahal be-Cheilav*. Tel-Aviv: Revivim.

Min-Hahar, S. 1971. *Hilkhot Tzavah u-Milkhamah*. Jerusalem: Haskel.

Ministry of Education 1991. *Israel Prizes, 1991: Citations* (Hebrew). Jerusalem: Government Printing Office.

Minka-Brand, H. 2005. 'To Set an Example'. Learning about the Assignment of Troops during the Disengagement Operation: A Description of the Case of the Golani Brigade (Hebrew), *Bein Ha-Zirot*, 4: 36–49.

Mor, S. 2011. *Tiqqun 'olam* (Repairing the World) in the Mishnah: From Populating the World to Building a Community, *Journal of Jewish Studies*, 62(2011): 284–310.

Morris, B. 1993. *Israel's Border Wars, 1949–1956*. Oxford: The Clarendon Press.

Moskos, C. and Wood, F. (eds) 1988. *The Military: More than Just a Job?* Washington D.C.: Pergamon-Brassey's.

Naor, A. 1999. The Security Argument in the Territorial Debate in Israel: Rhetoric and Policy, *Israel Studies*, 4: 150–177.

——. 2001. *Eretz Yisrael ha-Shelemah*. Haifa: Haifa University Press.

Newman, K. 2012. The Law of Obligatory War and Israeli Reality, in Y. Levin and A. Shapira, eds, *War and Peace in Jewish Tradition*. London: Routledge, 186–99.

Ohana, D. 2003. *Meshichiyut u-Mamlakhtiyut*. Beer-Sheba: Ben-Gurion University of the Negev Press.

Ostfeld, Z. 1994. *Tzavah Nolad*. Tel-Aviv: Ministry of Defense.

Pa'il, M. 1983. The Fighting Forces (Hebrew), in Y. Ben-Aryeh, ed., *Milkhemet ha-Atzma'ut*, Jerusalem: Keter, 109–50.

Passamaneck, S. 2003. *Police Ethics and the Jewish Tradition*. Springfield, Ill.: C.C. Thomas.

Peled, A. 2000. The Politics of Language in Multiethnic Militaries: The Case of Oriental Jews in the Israel Defense Forces, 1950–1959, *Armed Forces & Society*, 26: 587–605.

Penslar, D. 2008. An Unlikely Internationalism. Jews at War in Modern Western Europe, *Journal of Modern Jewish Studies*, 7: 309–23.

Peters, R. 1996. A Revolution in Military Ethics? *Parameters*, 26: 102–6.

Peretz, R. 2011. Interview (Hebrew). *Ba-Mahaneh*, 20 May 2011, 28–32

——. 2012. Interview (Hebrew). *Mekor Rishon*, 27 January 2012, 20–22.

Pfeffer, A. 2009. IDF Chief Wants to Enlist Arabs, Charedim in National Service. *Haaretz* 2 December, <http://www.haaretz.com/hasen/spages/1132161.html> (accessed 3 December 2009).

Plessner, Y. (2012). Report by MK Y. Plessner, Chair of Committee for Integration into Service and Burden-sharing (Hebrew). Jerusalem. <http://www.nrg.co.il/images/news1/plesner.pdf> (accessed 11 November 2012).

Polak, J. 1983. Torah and the Megabomb, *Judaism*, 32: 302–308.

Polak, U. 2013. Feiglin Proposes All-volunteer IDF (Hebrew). *Kipah*, 3 Feb. <http://www.kipa.co.il/now/50801.html> (accessed 17 February 2013).

Putnam, R.D. 2000. *Bowling Alone: The Collapse and Revival of American Community*. New York: Simon and Schuster.

Rabbinical Assembly 1944. *Proceedings 1941–1944*. New York: Jewish Theological Seminary.

Rabinovitch, N. 1994. *Melumedie Milkhamah*. Ma'aleh Adumim: Yeshivat Birkat Mosheh.

Rakover, N. 2000. *Mesirut Nefesh*. Jerusalem: Moreshet ha-Mishpat.

——. 1998. The Protection of Human Dignity, in N. Rakover, ed., *Jerusalem City of Law and Justice*. Jerusalem: Jewish Legal Heritage Society, 187–227.

Rappaport, A. 2005. An Existential Test (Hebrew). *Ma'ariv*, 14 August 2005, p. 7

Ravitzky, A. 1988. Exile in the Holy Land: The Dilemma of Haredi Jewry, *Studies in Contemporary Jewry*, 5: 89–125.

——. 1996. *Messianism, Zionism and Jewish Religious Radicalism*. Chicago: University of Chicago Press.

——. 1996. Prohibited Wars in Jewish Tradition, in Terry Nardin, ed., *The Ethics of War and Peace: Religious and Secular Perspectives*. Princeton: PUP, 115–127.

Raz, S. 1966. *Shalom Karniel. Hayyav u-Mishnato*. Tel-Aviv: The Religious Kibbutz Movement.

Rimon, Y. 2002a. 'Operation Defensive Shield' – *Halakhic* Guidelines (b) (Hebrew), *Bulletin of Har-Etziyon Yeshivah*, 859: 1.

——. 2002b. The Oath of Allegiance to the IDF, *Tzohar*, 13: 137–42.

——. 2010. *Halakhah Mimkorah – Tzavah*. Tel-Aviv: Yediot.

Rolbant, S. 1970. *The Israeli Soldier: Profile of an Army*. New York: Yoseloff.

Roness, A. 2007. Questions on Jewish Military Ethics and International Agreements (Hebrew), *Tzohar*, 29: 33–42.

——. 2009. Desecration of the Sabbath whilst Giving Encouragement to Soldiers about to go into Battle (Hebrew), *Techumin*, 29: 453–461.

——. 2010. Halakhah, Ideology and Interpretation: Rabbi Shaul Yisraeli on the Status of Defensive War, *Jewish Law Association Studies*, 20: 184–195.

Rontski, A. 1996–2003. *Ke-Chitzim be-Yad Gibor*. 3 vols. Itamar: Yeshivat Itamar.

——. 2006. Ethics and War (Hebrew), in Y. Ha-Levi, ed., *Ha-Milkhamah ba-Terror*. Kiryat Arba: Machon Rabbanei ha-Yishuvim, 217–27.

Rose, A. 2006. The Haredim: A Defense, *Azure*, 25: 29–60.

——. 2008. An Orthodox Revolution? *Azure*, 31: 125–135.

Rosen, S. 1995 Military Effectiveness: Why Society Matters, *International Security*, 19: 5–31.

Rossman-Stollman, E. 2005. Religion and the Military as Greedy Frameworks: Religious Zionism and the IDF (Hebrew), unpublished Ph.D. dissertation, Bar-Ilan University.

Rozen, I. 2002. Un-*halakhic* Apologetics (Hebrew), *Tzohar*, 12: 135–9.

——. 2010. Releasing Captives for 'an Exorbitant Price' that is Not Financial (Hebrew), *Techumin*, 30: 95–100.

Rozenak, A. 2007. War and Peace in Modern Jewish Thinking Concerning 'The Other' (Hebrew), *Da'at*, 62: 99–125.

Rozenfeld, S. 2003. The Distribution of Spoils and Booty in Contemporary Wars (Hebrew), *Techumin*, 23: 52–9.

Roumani, M. 1991. The Military, Ethnicity and Integration in Israel Revisited, in H. Dietz, J. Elkin and M. Roumani, eds, *Ethnicity, Integration and the Military*. Boulder, CO: Westview Press, 51–80.

Rubin, M. 1998. *Ha-Morim Ba-Keshet*. Hebron: Machon le-Rabbanei Yishuvim.

Rubinstein, A. 1984. *The Zionist Dream Revisited: From Herzl to Gush Emunim and Back*. New York: Schocken.

Rubinstein, S. 1975. Matters Forbidden and Permitted to Troops in War (Hebrew), *Torah Shebe'al Peh*, 17: 99–105.

Sagi, A. 1994. The Punishment of Amalek in Jewish Tradition: Coping with the Moral Problem, *Harvard Theological Review*, 87: 323–346.

Saperstein, M. 2008. *Jewish Preaching in Times of War 1800–2001*. Oxford: Littman.

Sasson-Levy, O. 2007. Contradictory Consequences of Mandatory Conscription: The Case of Women Secretaries in the Israeli Military, *Gender and Society*, 21: 481–507.

——. 2010. Where Will the Women Be? Gendered Implications of the Decline of the Citizen's Army, in S. Cohen, ed., *The New Citizen Armies*. London: Routledge, 173–95.

Schechter, Z. 1997. *Be-Ikvei Ha-Tzon*. New York: Flatbush Yeshivah.

——. (ed.) 1994. *Nefesh Harav*. Jerusalem: Flatbush Yeshivah.

Schiff, Z. and Ya'ari, E. 1984. *Israel's Lebanon War*. New York: Simon and Schuster.

Schweid, E. 1994. *Bein Churban le-Yeshuah*. Tel-Aviv: Ha-Kibbutz ha-Meuchad.

Schechtman, J. 1986. *Rebel and Statesman: The Life and Times of Vladimir Jabotinsky*. Silver Springs, MD: Eshel.

Schochetman, E. 2004. A Military Order to Desecrate the Sabbath (Hebrew), *Techumin*, 24: 373–82.

Sedan, E. 2005. *Ne'emanuteinu la-Torah ve-la-Tzavah*. Eli: Bnei David.

Seeman, D. 2005. Violence, Ethics and Divine Honor in Modern Jewish Thought, *Journal of the American Academy of Religion*, 73: 1015–1048.

Segev J. 2008. Relief in the Interest of Justice: Two Models of an Unconventional Functional Authority (Hebrew), *Kiryat Ha-Mishpat*, 7: 63–114.

Sela, Y. 2012. Female Religious Soldiers in the IDF (Hebrew), in: R. Gal & T. Libel (eds), *Bein Ha-Kipah la-Kumtah*, Modan: Ben Shemen, 529–540.

Selengut, C. 1994. By Torah Alone: Yeshivah Fundamentalism in Jewish Life, in M.E. Marty and R.S. Appleby, eds, *Accounting for Fundamentalisms*. Chicago: Chicago University Press, 236–263.

Shafat, G. 1995. *Gush Emunim. Ha-Sipur mei-Ahorei ha-Kelaim*. Bet El: Sifriat Bet-El.

Shafir, G. and Peled, Y. 2002. *Being Israeli: The Dynamics of Multiple Citizenship.* Cambridge: Cambridge University Press.

Shah, T.C., Stepan, A.C. and Duffy Toft, M. (eds) 2012. *Rethinking Religion and World Affairs.* New York: Oxford University Press.

Shapira, A. 2004. Interview. *Ba-Sheva* (Hebrew). 15 October 2004, p. 1

Shapira, A. 1992. *Land and Power: The Zionist Resort to Force, 1881–1948.* New York: Oxford University Press.

——. 1997. The Myth of the New Jew (Hebrew), in A. Shapira, *Yehudim Chadashim, Yehudim Yeshanim.* Tel-Aviv: Am Oved, 155–74.

——. 1997b. Ben-Gurion and the Bible: The Forging of an Historical Narrative? *Middle Eastern Studies*, 33: 645–74.

Shapira, N. 1998. The Call for Peace (Hebrew), *Torah Shebe'al Peh*, 39: 82–90.

Shapira, Y. and Elitzur, Y. 2010. *Sefer Torat Ha-Melekh.* Shechem: Yeshivat Od Yosef Hai.

Shapiro, David S. 1975. *Studies in Jewish Thought.* New York: Yeshiva University Press.

Sharir, A. 2005. Military Ethics According to the Halachah (Hebrew), *Techumin*, 25: 426–438.

Sharon, A. 1989. *Warrior: The Autobiography of Ariel Sharon.* New York: Simon and Schuster.

Shavit, Y. 1988. *Jabotinsky and the Revisionist Movement 1925–1948.* London: Cass.

Shaviv, Y. (ed.) 1977. *Eretz Nachalah.* Jerusalem: World Mizrachi Organization.

——. 1987. Conflicting Mitzva Obligations (Halakhic Aspects of the '*Hesder*'), *Crossroads* I: 187–99.

——. 1990. Analyses of Laws Concerning the Redemption of Captives (Hebrew), in: Shaviv, *Betzir Aviezer.* Gush Etziyon: Tzomet, 176–91.

——. 1994a. 'Loved in Life [II Sam. 1:23]' – and in Death? (Hebrew), *Techumin*, 14: 319–330.

——. 1994b. The Shechem Episode – Halachic Aspects (Hebrew), *Oz*, 279–280.

Sheikh, M.K. 2012. How does Religion Matter? Pathways to Religion in International Relations, *Review of International Studies*, 38: 365–392.

Shelach, O. 2003. *Ha-Magash ve-ha Kesef.* Tel-Aviv: Dvir.

Shelef, N.G. 2010. Evolving Nationalism: Homeland, Identity and Religion in Israel, 1925–2005. Ithaca: Cornell University Press.

Sheleg, Y. 2000. *Ha-Datiyim ha-Chadashim.* Jerusalem: Keter.

Shenwald, E. 2002. *Ad ridetah* [Until it is subdued] (Hebrew) in: Shenwald (ed.), *Sefer Harel: tzevaiyut yisra'elit be-aspeklariyah toranit.* Chispin: The Golan Hesder Yeshiva, 119–84.

Sherman, A. 1995. Israel's Wars – Their *Halakhic* Validity (Hebrew), *Techumin* 15: 23–30.

——. 2002. Law and the Ethic of War: The War on Terror in the View of Israel's Torah (Hebrew), *Torah Shebe'al Peh*, 43: 63–86.

Shimoni, G. 1995. *The Zionist Ideology.* Hanover: Brandeis University Press.

Shindler, C. 2006. *The Triumph of Military Zionism: Nationalism and the Origins of the Israeli Right*. London: Palgrave Macmillan.

Shushan, O. and Peltz, R. 2007. Activities During the Disengagement Undertaken by Officers of the Civilian Behavior Unit: A Model of Intervention in a Settlement (Hebrew), *Bein Ha-Zirot*, 6: 65–70.

Sivan, E. 1991. *Dor Tashach*. Tel-Aviv: Ma'arachot.

Soen, D. 2008. 'All Able-Bodies, to Arms!' – Attitudes of Israeli High School Students Toward Conscription and Combat Service, *European Journal of Social Sciences*, 6: 72–82.

Solomon, N. 2006. Judaism, in R. Sorabji and D. Rodin, eds, *The Ethics of War*. Aldershot: Ashgate, 108–37.

Soloveitchik, A. 1982. Waging War on Shabbat, *Tradition*, 20: 179–87.

Sprinzak, E. 1992. *The Ascendance of Israel's Radical Right*. Oxford: Oxford University Press.

State Comptroller and Ombudsman. 2012. Aspects of Education in the IDF (Hebrew), *62nd Annual Report*, 5 May 2012. Jerusalem: Government Printing, 1599–1626.

Steinmann, A. 2013. Open Letter to *haredim* (Hebrew), *Hadrei Haredim*, 19 February <http://www.bhol.co.il/Article.aspx?id=51116> (accessed 21 February 2013).

Stern, E. 2009. *Masa Kippah*. Tel-Aviv: Yediot.

Sullivan, K.M. 1992. Forward: The Justices of Rules and Standards, *Harvard Law Review*, 106: 22–123

Tal, I. 2000. *National Security: The Israeli Experience*. Westport: Praeger.

Tau, Z. 1983. *Sichot Ba-et Milkhamah*. Jerusalem: privately printed.

Twersky, I. 1980. *Introduction to the Code of Maimonides (Mishneh Torah)*. New Haven: Yale University Press.

Torgan, S. 2008. The Training of IDF Combat Leadership, 1949–1956 (Hebrew), unpublished Ph.D. thesis, Hebrew University of Jerusalem.

Ushpizai, M. 1983. Preventative War – Discretionary or Mandatory? (Hebrew), *Techumin* 4: 90–6.

Van Creveld, M. 1998. *The Sword and the Olive: A Critical History of the Israel Defense Force*. New York: Public Affairs.

———. 2008. *The Culture of War*. New York: Ballantine.

Vital, D. 1986. The afflictions of the Jews and the afflictions of Zionism: the meaning and consequences of the 'Uganda' controversy. in: S.A. Cohen and E. Don-Yehiya eds., *Conflict and Consensus in Jewish Political Life*. Ramat Gan, Bar-Ilan University Press, 79–81.

Vorspan, A. 1969. *Jewish Values and Social Crisis*. New York: Union of American Hebrew Congregations.

Wahrhaftig, I. 1988. The Position of the Rabbis in the Controversy over Partition 1939 (Hebrew), *Tehumin*, 9: 269–301.

Waldenberg, E. 1972. *Tzitz Eliezer*. Jerusalem: privately printed.

Walzer, M. 2006. *Law, Politics, and Morality in Judaism*. Princeton: Princeton University Press.

———. 2011. What is Just War Theory About? Unpublished paper presented to Kfar Blum conference on law and religion.

Watts, M. 2004. *The Jewish Legion and the First World War*. New York: PalgraveMacmillan.

Weinberg, D. 2013. Healing the Haredi Work Ethic. *The Jerusalem Post* 28 February.

Weisburd, D. 1989. *Jewish Settler Violence: Deviance as Social Reaction*. College Park, PA: Pennsylvania State University Press.

Weiss, Y. 2010. *Be-dam Libi*. Tel-Aviv: Yediot.

Wind, S. 1961. *Rabbi Yehezkel Landau*. Jerusalem: Daat Torah.

Wisse, R. 2007. *Jews and Power*. New York: Schocken Books.

Wiznitzer, A. 1956. Jewish Soldiers in Dutch Brazil (1630–1654), *Publications of the American Jewish Historical Society*, 46: 41–50.

Wong, L. 2005. Leave No Man Behind. Recovering America's Fallen Warriors, *Armed Forces & Society*, 31: 599–622.

Ya'alon, M. 2008. *Derekh Arukah Ketzarah*. Tel-Aviv: Yediot.

Yablonka, H. 1995. The Silent Partner: Holocaust Survivors in the IDF, in S. Troen and N. Lucas, eds, *Israel: The First Decade of Independence*. Albany: SUNY Press, 557–72.

Yadin, Y. 1950. General Order *Mivtzah Ma'aborot*, 17 November 1950. Tel Ha-Shomer: IDF archives, File 119/754.

Yaniv, A. 1985. Deterrence Without Bombs: A Framework for the Analysis of Israeli Strategy (Hebrew), *Medinah Mimshal ve-Yachbal*, 24: 63–85.

Yehezkeli, P. 2009. *Tzahal – Tzavah Ha'am o Tzavah Miktzoi?* Tel-Aviv: Ministry of Defense.

Yisraeli, S. 1954. The Qibya Incident in Halakhah (Hebrew), *Ha-torah ve-ha-medinah*, 6: 71–113.

_____. 1975. Is it Permissible to Give In to Extortion in [cases of] Redemption of Captives and Hostages? (Hebrew). *Torah She-be'al Peh* 17: 69–76.

———. 1990. Ceding Territory Because of Mortal Danger, *Crossroads*, 3: 29–46.

Yosef, O. 1977. The Entebbe Operation in Halakhah (Hebrew), *Torah Shebe'al Peh*, 19: 9–39.

———. 1990. Ceding Territory of the Land of Israel in Order to Save Lives, *Crossroads*, 3: 11–28.

Yoshor, M. 1943. *Israel in the Ranks: A Religious Guide of Faith and Practice for the Jewish Soldier*. New York: Yeshivah Choftez Chayim.

Zalkin, M. 2006. Between 'the Sons of God' and 'Human Beings': Rabbis, Yeshivah Students and Conscription into the Russian Army in the 19th Century (Hebrew), in A. Bar_Levav, ed., *Shalom ve-Milkhamah be-Tarbut ha-Yehudit*, Jerusalem: Shazar Center, 165–222.

Zamir, A. 2011. Report by Outgoing Head of IDF Manpower Directorate to COS (Hebrew), *Haaretz*, July 20, 2011.

Zerubavel, Y. 1991. The Politics of Interpretation: Tel-Hai in Israel's Collective Memory, *AJS Review*, 16: 133–60.

Zimmerman, S. 1971. Confronting the Halakhah on Military Service, *Judaism*, 20: 204–12.

Zoldan, Y. 2002. *Malchut Yehudah ve-Yisrael*. Or Etzion: Merkaz Shapira.

Index